SHELVES, CABINETS & BOOKCASES

The Editors of Fine Homebuilding & Fine Woodworking

The Taunton Press

The Taunton Press

The Taunton Press, Inc., 63 South Main Street, PO Box 5506, Newtown, CT 06470-5506
e-mail: tp@taunton.com

Editor: Matthew Teague, Helen Albert
Indexer: James Curtis
Jacket/Cover design: Renato Stanisic
Layout: Laura Lind Design

Library of Congress Cataloging-in-Publication Data
Shelves, cabinets & bookcases : from Fine homebuilding & Fine woodworking / the editors of
Fine homebuilding & Fine woodworking.
    p. cm.
 Includes bibliographical references and index.
 ISBN 978-1-60085-049-3 (alk. paper)
 1. Cabinetwork. 2. Shelving (Furniture) 3. Bookcases. I. Taunton's fine homebuilding. II.
Taunton's fine woodworking.
 TT197.S6423 2009
 684.1'6--dc22

                              2008013633

Printed in the United States of America
10 9 8 7 6 5 4 3 2

The following manufacturers/names appearing in *Shelves, Cabinets & Bookcases* are trademarks:
3M®, AquaMix®, Athlon®, Avonite®, Blum®, Blum Tandem®, Bulls Eye®, Cheng Design®,
Colorlith®, Conestoga®, Corian®, Cuisinart®, CWB Custom Woodworking Business®,
DuPont®, Europly®, Fountainhead®, Gibraltar®, Häfele®, Hardwood Plywood & Veneer
Assocation℠, Hettich®, Home Depot®, HPVA℠, Hydrocote®, John Boos®, Kitchen
Cabinet KCMA Manufacturers Association℠, KraftMaid®, Kreg®, Lee Valley®, Leigh®,
Livos®, Merillat®, Minwax®, NKBA℠, Pionite®, PlusWood®, Porter-Cable®, Rockler®,
RS Means®, Rutt®, Scotch-Brite®, Scotchgard®, SealCoat™, Shop-Vac®, Silestone®, SlateScape®,
Speed-Bloc®, Sugatsune®, Surell®, Swanstone®, TCA Tile Council of America Inc.℠, TopLab®,
Trespa®, Tru-Grip®, Veritas®, Vermont Structural Slate Company℠, Victrola®, Waterlox®,
Wilsonart®, Woodworker's Supply℠, Zinsser®, Zodiaq®.

Working wood is inherently dangerous. Using hand or power tools improperly or ignoring
safety practices can lead to permanent injury or even death. Don't try to perform operations
you learn about here (or elsewhere) unless you're certain they are safe for you. If something
about an operation doesn't feel right, don't do it. Look for another way. We want you to enjoy
the craft, so please keep safety foremost in your mind whenever you're in the shop.

Acknowledgments

Special thanks to the authors, editors, art directors, copy editors, and other staff members of *Fine Woodworking* who contributed to the development of the articles in this book.

Contents

Introduction

One hobby often leads to another. The hobby of reading is probably responsible for creating more woodworkers than any pastime I can think of—most of the woodworkers I meet got started in the craft because they found themselves with a stack of books and nowhere to put them. Whether you build your own bookcases (or shelves, or kitchen cabinets) because you're too persnickety to accept the ones for sale at furniture stores or because you're too thrifty to pay for them is a decision I'll leave up to you.

Originally published in the pages of *Fine Woodworking* and *Fine Homebuilding* magazines, the articles in this book feature designs, construction details, and tips from some of the top woodworkers in the field. Whether your tastes lean toward 18th century, Shaker, Arts and Crafts, or contemporary—and whether you're looking for simple pine shelving or a kitchen full of cabinets—one or more of this collection's wide array of designs is sure to suit your tastes. With a little attention to detail and armed with the guidance found in this book, you can create storage and display solutions that do the job with style.

If you're just getting started in woodworking, be careful. For some of us the woodworking bug takes on a life of its own. We might go on to build beds, chests of drawers, chairs and tables, but we never stop building shelves for our books. If we did, where would we put this one?

—Matthew Teague, furniture designer, builder, and author

Engineering a Bookcase

BY JEFF MILLER

Everyone can use a few more shelves. Indeed, in many homes, an available shelf can be as difficult to find as the TV remote. So if you build a set of bookshelves, they'll probably be filled as soon as the finish dries.

Bookshelves can work in any room. You can make them freestanding or built-in. They can be big or small. And they can take any form, from simple screwed-together and painted plywood for use in a utility room, to sophisticated formal library shelves made from beautiful hardwoods.

A Shelf Should Look Good

A successful bookshelf design must achieve a balance between appearance and function. A shelf with the perfect look might not be adequately strong. That often means making changes as you work out the design.

A good approach is to start by writing out a wish list that summarizes your ideal shelf design. The list should include the shelf depth, a factor determined by the width of the books going on the shelf. Next, choose a shelf length (bookcase width). Then, choose a shelf thickness— ¾-in. stock is readily available, but let your eye make the final determination. After that, decide if you want the shelves to be fixed, adjustable, or some of each. Finally, choose a joint or mounting system that offers the look you want.

The design process is just beginning once you've worked out your bookshelf design "brief." Now you must determine if your initial choices will be strong enough. If not, you'll have to make some design changes. But before we get to that, it helps to understand how a shelf reacts to load.

Sag Is the Main Enemy

As the load on a shelf increases, the weight eventually reaches a point where the shelf bends, or sags. The same factors that affect appearance also affect shelf sag: the thickness, width, and length of the shelf; the wood species used; and the method used to mount the shelf.

As a general rule, our eyes won't notice sag if it's less than 1⁄32 in. (0.031 in.) per foot. With time, even if the contents don't change, a shelf's initial sag could increase by 50% or more as the wood fibers "tire." Wood engineers call this "creep." To be on the safe side, design shelves to limit any initial sag to no more than 0.02 in. per foot under a load of full-size books.

In extreme cases (loading a bookcase with your anvil collection, for example), shelves can deflect so much that the wood actually fails. This is not a common worry. More common, especially on long shelves, is that sag causes the effective length of the shelf to become shorter, causing it to slip off the shelf supports. Or, too much weight on a long shelf can cause some adjustable shelf supports to crush the wood fibers in the case sides. As a result, the supports tilt downward.

Fixed or Adjustable

The method used to mount a shelf affects how much it will bend under a load. All else equal, a fixed shelf will bend less than an adjustable shelf. That's because on a well-secured fixed shelf, the ends resist both tilting and being pulled inward by the sag (see pp. 8–11 for fixed- and adjustable-shelf options).

Be aware that fixed shelves aren't immune to failure. With enough weight (perhaps adding your spouse's anvil collection to your own on the same shelf) and its consequential sag, even fixed shelves can fail at the ends. When that happens, the shelf curves and effectively shortens, the ends pull free, and everything can head south in a hurry.

JEFF MILLER builds furniture and teaches wood-working in Chicago.

Design Shelves for Maximum Load

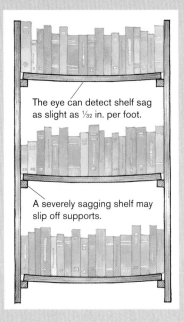

The eye can detect shelf sag as slight as 1/32 in. per foot.

A severely sagging shelf may slip off supports.

Approximate shelf loads:

Hardcover books (9 in. by 11 in.), 20 lb. per ft.

Magazines (9 in. by 11 in.), 42 lb. per ft.

You don't need to guess at how much a shelf is going to sag. The chart below provides a quick way to determine if your shelf will be sag-free. If the chart doesn't work for your shelf, you can use the Sagulator, an online program that makes it easy to determine sag. Both the chart and the Sagulator assume unfixed shelf ends. Fixed ends sag less.

The chart is easy to use. It provides the maximum shelf-weight limits (in pounds per foot) and works for most designs. You need to know the thickness of the shelf (3/4 in. or 1 in.) and its length (24 in., 30 in., 36 in., or 42 in.).

If the expected load exceeds the weight limit shown in the chart, you'll have to make compromises. To do that, use the Sagulator (www.finewoodworking.com/sagulator).

An answer of more than 0.02 in. per foot of shelf means you need to put less load on the shelf; use a stronger wood; make the shelf thicker, wider, or shorter; or add wide edging. With the Sagulator, you can adjust those values and calculate a new sag number.

MATERIAL MAKES A DIFFERENCE. Some shelf materials resist sag better than others. Red oak is one of the better ones, eastern white pine less so. MDF makes a weaker shelf.

SHELF WEIGHT LIMITS (pounds per foot)*

Species	Thickness	24 in.	30 in.	36 in.	42 in.
	TYPE		**LENGTH**		
RED OAK	3/4 in.	49	21	9	5
	1 in.	116	47	23	12
	3/4 in. with 2-in. edging	112	47	21	12
POPLAR	3/4 in.	42	17	8	4
	1 in.	101	41	20	10
	3/4 in. with 2-in. edging	97	39	20	10
EASTERN WHITE PINE	3/4 in.	33	14	6	3
	1 in.	74	32	15	8
	3/4 in. with 2-in. edging	76	32	14	8
FIR PLYWOOD	3/4 in.	32	13	6	3
	3/4 in. with 2-in. edging**	96	39	18	9
MDF	3/4 in.	9	4	2	1
	3/4 in. with 2-in. edging**	73	30	14	7

*Based on 11-in. wide shelves

**Edging is red oak; other edgings are the same wood as the shelf.

Confirmat Screws Add Strength

I'm not a fan of screwing shelves in place with the typical tapered woodscrew. They rarely hold up long-term. That said, I have found a specialized screw that works much better. Called a Confirmat screw, it has a thick body with sharp, deep threads. It's mainly used with particleboard, melamine, and MDF, but it also holds well in solid wood. When used in a dado or a rabbeted dado, the joint strength is excellent. Confirmat screws require a pilot hole and a shank hole. A special bit is available that does the drilling in one step (see "Sources of Supply" on p. 12).

Jig Speeds Biscuiting

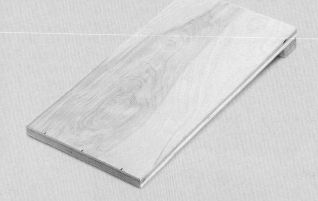

A jig for cutting slots in the sides makes it easy to locate shelves accurately. The jig has just two parts: a cleat and a fence. The cleat keeps the end of the fence square to the side. Centerlines for the slots are marked on the end of the fence. With each new set of shelf slots, the fence is crosscut to a shorter length. Toss the jig when done.

CLAMP AND CUT. Clamp the jig to the case. Cut one set of slots, then use the jig to cut the same slots on the other side. Crosscut the fence to the next shelf position, and repeat until all slots are cut.

Fixed Shelves Sag Less and Strengthen the Case

Fixed shelves attach to the sides of a case with either wood joinery, hardware, or a combination of both. Unlike adjustable shelves, fixed shelves help strengthen the entire case. And because they are attached to the case sides, fixed shelves sag less.

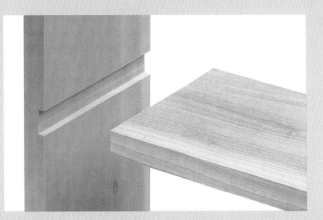

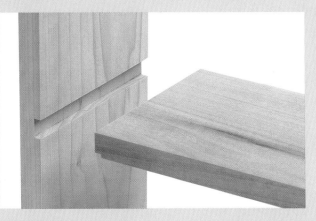

DADO

Strength: Good

Appearance: Good (excellent if using a stopped dado or if covered by a face frame)

A dado joint effectively houses the ends of the shelf in a long notch, providing some mechanical strength. Because a dado joint produces mostly end-grain surfaces, adding glue increases the strength only nominally. The attachment strength of a shelf can be improved further by combining Confirmat screws (see sidebar p.7) with either a dado joint or a rabbeted dado joint. The screws keep the ends of the shelves in the dado, and the dado adds extra shear strength.

RABBETED DADO

Strength: Good

Appearance: Good (excellent if using a stopped dado or if covered by a face frame)

A minor variation on the dado joint is to rabbet the ends of the shelf to fit into a narrower dado. The main advantage is the ability to fit the joint more easily, especially if the shelf thicknesses are inconsistent.

This joint is useful when working with hardwood plywood, a material that typically measures less than ¾ in. thick. In this case, a dado cut by making a single pass with a ¾-in.-dia. straight router bit ends up too wide. However, with a rabbeted dado, you cut a narrow dado first, then the rabbet for a perfect fit.

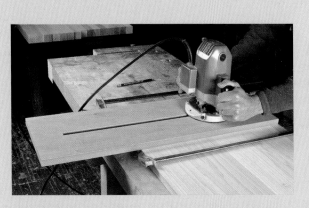

RABBETED DADO STARTS WITH A DADO. A T-square jig helps cut a dado across the side. The slot in the jig is just wide enough to accept the bearing of a top-mounted bearing-guided straight bit.

MARK AND CUT THE RABBET. First, mark the rabbet location on the end of the shelf (above left), then use a bearing-guided rabbeting bit to cut the rabbet (above right).

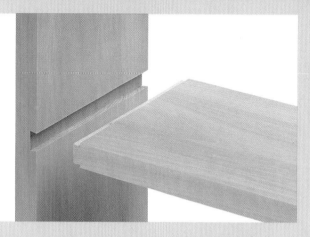

BISCUITS

Strength: Fair

Appearance: Excellent

It's easy to fix a shelf in place using a biscuit joiner. And, because the biscuits are hidden when assembled, there is no joinery, support parts, or hardware to distract the eye. Use at least two biscuits on each end of the shelf. Add a third biscuit if there's room. The jig shown on p.7 is a good one to use here. Invest a few minutes making it and you'll be rewarded many times over by the time saved.

SLIDING DOVETAIL

Strength: Excellent

Appearance: Very good (excellent if stopped, or covered by a face frame)

A sliding dovetail adds considerable mechanical strength, but sliding a 10-in.-long dovetail into a tight-fitting slot before the glue sets up is a challenge. Using a fairly slow-setting epoxy glue will help considerably. Epoxy is a slippery glue that helps get this type of joint together without excessive expansion and stress.

SCREWED CLEATS

Strength: Very good

Appearance: Fair

Screwed cleats let you add shelves without too much fuss, but they come up a little short in the appearance department. With the exception of the hole closest to the front, all of the holes in the shelf should be slotted to accommodate wood expansion. For the same reason, if you wish to glue this joint, bear in mind that you should glue only the front inch or so.

Adjustable Shelves Add Versatility

Adjustable shelves make it easy to change the spacing as needs change. But there is a structural cost: These shelves do nothing to hold the cabinet sides together. So on taller bookcases it's a good idea to have one fixed shelf to help anchor the case sides.

SLEEVE ADDS REFINEMENT AND STRENGTH. You can improve both the appearance and strength of a shelf pin simply by slipping a brass sleeve into the pin hole.

SHELF PINS

Strength: Good (very good with sleeves)

Appearance: Good

Shelf pins come in a wide variety of shapes, sizes, materials, and finishes. My favorites are the machined solid brass ones from Lee Valley®. I also like the very small round pins by Häfele® for smaller cases. Shelf pins also come with special clips for securing the shelves or for holding glass shelves. Sleeves are a great way to recover from poorly drilled holes. Stamped sleeves (short tubes with a flared and rounded-over end) tend to look like shoelace eyelets when installed in a cabinet. Solid brass machined sleeves look better, even though they accentuate the row of holes in the case sides somewhat. Some sleeves are threaded for specially threaded shelf pins (See "A Jig for Pin Holes" on p.12).

HIDDEN WIRES

Strength: Good

Appearance: Very good

These bent-wire supports fit into holes drilled in the case sides. A stopped kerf cut in the ends of the shelf slips over the support, hiding the hardware. Structurally, this means the end of the shelf is thinner. This affects the shelf's shear strength, but will have little effect on sag.

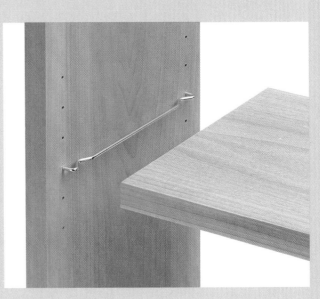

WOODEN STANDARDS

Strength: Very good

Appearance: Very good

Wooden shelf standards have been around in various styles for generations. They are easy to make and add an interesting look to almost any bookcase. The style shown in the upper left photo (I call it zigzag) is one of the more common forms. For more on cutting zigzag supports, see p.12.

Another style (I call it half-moon) is shown in the upper right photo. To make a pair, you'll need a piece of stock that's at least double the width of each standard. Scribe a lengthwise centerline along the stock, then lay out the shelf spacing by making a series of evenly spaced marks along the centerline. Use a spade bit or a Forstner bit to drill a through-hole at each marked centerpoint. Finally, using a tablesaw, rip the stock down the middle. The net result is a pair of standards, each with a series of half-moon shapes. Make the cleats just loose enough to slip in and out with ease.

METAL STANDARDS

Strength: Very good

Appearance: Fair

It's hard to beat metal shelf standards for ease of installation. Just run a pair of dadoes down each side of the case, and nail, staple, or screw the shelf standards into place. Shelf supports usually just hook into place, although one new version has brass support pins that screw into threaded holes in the brass standards. In general, shelf standards seem out of place on finer furniture. But they are great for utilitarian pieces, and even in larger bookcases, where any support system will be pretty much invisible once the shelf is full of books.

A Jig for Pin Holes

SHELF-PIN HOLES IN A JIFFY. Thanks to this shopmade jig, Miller quickly drills shelf-pin holes that are the same depth and perfectly spaced.

Sources of Supply

HÄFELE
800-423-3531
www.hafele.com

McFEELY'S
800-443-7937
www.mcfeelys.com

**LEE VALLEY/
VERITAS®**
800-871-8158
www.leevalley.com

ROCKLER®
800-279-4441
www.rockler.com

Zigzag Support in Three Steps

Start with stock wide enough to make four standards. Using the tablesaw, make a vertical cut at each shelf location (1). An auxiliary miter-gauge fence with a location pin in front (much like a finger-joint jig) makes it easy to position the stock for subsequent cuts. Follow with 45° cuts (2) after relocating the location pin. Remove the triangular waste piece, then clean the resulting flat with a chisel. Rip the stock to create four standards (3).

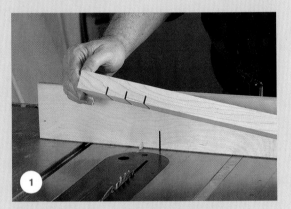

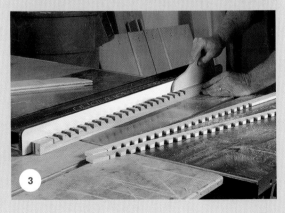

Biscuit Basics

BY TONY O'MALLEY

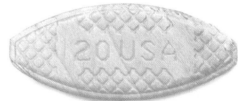

QUICK CASE JOINERY. A biscuit joiner makes fast work of assembling plywood cases. Laying out and cutting the basic slots is easy, especially when using simple alignment jigs.

When I started my first wood-working job in 1984, the biscuit joiner, also called a plate joiner, was just arriving on the shop scene. The company where I learned the trade still was using rabbet and dado joints to assemble plywood case goods. It's a tried-and-true system but one we abandoned forever after discovering the manifold benefits of biscuit joinery.

First, by using biscuit joints instead of rabbets and dadoes, every joint is a butt joint, which makes calculating dimensions from a measured drawing much less painful and error-prone—no more adding and subtracting to account for dadoes and rabbets. Second, biscuit joinery allows you to move a stack of freshly cut parts directly from the tablesaw to the workbench, where all of the joinery work can be done (maybe not a big deal in a one-person shop, but a definite advantage in a shop where coworkers are waiting to use the saw). Third, there's no need for dado blades and the finicky process of getting the fit just right. Fourth, biscuit joinery eliminates the frustrating task of sliding large workpieces across the saw to cut joinery. Sure, you can

THE BASE IS A CONSTANT REFERENCE

Try to rely on the base of the machine as the reference surface. This generally is a better approach because the distance between the blade and the base does not change, whereas the fence is movable.

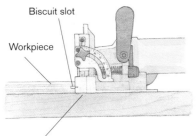

The base serves as the reference surface.

THE STANDARD POSITION IS SHOWN AT LEFT. To cut the mating slots, the workpieces or the tool (above, with the help of a jig) must be positioned vertically.

THE FENCE OFFERS FLEXIBILITY

Make sure your fence is reliable, and be sure the base isn't getting hung up on the benchtop or another workpiece below.

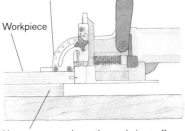

Use a spacer or hang the workpiece off the edge of the bench to ensure that the base is not resting on the benchtop.

FENCE ADDS CONVENIENCE. If the fence is used for both cuts (left and above), the workpieces can remain flat without the need for jigs.

HOW MANY BISCUITS?

A good rule of thumb for carcase construction is to use at least one biscuit for every 6 in. of width. Locate them close to the front and back edges to keep the corners aligned, unless screws are used for assembly.

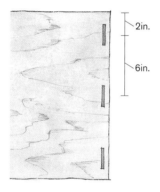

2in.

6in.

LAYOUT TRICKS. For this carcase, only the center of three biscuits must be marked. To locate the outside biscuits, line up the edge of the tool with the edge of the stock. Mark the pieces as a group, first on their ends (above left), carrying the marks onto the faces where necessary (above right).

DRAWER-BOX CONSTRUCTION

Use as many biscuits as possible for strength; configure butt joints as shown to resist stresses of use.

Drawer side

Drawer front

False drawer front, applied afterward, hides plywood edges.

CARCASE CONSTRUCTION

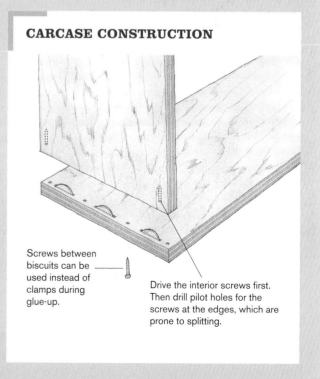

Screws between biscuits can be used instead of clamps during glue-up.

Drive the interior screws first. Then drill pilot holes for the screws at the edges, which are prone to splitting.

CUT SLOTS FOR A SINGLE SHELF OR DIVIDER ALL AT ONCE. **After laying out all of the pieces and cutting slots in the divider or shelf, clamp the case parts together and use a long straightedge as a fence for the tool.**

A JIG TO LOCATE MULTIPLE FIXED SHELVES. **For a symmetrical series of shelves, use a piece of sheet stock that reaches to the center shelf. A small cleat at the end locates the jig accurately each time.**

avoid these last two problems by cutting rabbets and dadoes with a router and T-square guide, but biscuiting is much faster. Fifth, assembling a case with rabbets and dadoes, no matter how finely fit, always requires some extra effort to get the case clamped up squarely—the joints just seem to lean a little bit on their own. A biscuit-joined case, in contrast, almost always clamps up squarely right from the get-go (assuming your crosscuts are square, of course).

But the biscuit joiner's usefulness goes far beyond joining carcases. From strengthening miters to joining panels, from assembling face frames to attaching them to cabinets, this versatile tool can be a major player in your shop's lineup. As a colleague recently observed, the biscuit joiner may be the most significant tool development for the small-shop woodworker since the invention of the router.

I should point out that dovetails and mortise-and-tenon joinery remain the best approaches for solid-wood furniture construction. But the biscuit joiner can handle all of the joints in a basic plywood cabinet—from the case to the shelves or dividers to the face frame, the base molding, and even a drawer—with the exception of the door, which requires traditional joinery for additional strength.

What to Look For in a Biscuit Joiner

Most of the time, the base of the machine can be used as the reference surface for making a cut. In most machines this positions the slot in the center of ¾-in.-thick stock. However, a fence mounted onto the face of the tool provides more versatility in positioning the slot. So it is very important that the machine cut a slot parallel to both its base and its fence; otherwise, joints won't line up properly.

Not all machines are created equal, and it's worth the time and effort to check that a new machine is accurate, and return it if it's not.

Joining Cases and Boxes

When joining parts to form a case or drawer box, the first step is to mark the slot locations on all of the parts. Often, this can be done simply by aligning the two pieces as desired and then drawing a small tick mark across the mating edges. However, for casework, where there are several of the same type of piece—sides and shelves, for example—it helps to develop a system (see the drawings and photos on pp. 14–15).

How many biscuits and where?–Biscuit joints in case goods supplant conventional joints like the dado, the rabbet, and the splined miter. These are long joints, and it seems logical to cram in as many biscuits as possible, but it's not necessary. Biscuits are manufactured by compressing the wood slightly so that upon gluing there will be a predictable amount of swelling. This swelling makes the joint at every biscuit stronger than a conventional wood-to-wood bond. My loose rule of thumb for case material is to use one biscuit for every 6 in. of width.

This is fully adequate, especially when using screws instead of clamps to pull together the cabinet during glue-up. When I can't use screws to clamp and reinforce the joint—when the sides will be exposed—I don't use more biscuits; instead, I position the end biscuits as close to the edge as I can.

Whenever possible, use the base of the tool as a reference–To cut biscuit slots along the edge of a workpiece, you have two choices: You can use the machine's fence or the machine's base to position the slots. Whichever you choose for any given joint, you need to use the same reference for both sides of the joint. Remember, too, that the reference surfaces on the workpieces should be the outside face and edge because they must end up perfectly aligned.

For most biscuiting tasks, you can rely almost solely on the base of the machine as the reference surface. Even on inexpensive biscuit joiners, the base usually is parallel to the blade. However, some fences are less reliable than others in terms of being perfectly aligned with the blade and staying locked in position. It's also easy to rock most biscuit joiners out of alignment when using the fence on the edge of a ¾-in.-thick panel; cutting those same slots with the base of the machine flat on a bench is a more stable and reliable approach.

When using the base as a reference, a biscuit joiner automatically places the center of the slot ⅜ in. from the bottom edge of the stock. To change that dimension, use thin stock such as hardboard to shim the machine or the workpiece to the proper position.

When joining box sides, cutting slots in the ends of panels is simple using the base, but cutting the opposite side of the joint—into the face of the panel—requires either holding the part on end or laying the part flat and orienting the machine vertically. For tall pieces the latter option is easier; so make a simple L-shaped guide to keep the machine perpendicular to the workpiece (see the top right photo on p. 14).

Building and Attaching a Face Frame

Biscuits can be used both for joining face frames and for locating a face frame on a cabinet. When assembling a face frame, use the largest biscuit that the stock will accommodate. In most situations, you don't want part of a cut-off biscuit showing at the corner of the frame. So narrow face-frame stock may require using the small biscuits designed for face frames (they require a smaller cutter). On wider stock, one of the standard three sizes should work fine.

Just a few biscuits to locate a face frame–When attaching face frames to cases, I generally rely on the long glue joint for strength, using a few biscuits to keep the frame from sliding around during the glue-up. A complete row of biscuits up and down every side would be overkill and would make it harder to fit the face frame to the case.

First, cut the slots in the case sides. This can be done before or after the case is assembled. Then glue up the face frame and lay it on the case to check the fit around the edges. Sometimes I build the frame to create a ⅛-in. to ¼-in. overlap on the outside of the case, which is fairly typical of kitchen-cabinet construction. Other designs require that the face frame be flush on the outside. Still other times I allow a very large overlap for scribing a built-in cabinet to a wall. If there is overlap, use plywood or medium-density fiberboard (MDF) shims to raise the base of the biscuit joiner the appropriate amount when cutting the slots in the face frame.

Mitered joints

Miters provide clean-looking joinery in numerous situations. However, having an equal combination of end grain and long grain, miters need more than glue to hold them together for the long run. Biscuits are the perfect way to reinforce them.

There are two different types of biscuited miters, and plywood cabinets use both of them. Face frames often feature flat miters for a picture-frame effect. And base moldings usually have standing miters at their corners. Of course, both types of miters are used elsewhere in woodworking—in boxes, frames, and other moldings—and biscuits can be used for these, too.

Biscuiting flat miters–Once the stock has been mitered, determine which size biscuit will fit best. Be sure to factor in any shaping that may be in store for the assembled frame (rounding over or rabbeting, for instance). Usually, it's necessary that the biscuit be concealed in the stock. Remember that even a #0 biscuit is better than no reinforcement at all.

Biscuiting standing miters–The outside corner on a base-molding assembly is a typical situation for a standing miter reinforced with biscuits. I also use biscuits to reinforce mitered case corners, instead of the more conventional continuous spline. With base moldings, the bottom edge of the stock won't show, so you can use a larger biscuit and let it extend out the bottom. A bigger biscuit gives you a deeper and stronger joint, and the excess is easily trimmed with a flush-cutting saw or utility knife.

The main layout principle is to position the biscuit slots off center, closer to the inside of the miter; otherwise, you risk cutting through the face of the stock.

The best technique for biscuiting standing miters depends on the size of the stock and the configuration of the fence on your machine. Some fences offer a fixed 45° position, while others are adjustable. Some fences have a solid face, while others are an open frame. And the thicker and wider the stock, the more bearing surface you have for the fence to register on.

TONY O'MALLEY makes furniture and built-in cabinetry in Emmaus, Pa.

STANDING MITERS

To use the trusty base as a reference, clamp two pieces with their inside faces together, aligning them carefully. Then the biscuit joiner can rest in the 90° notch to cut slots in both miters.

Biscuits are sized and located to avoid breaking through the outside faces.

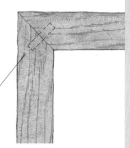

FLAT MITERS

Clamp down workpieces for safe and accurate results. Be sure to keep the tool pressed firmly in place throughout the stroke.

Locating biscuits closer to the inside of the miter allows the outside edges to be profiled or molded.

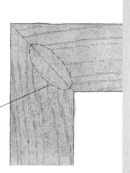

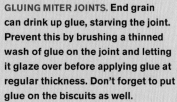

GLUING MITER JOINTS. End grain can drink up glue, starving the joint. Prevent this by brushing a thinned wash of glue on the joint and letting it glaze over before applying glue at regular thickness. Don't forget to put glue on the biscuits as well.

DETERMINE WHERE THE BISCUIT WILL BEGIN AND END. Allow extra room at edges that might be molded later, which could expose the biscuit. Mark the center of the slot, and then transfer the mark to the mating piece.

BISCUITS KEEP PIECES FLUSH

NARROW FRAME PIECES REQUIRE SMALLER, NONSTANDARD BISCUITS. The Porter-Cable 55K Plate Joiner includes a smaller blade for joining pieces as narrow as 1½ in.

BISCUITS ALIGN THE FRAME AND CASE

For an overlapping face frame, offset the biscuits. The stiles on this shop cabinet will overhang the sides by ¼ in., which must be factored in when locating the biscuit slots.

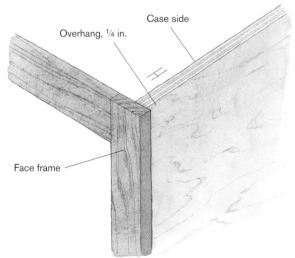

Case side

Overhang, ¼ in.

Face frame

ONLY A FEW BISCUITS ARE NECESSARY. These serve primarily to keep the frame and case aligned during glue-up. Use plenty of clamps to distribute pressure. The glue-up will go more easily if the piece is on its back with room all around for clamps.

A User's Guide to Plywood

BY ROLAND JOHNSON

As much as I enjoy building furniture out of solid wood, there are times when it is not the best choice of material. When I make built-in cabinets or large tabletops, I turn to plywood. Its sandwich structure of thin veneer layers, with the grain oriented at right angles, makes plywood flat and stable. When faced with a high-grade hardwood veneer, plywood looks good and saves time and money.

Plywood also is structurally stronger than natural wood and has excellent screw-holding capabilities. It is also ideal for door panels, frame panels, drawer bottoms, and cabinet backs. As a shop resource, plywood makes strong and stable jigs and fixtures that are inexpensive to build and easy to modify.

How Plywood Is Graded

The best way to buy plywood is to select sheets individually from a dealer with a good inventory. If that is not possible, it helps to know what to ask for.

If you're ordering plywood sight unseen from a distributor, you'll want to specify several things, including the quality of the veneer on the sheet's face and back (the face is generally better looking) and the composition and quality of the plywood's inner core.

The Hardwood Plywood and Veneer Association[SM] (HPVA; www.hpva.org) sets standards for grading hardwood-veneer plywood based on how free the surfaces are of defects such as knots, patches, and color variations. Grades for face veneer begin with AA for the best quality and run down to grade E, which can include unlimited color variations and patches. The back veneer is number graded, with grade 1 being the best and grade 4 allowing knotholes, splits, and other defects.

You also should select plywood with a core that's as uniform and free of voids as possible. In the HPVA grading system, J signifies the best core material with no voids in the plies. Cores step down in quality to grade M.

This system occasionally changes, and other types of plywoods, such as Baltic birch, or ApplePly, use their own grading systems. When in doubt, ask your distributor how the product is graded.

When I order plywood, I prefer to let the lumber dealer determine the correct grade for my application. I tell him what I need, such as cherry veneer-core plywood with plain-sliced veneer, both sides good. Most likely the product will be A1,VC (veneer core) Cherry PS (plainsawn), but that may be simply how my sheet-goods distributor has it set up in the inventory system.

Options for Hardwood-veneer Plywood

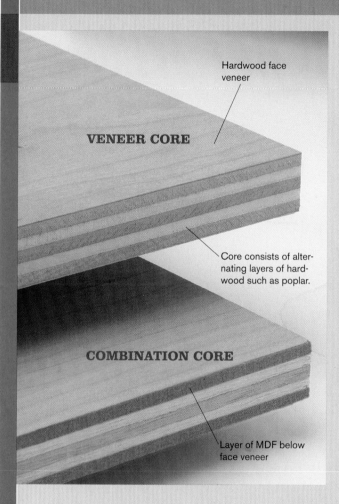

VENEER CORE

Hardwood face veneer

Core consists of alternating layers of hardwood such as poplar.

COMBINATION CORE

Layer of MDF below face veneer

Furniture makers are most likely to use plywood made with a hardwood face veneer. Domestic hardwoods are the most readily available as face veneers, although exotic species may be special ordered.

Veneer-core plywood stays flat, holds a screw well, and is reasonably lightweight. This material is ideal for building cabinet cases. Panels, partitions, and cabinet floors can be cut to size quickly and assembled into strong, light boxes. Veneer-core plywood also can be used to make cabinet tops and tabletops, but they'll need solid-wood edging and a durable finish to protect the thin face layer.

Combination-core plywood has an MDF layer between the inner plies and the hardwood face veneer, which eliminates voids and ensures that grain from underneath won't cause imperfections in the top layer. Combination core can be used anywhere veneer core is used. It's not much heavier than veneer core, with similar screw-holding ability and less tearout when sawing.

Veneer can be taken off the log in several different ways, and each method yields its own distinctive look. The most common types of face veneer are rotary cut; plain, or flat sliced; and rift cut. There are also several methods for matching the veneer on a panel face: book matching, slip matching, and random matching.

CHOOSE FACE VENEERS BY CUT AND MATCH

Book matching is accomplished by turning over every other sheet of veneer for a face that resembles the opened pages of a book, with opposite patterns identical.

Slip matching uses progressive veneer sheets joined side by side, with the same sides facing up. Book matching accentuates the grain, while slip matching tends to appear uniform, more like solid wood.

Random matching is as it sounds. Sheets are randomly assembled, with the chance of veneer from several logs on one face. This method can lend a very real laminated look, but it also can lead to multiple color and grain patterns in one face.

ELEGANCE IN SHEET GOODS. The back and door panels of this cherry cabinet were made from ½-in.-thick veneer-core plywood with a book-matched face.

Choose the Best Core for the Job at Hand

BALTIC BIRCH

Numerous layers of birch, alder, or both yield exceptional stability, strength, and density. Baltic birch is especially suited for building drawers. Check sheet sizes before ordering; several manufacturers produce only 5x5 sheets. Similar products are known as ApplePly, Europly®, Russian, or Polish birch.

MEDIUM-DENSITY OVERLAY (MDO)

MDO combines a veneer core with a top layer of kraft paper impregnated with waterproof glue. This provides a flat, smooth surface favored by outdoor sign makers; it is absolutely waterproof. MDO is great for furniture panels that will be painted or that don't require the look of wood grain. It is ideal for painted outdoor furniture.

BENDING PLYWOOD

Bending plywood can conform to a tight radius without splitting because the grain in all of the veneer layers runs in the same direction. This material is indispensable for making curved doors and panels. Once laminated or veneered (a vacuum bag is best), it will hold the intended shape. Thicknesses range from ⅛ in. to ⅜ in., and species include poplar, birch, okume, and lauan. It comes in 4x8 sheets with grain running either the length or width of the sheet.

Tips on Cutting Big Sheets Safely and Without Tearout

Plywood sheets are awkward and heavy. It's always a good idea to work with a helper while making your first cuts in a full sheet. If help is not available, set up sawhorses with height extensions, movable workbenches, or whatever it takes to support the sheet both before and after the cut.

The worst kickback I have experienced occurred when I tried to rip an edge off a half sheet of plywood without adequate support. The tablesaw sent the half sheet and me flying to the shop floor with damage to both me and the plywood. The floor survived intact.

For ripping or crosscutting plywood cleanly, use a triple-chip blade with a high tooth count (80 teeth on a 10-in. blade is not uncommon). Be aware of the rotation of the blade and the good veneer face of the plywood. When cutting on a tablesaw, the good veneer should face up; with a circular saw, the good veneer should face down.

For especially delicate face veneers that are prone to tearout when crosscutting, I sometimes scribe the face veneer with a sharp utility knife before cutting. This procedure is very fussy, and absolute accuracy is a must, but it does work.

A handheld circular saw will quickly reduce full sheets of plywood into more manageable sizes. If possible, cut the pieces about ⅛ in. to ¼ in. oversize and make the finish cuts on a tablesaw. I use a straightedge clamp (Tru-Grip®) as a guide for the saw.

On the tablesaw, a zero-clearance throat plate will help control tearout, at least when the plate is new and the clearance is

Cutting It Down to Size

RIPPING. **Large sheets can be ripped safely on the tablesaw, but make sure you have plenty of room on the out-feed table.**

WHICH SIDE IS UP?

To minimize tearout, orient the show face down when cutting with a circular saw and up when cutting with a tablesaw.

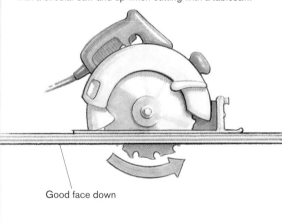

Good face down

Good face up

CROSSCUTTING. **For longer pieces, use a circular saw with an edge guide clamped to the stock (upper right). Shorter stock can be cut on the tablesaw with a crosscut sled (lower right).**

JOINERY FOR PLYWOOD

Plywood cases can be assembled using a variety of joinery techniques, including rabbets, dadoes, and biscuits. A rabbet joint's structure maks a stronger corner than a simple butt joint. Dadoes provide great strength in edge-to-face joinery. Biscuits work well for edge-to-edge or edge-to-face joints. They aren't as strong as dadoes or rabbets, but they're useful for keeping adjoining surfaces properly aligned.

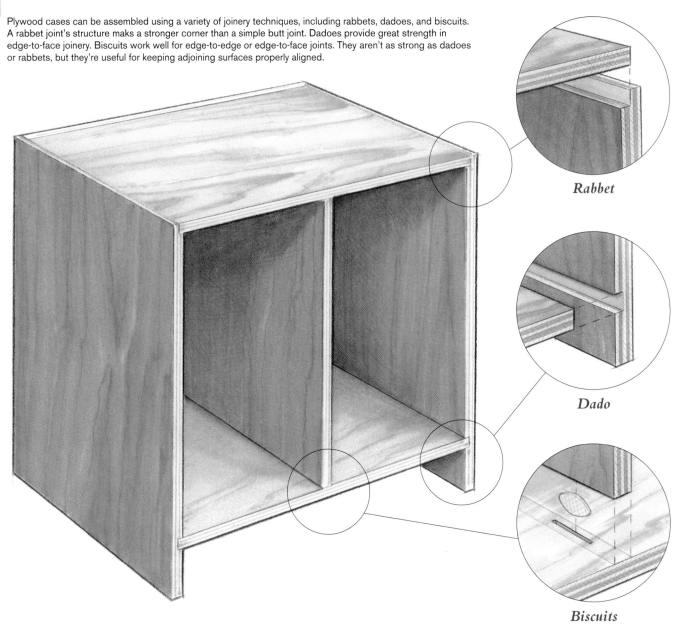

Rabbet

Dado

Biscuits

still close. If you have a large production run that justifies the expense, you might consider a scoring-blade attachment (a small-diameter blade that rotates opposite the main blade and precedes it during the cut) that helps minimize crosscut tearout.

Best Joints for Plywood

Because plywood does not have continuous grain orientation throughout its thickness, it does not lend itself to all of the same construction techniques as solid wood.

Plywood faces can be glued together with good results, but edge-to-edge or edge-to-face joinery must be mechanically or structurally secured.

For joining two edges or an edge to a face, biscuits provide moderate strength. However, because the joint is shallow, it can be pried apart by leverage (heavy books in the midspan of a biscuited shelf, for instance).

Dadoes add great strength in edge-to-face joints, so they are especially effective for use in shelving or cabinet partitions.

Cutting Accurate Dadoes

Plywood rarely measures up to its stated thickness, so standard dado-head widths can yield sloppy joints. For a snug dado, start by gauging the thickness of the shelf or partition. Then install enough chippers to get close to this mark, and use shims to fine-tune the width of the dado.

Another option is to cut dadoes with a router, using a straight bit sized specifically for plywood. A number of manufacturers offer undersize bits to accommodate common plywood widths.

SHIM FOR A PERFECT FIT. Because plywood is often narrower than its stated size, shims are needed to create a dado of the correct width.

Butted corners and edge-to-face joinery without a dado or biscuits need to be mechanically fastened with screws or nails to provide a secure joint.

Half-lap or rabbet joints work reasonably well as long as there is not great twisting pressure applied to the joint, which could cause splits to develop in one or more of the cut veneer layers. This joint has good shear strength, meaning it won't tend to fail when loaded heavily at the point where the two pieces meet.

Edging Hides the Ugly Layer Lines

Because of the layered core, the edge of a sheet of plywood is not particularly attractive. Fortunately, there are several ways to conceal it. Cabinets typically are covered with face frames. Solid or veneer edge-banding usually is applied to shelves or tabletops.

Edge-banding with a heat-sensitive glue back can be purchased in most domestic and some exotic woods. Shopmade solid edge-banding usually is attached to plywood with yellow glue (aliphatic resin). When using thick edge-banding, apply glue to both the banding and the plywood because the end grain readily absorbs glue.

Edge-banding typically is wider than the plywood is thick, so it must be trimmed flush to the plywood's edge. Sounds easy enough, but the process is always a nail-biting experience because of the fear of damaging the plywood. Most often, I trim the edge-banding flush with a well-tuned block plane, working from the sheet out across the banding. With a little practice, it's relatively easy to trim the edge perfectly flush without gouging the face veneer. A router with a flush-trimming bit will work fine, but it's often not as handy to use as a block plane.

A clean surface is an important starting point if the cut edge will be banded. The edge of a sheet of plywood is often damaged or dirty. Try to cut away these

Hiding Unattractive Edges

There are a few ways to hide the wood-sandwich edges of plywood. Solid-wood edging is appropriate for high wear edges, such as on tabletops, and can be profiled with a router after installation. Iron-on veneer tape is adequate for shelving or case partitions. A face frame will give a more refined look.

SOLID-WOOD EDGING

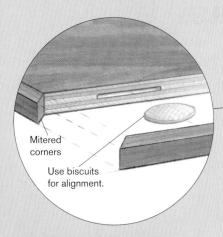

Mitered corners

Use biscuits for alignment.

BISCUITS ALIGN SOLID EDGING. Use card stock as a shim when slotting the plywood (above), but not on the edging. Milled slightly thicker, the edging will stand proud of the top. Plane each edge flush before gluing (below).

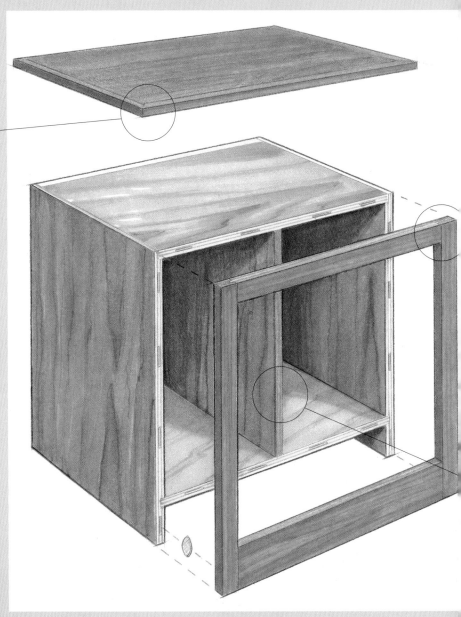

FACE FRAME

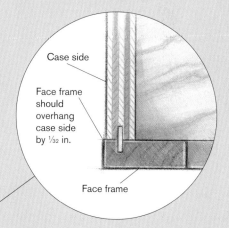

Case side

Face frame should overhang case side by $\frac{1}{32}$ in.

Face frame

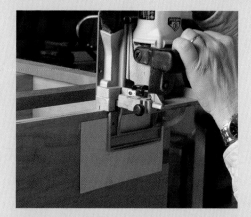

ATTACHING THE FACE FRAME.
To create an even overhang
on each side, use a card-
stock shim when biscuiting
the case (left). Glue and
clamp the face frame to the
case (below).

IRON-ON VENEER

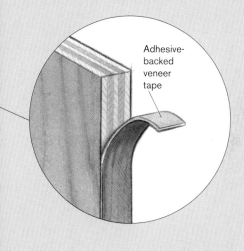

Adhesive-backed veneer tape

IRON-ON VENEER EDGE-BANDING.
The material may be bonded with
the use of a household iron. Trim
the edges flush with a handplane
or specialty trimmer.

damaged edges as you're cutting the plywood to size. Start by ripping a little wider than needed, and then trim the edges for a final cut.

I used to use a belt sander to level edge-banding with the plywood, a risky procedure because it's easy to ruin the plywood face with this aggressive machine. My technique was simple. I scribbled on the plywood with a graphite pencil, making lines that came up to the back edge of the banding and extended 5 in. or 6 in. into the plywood. These reference lines let me know whether the belt sander was staying flat or tipping into the plywood, and saved me lots of veneer sand-through.

Sand With Care

Generally speaking, I'd stay away from sanding plywood with a belt sander. If you're not careful, you could sand through the face before you know it. On the edges, the sander can tip over easily and erase the thin veneer there. I use a random-orbit sander instead.

Always follow the grits in order, and don't skip any. Start with P120 grit to clean up marks and small dings, work quickly up to P150, and finish with P180.

Sand with relatively slow, even strokes. Swirl marks are hard to remove from the thin veneer without doing damage.

ROLAND JOHNSON is a contributing editor to *Fine Woodworking* magazine.

Six Ways to Edge Plywood

BY MARIO RODRIGUEZ

To the world of woodworking, the innovation of plywood ranks right up there with the invention of the tablesaw. It's hard to imagine building some furniture and cabinetry without it. Plywood gives you the relative stability and flatness of a 4x8 panel, combined with the beauty of select veneers. You also get a variety of thicknesses, from ¼ in. to ¾ in. on stock items and up to 1½ in. on special orders—and you get all of this at a reasonable price. The challenge when using plywood is, of course, what to do about that ugly laminated edge. The goal is to create an edge treatment that looks like a continuation of the veneered surface without an obvious seam. You can achieve that goal with a simple layer of veneer or a more complex edge treatment that requires sophisticated joinery techniques.

The decision about how to treat a plywood edge can be influenced by a number of factors—aesthetic and design considerations (how do you want it to look?), function and durability (what kind of wear and tear will this edge face?), time and labor (how much of either do you want to spend?). The choice should depend on the planned use of the furniture piece or cabinet component. For example, a thick, solid edge would be appropriate for the exposed edge of a cabinet carcase. But for shelves contained and protected within a cabinet, an iron-on veneer edge would probably be sufficient. What follows is a look at the choices, from the easiest to apply but least durable to the more complicated versions that take longer but offer more protection.

MARIO RODRIGUEZ is a contributing editor, to *Fine Woodworking* magazine.

Iron-On Veneer Is Easy to Apply

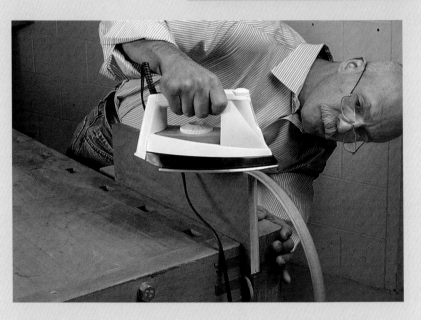

This material, also called edge tape or edge-banding, commonly measures $^{13}/_{16}$ in. wide for use with ¾-in.-thick plywood. It is sold in rolls from 8 ft. to 250 ft. long, and it is available in a number of different woods. Birch, cherry, mahogany, red oak, and walnut are fairly easy to find, but you can also buy it in ash, maple, pine, white oak, teak, and just about any other species of hardwood plywood that is made. Because it's so thin, edge-banding isn't suitable for furniture components that will be subject to heavy use. But once the heat-sensitive glue has melted and cooled and the edge-banding has been trimmed, the seams are virtually invisible. Just remember that heat causes the glue to release, so don't choose edge-banding for pieces that will be exposed to heat.

A standard household iron is the tool of choice for most people who use edge-banding. Set the iron to a medium heat level. While it's warming up, you can cut lengths of banding to size, allowing a little overhang on both ends. Move the iron slowly back and forth, applying a steady pressure until the heat-sensitive glue melts and bonds the edge-banding to the plywood. Some people burnish the banding with a scrap of wood, but I haven't found that technique necessary to get a good bond.

The glue needs to cool before you can trim the banding; otherwise, you end up with a gooey mess. You can trim the edge-banding overhang with a razor blade, a veneer saw, a file or a specialty tool designed for the job (see the photos at right).

IRONING IS SIMPLE AND STRAIGHTFORWARD. A regular household iron set on medium heat is all you need to melt the heat-activated glue on the back of manufactured edge-banding. The material is available in just about any hardwood veneer that is also used to make plywood.

PLYWOOD GUIDES THE CUT. Rodriguez uses a sharp veneer saw to trim edge-banding on small workpieces that he can easily hold with one hand. To direct the cut he keeps the bottom of the saw flat against the plywood.

THE RIGHT TOOL FOR THE JOB. For trimming large quantities of edge-banding, invest in a spring-loaded edge trimmer designed for this task. The one shown here is made by Virutex and sells for about $10*.

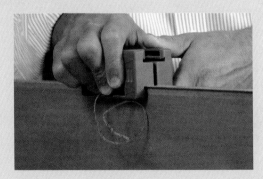

Solid Edging

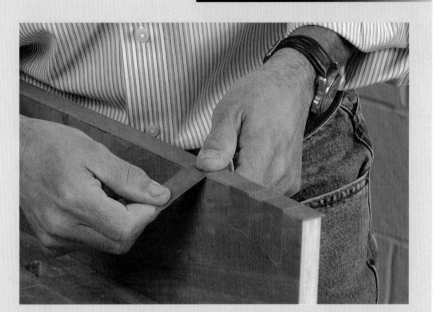

With solid edging you get a thicker edge than you do with iron-on edge-banding, and it requires only a little more work. For ¾-in.-thick plywood, begin by jointing a straight, square edge on a ⅞-in.-thick piece of solid lumber, then rip as many ⅛-in.-thick strips of lumber as you'll need.

I use a sharp 40-tooth rip blade, but a good alternate top bevel (ATB) blade can also do the job. Be sure to back up the cuts with a sturdy push stick to prevent the thin strips trapped between the spinning blade and the fence from shooting back at you. Before ripping each ⅛-in.-thick strip, joint the edge of the lumber. Place the jointed edge against the plywood edge when you glue it up.

After applying a swath of glue to the plywood edge, use a good-quality masking tape to clamp the edging strips in place. Inspect each edge after you tape it. A tight seam with a little bit of glue squeeze-out along the length of the joint indicates a good job. After the glue has dried, trim down the overhang with a block plane and a cabinet scraper.

MASKING TAPE MAKES A GOOD CLAMP. Numerous short pieces of masking tape provide plenty of pressure for gluing wood edging.

TOOLS FOR TRIMMING. Use a block plane to trim most of the excess edging flush to the plywood surface (above). Angle the sole of the plane to achieve a cleaner cut. A cabinet scraper finishes the job (left).

V-Shaped Edging Is Durable and Practically Seamless

This method offers a couple of important benefits. The V shape has an extremely low profile at the seam, making it nearly invisible; and the increased thickness toward the center offers more durability than you get with edge-banding (see the sidebar on p. 32) or even the ⅛-in.-thick treatment (see the sidebar on p.33).

Shape the solid-wood edging first, using a board wider than you need, which makes the process easier and safer. First mark the exact center of the edging material with a marking gauge, then transfer that mark to the bottom edge of a sacrificial plywood fence. Set the tablesaw blade to an angle of 25°, and set up the fence so that the spinning sawblade advances into the sacrificial fence just below the scribed line. Once this setup is ready, you can shape as many edgings as you need, beveling the top and bottom of each piece of lumber by flipping and turning each board around and passing it against the sawblade.

To cut the V shape into the edges of the plywood, leave the blade set at 25° and shift the fence to the other side of the blade. As with any finicky setup, it's best to have some scraps on hand to make adjustments as needed until the cut is aligned. When all of the angled cuts have been made, return the blade to 90° and rip the final pieces of V-molding from all of the lumber that you shaped. You can use masking tape to hold the V-molding in place when you glue it up. Once the glue sets, trim the edges with a block plane and a cabinet scraper.

CUTTING THE BEVELS

Use a ⅞-in.-thick piece of lumber to make a V-shaped edging for ¾-in.-thick plywood.

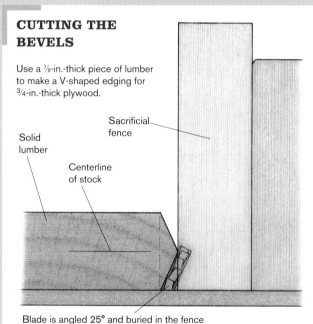

Solid lumber

Sacrificial fence

Centerline of stock

Blade is angled 25° and buried in the fence just below the centerline of the stock.

SHAPING THE PLYWOOD

Move the fence to the other side of the blade to set up the cuts for the V-shape into the edge of the plywood.

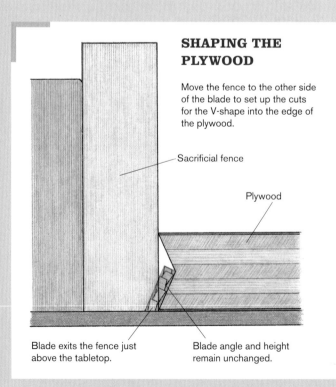

Sacrificial fence

Plywood

Blade exits the fence just above the tabletop.

Blade angle and height remain unchanged.

THIS SETUP IS PRECISE. Transfer the lumber marking-gauge setting to a scrap of plywood. The scrap serves as a sacrificial fence for making the bevel cuts.

A NEARLY INVISIBLE SEAM AT THE EDGE. This alternative edging offers the advantage of showing very little wood at the edge where veneer meets lumber, unlike the effect you get with tongue-and-groove edges (see pp. 36-37).

Three Tongue-and-Groove Edge Treatments

The three common versions of a tongue-and-groove lumber edge for plywood offer the most protection for a plywood edge. A significant advantage of adding a substantial piece of lumber to the edge of plywood is that you can shape that edge in any number of decorative configurations, such as a bullnose, an ogee, or a bevel.

But these edge treatments have a couple of drawbacks. They are time-consuming to carry out, and each of them produces a visibly discernible seam.

You can go about cutting these joints a couple of different ways. You can buy a matched set of router bits to make the required cuts, or you can make all of the necessary cuts on a tablesaw using either a combination blade or a stacked dado set, or both. There's not a lot of room for mistakes when you're setting up these cuts—you must be precise.

I usually begin by plowing the grooves first, using a stacked dado set. Naturally, you must be prepared to make allowances for plywood that is not a full ¾ in. thick, because it rarely is. Plowing the groove from both sides guarantees that it will be perfectly centered, regardless of the actual thickness. After plowing the grooves, clamp a plywood scrap to the fence and reposition it to cut the tongues to fit. I prefer to make the shoulder cuts first, using a combination blade for a clean cut. When gluing up any of the three versions shown here, a clamped, slightly concave batten will give you tighter seams, distribute the pressure more evenly across the span of the edge, and require fewer clamps.

1. GROOVED PANEL

This version provides the most solid wood at the center, for shaping the edge later.

TWO OPTIONS FOR PLOWING GROOVES. A stacked dado set or a straight-toothed rip blade each works well at cutting grooves into the edges of either plywood or solid lumber.

SHAPING LUMBER TONGUES ON THE TABLESAW. Make the shoulder cuts first, with the edge stock flat on the tablesaw. Then turn the stock to a vertical position and run it through the blade again to cut the tongue to size.

START WITH LUMBER LARGER THAN NEEDED. When cutting joints in lumber edge stock, use wider boards and rip the edging down to width later, after shaping all of the joints.

2. GROOVED LUMBER

This method is a little simpler to make but might limit the shapes you can mill into the edge.

SAME PROCESS, BUT THE MATERIALS ARE REVERSED. A grooved lumber edge fitting over a plywood tongue is set up and cut just like its mirror-image cousin.

CUT THE SHOULDERS CAREFULLY. The quality of the joint where the plywood veneer meets the lumber edge is defined by how well the two materials come together. Maintain an even, steady cut for the best results.

3. PLYWOOD SPLINE

A separate spline serves as the tongue to join plywood to lumber.

MATCHING GROOVES. This is the easiest and fastest of the three tongue-and-groove edge treatments to set up and cut. It reduces the joint-making time by half. Properly glued in place, the ¼-in.-thick plywood spline is plenty strong.

Concave Batten Aids Clamping

A CONCAVE BATTEN MINIMIZES THE NUMBER OF CLAMPS. A scrap of wood with a slight bow in it (left) requires fewer clamps to get even pressure along an edge being glued up. A block plane (below) makes quick work of leveling the solid wood.

Shelving, Plain and Simple

BY M. FELIX MARTI

A VERSATILE DESIGN FOR A VARIETY OF USES. These shelves can be sized to fit any location.

A s unassuming as these shelves are, they have many of the features that I like most in furniture. They're lightweight, sturdy, and use simple, effective joinery. The design I use evolved partly from childhood memories of shelves in our house and partly from the built-in storage-shelf system that I now install in houses. Plastic laminate glued to both sides of medium-density fiberboard (MDF) or particleboard makes the shelving stiff. Tight-fitting dado joints and front and rear uprights at right angles to each other make the assembly strong and resistant to racking.

Laminate Shelf Stock First, and Then Cut to Size

I glue the plastic laminate to a sheet of ⅝-in. particleboard or MDF. Melamine could be a less-expensive and, perhaps, a less-stiff alternative, but I have not used it for my shelves. A cabinet-component manufacturer is a good source of laminated stock if you don't want to make it yourself.

With a new shopmade throat plate in my tablesaw, I cut the shelves to size using a Forrest Duraline HI-A/T blade made specifically for cutting double-sided laminated stock (Forrest Manufacturing Company, Inc.; 457 River Road, Clifton, NJ 07014; 800-733-7111). There is virtually no chipping on the down side of the shelf stock.

Dado Material for Corner Uprights

I lay out the shelf spacing on a 9-in.-wide oak board. This width will yield four 2-in.-wide upright corner posts with allowance for kerfs and some cleanup. Using a ½-in. down-shear bit in my router and the jig shown in the top sidebar on the facing page, I plow ¼-in.-deep dadoes across the full 9-in. width. The down-shear bit makes a clean cut, and careful jig construction yields a dado so tight I have to tap the uprights onto the shelf stock. Then I rip this board into pieces a little wider than 2 in., which I feed on edge through a planer to produce uniform finished widths. Finally, I round over the corners and edges.

Assemble Shelves and Uprights

I now fit the shelf into the dadoes of the upright pieces, so the shelf is flush with the edge of the upright. I drill through the corner uprights using a tapered bit and counterbore. I use a 2-in. particleboard (not drywall) screw to fasten the pieces together. The deeper thread of the particleboard screw makes a strong joint. An oak plug glued into the counterbore finishes this simple connection.

For the shelf-nosing stock, I plane a wide board a hair thicker than the thickness of the shelves and cut it to length. On my router table, I round over the ends and edges

of this board for the front nosing and rip the rounded edge to a ¼-in. thickness. I round over this fresh edge on the router table and rip the next ¼-in. piece, alternating between router table and tablesaw until I have enough nosing for the job.

I glue and staple the nosing to the shelf edges using a narrow-crown pneumatic stapler. The nosing is applied as shown in the bottom sidebar on the facing page. To me, the effect is a fully nosed shelf let into the uprights. A scraper flushes the nosing to the shelf surface. Using dry stock for the nosing guarantees that it won't shrink away from flush later.

By maintaining sharp planer knives and feeding stock slowly on the router table, I've just about eliminated any sanding. To complete the job, I apply a penetrating oil finish and fill the small wounds left by the staples with a crayon-type putty stick.

Try Different Materials or Knockdown Construction

I could get very different results by using the same basic idea and unusual materials. Marble or glass could be epoxied into dadoes in wood or metal uprights, or different woods could be used for the shelves and uprights (although I'd be concerned about shrinkage in the shelf thickness, which would reduce the effectiveness of the dado joint). For a knockdown version, I'd use threaded inserts in the shelves and machine screws instead of particleboard screws. Buttons would conceal the screws.

I'm pleased with the low cost, appearance, and strength of these units—happily, so is my wife, who has surrounded her weaving studio with them.

M. FELIX MARTI is a designer and builder in Ridgway, Colo.

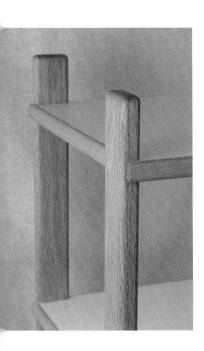

DESIGN GUARANTEES STRENGTH. Front and rear uprights, oriented at right angles to each other, provide lateral stability.

Router Jig Ensures Tight-Fitting Joints

To rout dadoes in stock for corner uprights, the author builds a jig to suit the exact shelf thickness. The stock is then ripped to width.

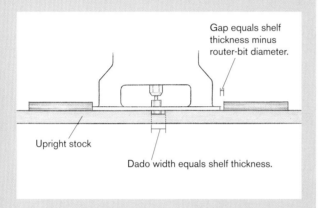

Gap equals shelf thickness minus router-bit diameter.

Upright stock

Dado width equals shelf thickness.

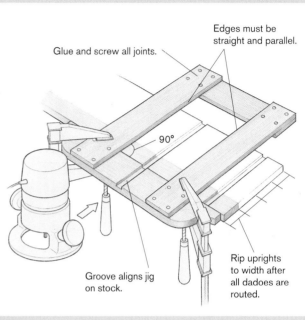

Glue and screw all joints.

Edges must be straight and parallel.

90°

Groove aligns jig on stock.

Rip uprights to width after all dadoes are routed.

Shelf Assembly

Align shelves flush with uprights, as shown, and fasten with a particleboard screw. A plug covers the screw head. Glue and staple (or brad) the nosing to cover the raw edges and dadoes.

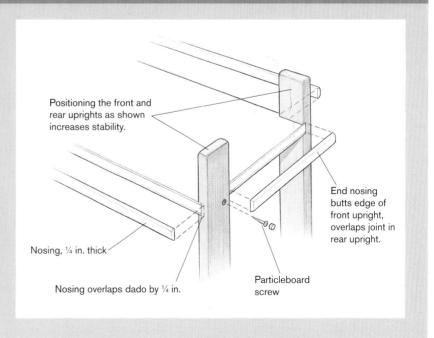

Positioning the front and rear uprights as shown increases stability.

End nosing butts edge of front upright, overlaps joint in rear upright.

Nosing, ¼ in. thick

Nosing overlaps dado by ¼ in.

Particleboard screw

Shaker Wall Shelf

BY PETER TURNER

SHAKE UP YOUR WALL WITH A SHELF. This simple wall-hung shelf, perfect for a spice rack or seashells, was adapted from a traditional Shaker design. The shelves are joined to the sides with sliding dovetails.

My wife, Colleen, occasionally asks me to build a piece of furniture for our home. I would love nothing more than to honor these requests, but there never seems to be time. But a hanging shelf is one project that I figured I could finish quickly.

I got the inspiration from a drawing of a peg-hung Shaker shelf in Ejner Handberg's book, *Shop Drawings of Shaker Furniture and Woodenware, Vol II* (Berkshire Traveller Press, 1975). The shelf sides in Handberg's drawing are curved on top, but the bottom is straight. I added another curve at the bottom, experimenting with different curves until one satisfied my eye. Handberg's Shaker shelves also hung from a wall-mounted peg rail. I don't have a peg rail at home, so the first time I made this piece, I used brass keyhole hangers. In later versions, including the one shown on the facing page, I used simpler brass hangers mortised into the second shelf from the top. These are less expensive, easier to install and make hanging the shelf a snap. We use one hanging shelf as a spice rack. The varying heights and sizes of our spice jars helped establish the shelf spacing and overall width.

Consistency is the key to this piece. If you start with flat stock of uniform thickness and length, the joinery follows smoothly. To ensure consistency, do all your milling at once (all the stock is ½-in. thick), and use a plywood pattern and flush-trimming router bit for making identical curved and tapered sides.

The trickiest parts of this piece are the sliding dovetails. Routing the grooves is easy, but the long tails on the ends of each shelf take some patience and finesse. I use a router setup in which the router is mounted horizontally; it seems to make it easier to get a straight, even cut (see the drawings on p.45).

By holding the pieces flat on the router table, I have more control as I slide the piece past the bit. I make test pieces out of scrap, which I milled at the same time as the final pieces.

The Shakers housed the shelves in dadoes, rather than sliding dovetails, and you can do the same. It won't be as strong, but if you're worried about the shelves, you can toenail them from the bottom with finish nails or brads.

PETER TURNER builds custom furniture in Portland, Maine.

Shaker Shelf Updated

Traditional, peg-hung Shaker wall shelves often have a slight curve at the top and taper from top to bottom. This shelf has a curve at the bottom also, and only the top half is tapered. The piece can be modified by changing the width or the shelf arrangement.

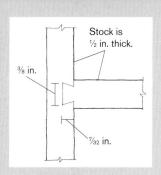

Stock is ½ in. thick.

⅜ in.

⁷⁄₃₂ in.

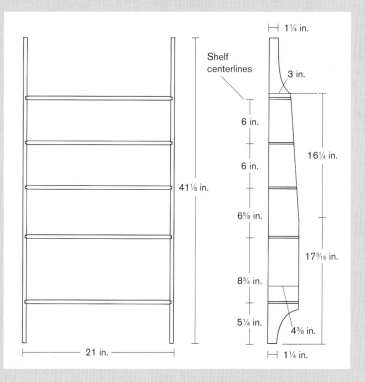

1¼ in.

Shelf centerlines

3 in.

6 in.

6 in.

16¼ in.

41⅛ in.

6⅝ in.

17³⁄₁₆ in.

8¾ in.

5¼ in.

4⅜ in.

21 in.

1¼ in.

Wall Shelf Step-by-Step

STEP 1

ROUTING DOVETAIL GROOVES IN THE SIDES: After mill-ing all the material to a thickness of ½ in., cut the sides to length, but leave them at least ¼ in. wider than the widest dimension (4⅜ in.). Then mark the centerlines for each shelf on both pieces. Using a slotted piece of plywood to guide a ½-in. router template insert, cut the dovetail slots. First rough the slots with a ¼-in. straight bit, and finish them off with a ⅜-in. dovetail bit.

STEP 2

TRACE THE PATTERN, AND BANDSAW THE SIDES: With the grooves routed, cut the curved and tapered sides. First make a plywood pattern matching the shape of the sides of the shelf, trace the pattern onto the back of each side, and bandsaw the shape close to the line.

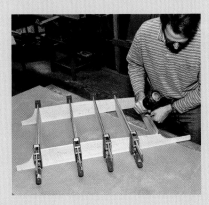

STEP 3

FLUSH-TRIMMING BIT MAKES BOTH SIDES IDENTICAL: After roughing out the sides on the bandsaw or jigsaw, clamp each side into the plywood pattern using hold-down clamps fastened to the ply-wood. Then rout the edge with a ½-in. flush-trimming bit, either using a router table or a hand-held router setup. This step will remove any tearout created when you routed the dovetail grooves, and it makes each side identical.

STEP 4

ROUTING THE DOVETAILS ON THE SHELVES: To cut the dovetails, mount your router horizontally on the router table (see the drawing on the facing page). This makes it easier to adjust the height of the cut. It also lets you hold the workpiece flat on the table rather than against a fence. Adjust the depth and height of the router bit to match the depth of the slots. I cut the tails to fit by trial and error, test-ing on scrap stock milled at the same time as the shelf parts.

STEP 5

CUT SHELVES TO WIDTH AND ASSEMBLE: Don't cut the shelves to width until after you cut the dovetails on the ends, so you can remove any tearout caused by the router. The front edge of the top three shelves is angled to match the tapered sides, which you can do by transferring the angle to the jointer fence. After sand-ing all the pieces, slide each shelf into the sides, starting at the bottom and clamp-ing each shelf as you go.

HORIZONTAL DOVETAILING FIXTURE MAKES A DIFFICULT JOINT EASY

Cutting sliding dovetails can be tricky. To get a long tail to slide snugly into its groove requires a uniform cut. Rather than holding the shelves vertically to cut the dovetails, you can mount the router horizontally on a standard router table, as shown. Holding the workpiece flat on the table, cut one side of the tail; then turn the piece over, and cut the other side. Use scrap of the same thickness to establish the exact height and depth of the dovetail bit, and then fit them in a test groove to prevent marring the final pieces.

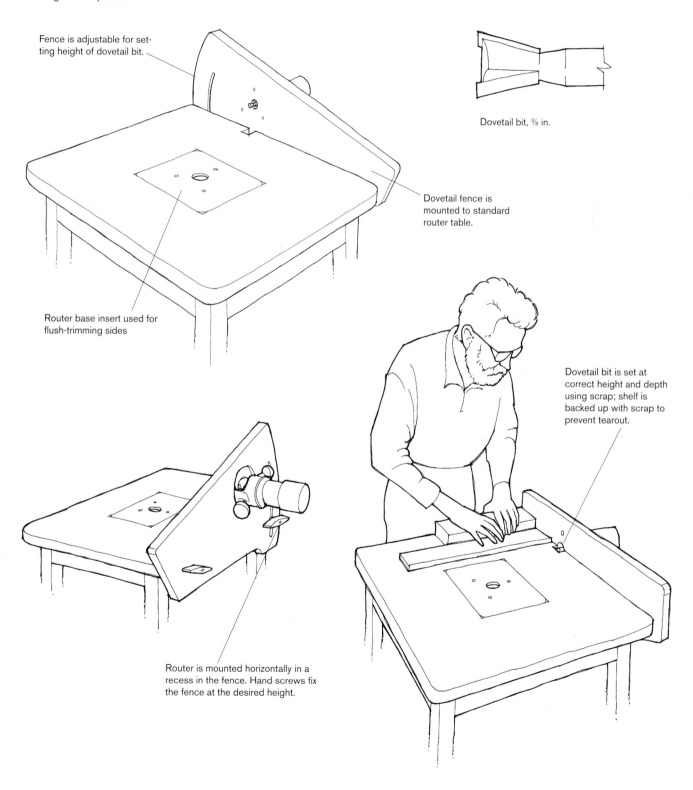

Fence is adjustable for setting height of dovetail bit.

Dovetail bit, ⅜ in.

Dovetail fence is mounted to standard router table.

Router base insert used for flush-trimming sides

Dovetail bit is set at correct height and depth using scrap; shelf is backed up with scrap to prevent tearout.

Router is mounted horizontally in a recess in the fence. Hand screws fix the fence at the desired height.

Arts and Crafts Wall Shelf

BY NANCY HILLER

While looking through a book on home design several years ago, I noticed a small cabinet hanging above a claw-foot bathtub. With its inlaid columns and beveled caps, the shelf was wonderfully British in style and was quite distinct from American interpretations of Arts and Crafts design. Although the original cabinet had a pair of doors, its shallowness seemed more suited to open shelves.

The design of this cabinet may be simple, but making it involves using a number of valuable techniques such as mitered joints for the columns, decorative inlay, and a finish for quartersawn oak that makes new work look old. Although quartersawn oak is the traditional choice for English Arts and Crafts furniture, this piece would look equally good if it were made of cherry or nonfigured maple.

Mitered Columns Showcase Oak Grain

The columns are the focal point of this piece. They are hollow, made of three vertical boards mitered together at the front

ANATOMY OF A WALL SHELF

The foundation of this simple but stylish wall shelf is the columns, which are dadoed for the shelves, mortised for the stretcher, and rabbeted for the backboards. The British-flavored end caps are also anchored to the columns.

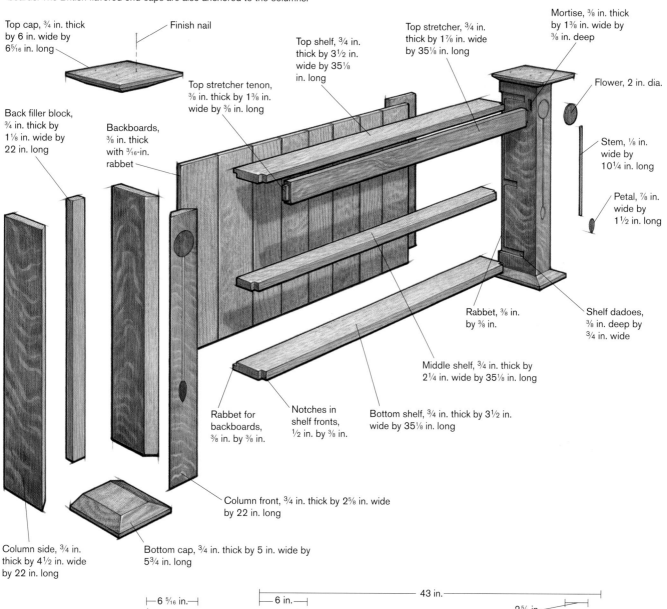

Top cap, ¾ in. thick by 6 in. wide by 6⁵⁄₁₆ in. long

Finish nail

Top shelf, ¾ in. thick by 3½ in. wide by 35⅛ in. long

Top stretcher, ¾ in. thick by 1⅞ in. wide by 35⅛ in. long

Mortise, ⅜ in. thick by 1⅜ in. wide by ⅜ in. deep

Flower, 2 in. dia.

Top stretcher tenon, ⅜ in. thick by 1⅜ in. wide by ⅜ in. long

Back filler block, ¾ in. thick by 1⅛ in. wide by 22 in. long

Backboards, ⅜ in. thick with ³⁄₁₆-in. rabbet

Stem, ⅛ in. wide by 10¼ in. long

Petal, ⅞ in. wide by 1½ in. long

Rabbet, ⅜ in. by ⅜ in.

Shelf dadoes, ⅜ in. deep by ¾ in. wide

Middle shelf, ¾ in. thick by 2¼ in. wide by 35⅛ in. long

Rabbet for backboards, ⅜ in. by ⅜ in.

Notches in shelf fronts, ½ in. by ⅜ in.

Bottom shelf, ¾ in. thick by 3½ in. wide by 35⅛ in. long

Column front, ¾ in. thick by 2⅝ in. wide by 22 in. long

Column side, ¾ in. thick by 4½ in. wide by 22 in. long

Bottom cap, ¾ in. thick by 5 in. wide by 5¾ in. long

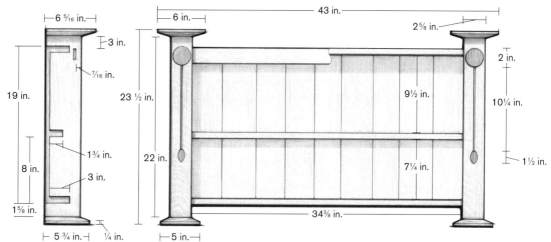

6⁵⁄₁₆ in.

3 in.

⁷⁄₁₆ in.

19 in.

1¾ in.

8 in.

3 in.

1⅝ in.

5 ¾ in.

¼ in.

6 in.

43 in.

2⅝ in.

23 ½ in.

2 in.

9½ in.

10¼ in.

22 in.

7¼ in.

1½ in.

5 in.

34⅜ in.

Miter and Glue Up Hollow Columns

This method of construction allows the hallmark Arts and Crafts ray-fleck figure to appear on each face.

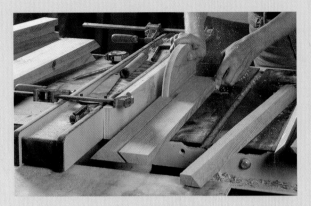

ATTACH AN AUXILIARY FENCE. Using a supplemental fence on a right-tilt saw prevents the thin, already mitered edge from creeping under the sliding rip fence (above).

INSERT THE FILLER PIECE IN THE BACK. Once the back is in place, use bar clamps to apply pressure (left).

START CLAMPING AT THE FRONT OF THE COLUMN. Because the pieces that form the column are now cut to length, make sure to get the ends level with each other (above).

corners so that the quartersawn figure is visible on each face, with a fourth board inserted as a back filler.

Even if you are not using oak, these mitered corners will give the columns a much cleaner look than simple butt joints. While you certainly could use a single, thick block of wood for the columns, doing so seems clumsy for a delicate piece of furniture, and the columns would be less stable when subjected to seasonal changes in humidity.

Cut the miters in one pass on the tablesaw, holding the board down firmly all the way along the cut. If it lifts even a little or wanders away from the fence, the mitered edge will not fit tightly.

After cutting the miters, you can go ahead and cut the pieces to length. Dry-clamp one of the columns to work out any kinks in the process. Now you are ready to glue them.

There are a number of ways to approach this glue-up, but the method I use has proven efficient and easy for somebody working alone, and it yields great results. I use Ulmia picture-framing miter clamps (www.garrettwade.com or www.collinstool.com)

because they are lightweight and easy to handle. While the pointed ends of the wires do leave small indentations in the wood, the coarse grain of the oak distracts the eye enough that the marks disappear when filled with wood putty.

I match the putty to the piece only after the third step of the finishing process. If you don't want to buy Ulmia clamps or if you are using a finer-grained lumber such as maple or cherry, you can use tape or picture-framer's miter clamps to avoid these marks.

As soon as each column's miters are clamped, insert and clamp the filler board at the back. After the glue is dry, run the back face of each column over the jointer to level the joints.

Rout the Shelf Dadoes, Rabbets, and Stretcher Tenons

The shelves will be housed in stopped dadoes routed into the columns. Mark the columns and rout the dadoes while the two

Cut the Dadoes and Rabbets

ROUT SHELF DADOES WHILE COLUMNS ARE CLAMPED TOGETHER. **Clamp a straightedge to the columns to guide the router (above).**

ROUT A RABBET FOR THE BACKBOARDS. **A rabbeting bit works well, with the guide bearing running against the side of the column. Stop the rabbet in the shelf dadoes.**

SQUARE THE DADO. **Use a chisel to square up the front edge of the dadoes by hand (above).**

Assemble the Shelf

CLAMPING THE CASE. Use enough pressure to pull the shelves into their housings, but avoid excessive strain on the hollow columns (left). Apply finish to the parts before screwing the backboards in place (above).

columns are clamped together. When marking the dadoes, there are two things you must remember: Because the center shelf is set back more than the other shelves, its dado begins farther back than the dadoes for the top and bottom shelves; and all of the dadoes are stopped short of the shelf fronts to accommodate the notch in the front of the shelf.

Cut the dadoes in one or two passes using a ¾-in. straight bit, guiding the router with a straightedge clamped to the work. With a chisel, square up the front ends of the dadoes.

While milling stock for the shelves (after you have finished cutting the dadoes), be attentive when you get close to ¾ in. thick and keep checking the stock against the dado. The fit should be hand-tight, requiring some pressure to push the stock home but not so tight as to need heavy pounding with a mallet.

Next, rout a rabbet for the backboards on the underside of the top shelf and on the upper side of the bottom shelf. The columns also need a rabbet to hold the backboards. When cutting the rabbets in the columns, stop them in the upper and lower shelf dadoes. Check how everything lines up.

The top stretcher will be tenoned into the columns. The small mortises for these stub tenons can be cut using a router guided by its own fence or just drilled out and then finished with a chisel. I cut the stub tenons by hand with a backsaw.

Fit the Shelves

When the piece is finished, there will be three distinct shelf setbacks. The top shelf will have a stretcher in front of it, so even though the top and bottom shelves are cut to the same depth, the top shelf will sit nearly at the front of the column. The bottom shelf, which does not have a stretcher,

ROUTE TWO DEPTHS FOR HANGING HARDWARE. The first step will hold the hardware, while the deeper step allows the hanging screw to be inserted.

ATTACH THE END CAPS. Countersink the finish nails and fill the holes with matching wood putty.

will be set back about ¾ in. more, and the center shelf will be the farthest back.

Cut the shelves to size, remembering to rip the center shelf narrower than those at the top and bottom in order to accommodate the extra setback as well as the backboards. Mark out for the notch on the front edge and use a backsaw to remove the waste, or you can cut these notches and the joints for the stretcher on the tablesaw. Test-fit the shelves in their dadoes.

Create the Decorative Inlay and Assemble the Case

I do my inlay with the aid of a magnifier that mounts to my workbench. The first step is cutting out the templates (using card stock) for the flower and the leaf. Select a species that will show up against the background wood (for more about the inlay technique, see the sidebar on pp. 52–53).

At this point, the piece should be ready to dry-fit. First, sand all of the parts to P180

grit. Dry-fit first and then glue the front stretcher and the shelves into place at the same time. The stretcher should also be glued and clamped to the front edge of the top shelf. When the assembly is dry, sand the entire piece to P180 grit.

While the columns are the visual anchor, the beveled end caps give the piece its British flair. Cut the caps and bevel them on the tablesaw.

Now mill the backboards, rabbeting alternate edges on the tablesaw. Sand the backboard faces and use a block plane to work a small bevel on the front edge of each board. Apply finish to the backboards. Once all the other parts also have been finished, attach the backboards using small screws.

When the shelf is completely assembled, rout the slots for hanging and install the hardware. Attach the caps to the columns with finish nails.

NANCY HILLER owns and operates NR Hiller Design Inc. in Bloomington, Ind.

A Simple Inlay Technique

Prepare the inlays by resawing stock (on the tablesaw or bandsaw) to ³⁄₃₂-in. thickness. Regular commercial veneer is too thin and doesn't leave any margin for error.

Trace the outline onto the inlay stock and cut each part to shape, using a scrollsaw or a coping saw, files, and coarse sandpaper. After the inlays are shaped, mark the position of the flower and leaf on each column, taking care to center them in the width and align each element with the other. You can use double-sided tape to ensure that the inlays don't slip out of position while you are scribing around them. Score the outline with a sharp knife or awl. Carefully rout out the main portion of the recess, using a ¼-in. straight bit set at just less than ³⁄₃₂ in. deep.

Pare away the remaining waste with carving gouges and a knife, making sure the bottom of the recess is uniformly flat. Cut the recess for the stem using a ⅛-in. straight bit (also set at slightly under ³⁄₃₂ in.), and a router equipped with a fence.

Using yellow glue, with cauls to distribute clamping pressure, glue in the flower and leaf. After the glue is dry, sand them flush. Finally, trim the stem to fit and glue it in place.

SCORE THE OUTLINE. Press lightly at first to avoid getting caught in the grain, then more deeply a second and third time.

REMOVE MOST OF THE RECESS. Rout close to the inlay border, leaving a bit of waste to clean up by hand.

PARE TO THE LINE. Carving gouges make it easy to clean up and shape the recess accurately.

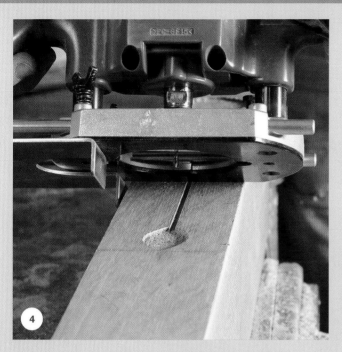

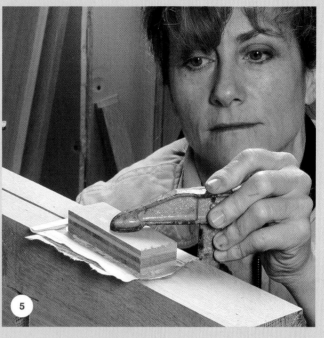

ROUT FOR THE STEM. After routing the groove, rip stock to fit tightly into it.

GLUE IN THE FLOWER AND LEAF. Use a caul to apply even pressure. Newspaper prevents the caul from sticking to the inlay.

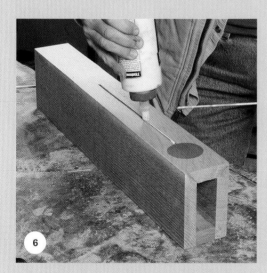

INSERT THE STEM AND FINISH UP. Glue and clamp the stem in place (above). Once the glue is dry, scrape and sand the inlay flush (right).

Bookcase Made With Biscuit Joinery

BY PETER TURNER

A SMALL BOOKSHELF.
This bookcase is made of
solid cherry, joined with
#10 biscuits.

BOOKCASE WITH V-SHELVES

All parts of this bookcase are made from ½-in.-thick material. The shelves are joined to the sides with #10 biscuits. The lengths of all three shelves should be the same and the ends of the V-shelves dead even.

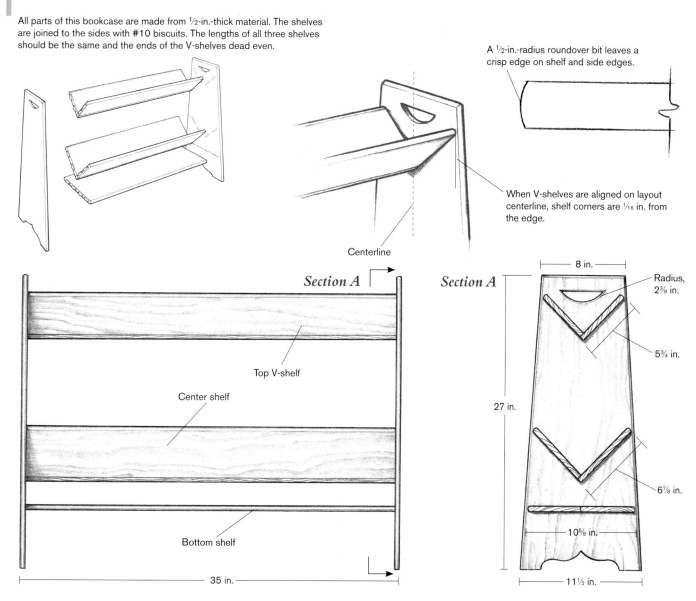

A ½-in.-radius roundover bit leaves a crisp edge on shelf and side edges.

When V-shelves are aligned on layout centerline, shelf corners are ¹⁄₁₆ in. from the edge.

Centerline

Top V-shelf

Center shelf

Bottom shelf

Section A

35 in.

Section A

8 in.

Radius, 2⅜ in.

5¾ in.

6⅞ in.

10⅝ in.

27 in.

11½ in.

urniture with few design flourishes benefits from wood that has lots of figure. When I build simple bookcases like this one, I look for cherry with bold grain patterns, which I often find when sifting through stacks of No. 1 and No. 2 common grades. Using lumber with beautiful figure, selecting and matching all the stock, is really my favorite part of furniture making. I modeled this bookshelf after one that once belonged to my great-grandmother. It's a small, easy-to-build piece whose few design details are quite simple. For the joinery, I use #10 biscuit joints for everything. All the pieces are ½ in. thick, which gives the bookshelf a light and delicate look.

Roughing Out All the Pieces

When picking lumber for this project, I select stock that's at least 7 in. wide, so each half of a V-shelf requires only one plank (see the drawing above). You can edge-join two boards for the sides and bottom shelf, or you can use single boards if your stock is wide enough. If I edge-join two boards for the sides, I make sure that the glueline ends up in the exact center.

THESE JOINTS HOLD THE CASE TOGETHER. The V-shelves are joined at 90° to each other. Biscuit slots cut in the ends of the shelves join them to the case sides.

I begin by flattening, edge-jointing, then thickness-planing all my stock down to ⁹⁄₁₆ in. Then I pick through the boards and find the best matches to make up the two sides and bottom shelf. I glue up the sections using pipe clamps. After the glue is dry, I clean up any squeeze-out and joint one edge of each side and the bottom shelf. Then I select the boards for the two V-shelves, joint one edge and rip them slightly oversize on the tablesaw.

At this point, I run the lumber through a thickness sander until everything is ½ in. thick. I prefer a sander because on highly figured woods, my planer produces tearout. You could, of course, thickness-plane the boards, and take care of any blemishes with handplanes and scrapers. Once all the stock has been sanded to ½ in., I rip it to final width on the tablesaw.

Using the sliding crosscut sled on my tablesaw, I cut the sides and shelves to length. It's critical that the shelf components all be square and exactly the same length. The joint between the shelves and ends are what will make or break this piece, so be sure your crosscut sled is right on.

I taper the sides using a homemade jig on my tablesaw (see the sidebar on the facing page). The jig is just a piece of plywood with a few guides screwed to it at an angle. To use the jig, I place it flush against the tablesaw's fence and nudge the fence toward the blade until the left side of the jig just touches the blade. I lock the fence, place one of the sides in the jig and screw a piece of scrapwood onto the right-side guide to act as a hold-down. I cut the taper by pushing the jig along the tablesaw fence (see the top photo on the facing page).

To cut the opposing taper, I flip the workpiece on its other face, place the cutoff against the right edge of the workpiece and, finally, place a shim the same thickness as my tablesaw blade between the cutoff and the jig guide (see the lower photo on the facing page). I make sure all the pieces are snug, attach a hold-down and cut the taper.

Join V-Shelves and Shape Edges

With all the pieces cut to size, it's time to join the V-shelves and cut the biscuit slots in the sides that will fasten the shelves. First I join the V-shelves. I use four biscuits per shelf, evenly spaced. For each V-shelf, one set of slots is cut in the edge of one board, and the mating set is cut into the face of the other board.

To glue up the V-shelves, I use scrap along the faces where the clamps are positioned to protect the wood. I'm not worried about the edges because they get shaped later. When I tighten the clamps, I use a try square to check that the pieces stay 90° to each other (see the left photo on the facing page). I use four clamps for each shelf, each clamp positioned over a biscuit joint. The ends of each V must be dead even. When the glue is dry, I rip each wing of each V-shelf to its final width on the tablesaw.

The long edges of both V-shelves and all edges of the sides, excluding the feet and cutouts, are rounded over leaving a crisp edge where the roundover meets the edge of the board. To get that shape, I set my router-table fence slightly past the outside edge of the pilot bearing on a ½-in.-radius roundover bit. I use hold-downs and featherboards to make sure the stock passes firmly and squarely over the bit. Because all the stock for this project is ½ in. thick, I only have to set up once. When all the edges are machined, I lightly scrape and sand them to get a fair roundover, being careful not to soften the edges.

Slots in Sides and Shelves Need to Match

I first cut all the slots in the shelves with the biscuit joiner. The shelves have four slots cut on each end. After I cut these, I'm careful not to get carried away and erase the layout marks until I have transferred them onto the sides.

To mark the location of the mating slots on the bookcase's sides, I use the V-shelves as layout guides. First I draw a vertical centerline on the inside face of each side.

Simple Jig for Cutting Tapers

RIP ONE SIDE. A hold-down screwed to the right guide of the jig keeps the workpiece snug when sawing (above).

CUTTING THE OPPOSITE TAPER. Place a shim the thickness of the sawblade against the right guide, then the cutoff and, last, the workpiece, which is turned over on its other side.

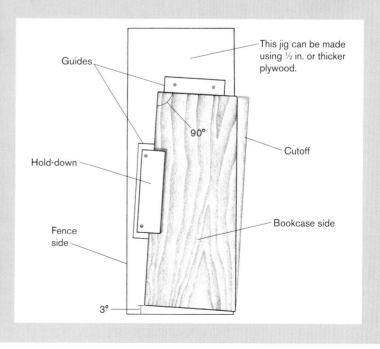

Guides

This jig can be made using ½ in. or thicker plywood.

90°

Cutoff

Hold-down

Fence side

Bookcase side

3°

Use V-Shelves as Layout Guides

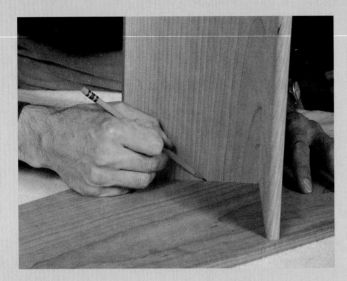

MARK THE INSIDE FACES OF THE SIDES. Transfer the biscuit slot marks from the shelves to the sides (above).

MARK THE OFFSETS FROM THE LINES JUST TRACED. These new marks are used to position a straightedge for the biscuit joiner (right).

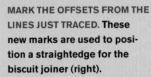

A STRAIGHT BOARD GUIDES THE BISCUIT JOINER. The author places the base of the tool against a board clamped to the side to cut the slots for the shelves (left).

To locate a V-shelf, I place it on end against a side, keeping the apex of the V on the centerline, and slide it along the centerline until both edges are inset $\frac{1}{16}$ in. from the case side. I hold the shelf in place and trace along the bottom edge with a pencil. I also transfer to each side the layout marks showing where the biscuit slots should be cut.

To cut the slots in the sides, you need something to register the biscuit joiner against because you can't use the tool's fence as you did on the shelves. I clamp a straight block of wood parallel to the lines I traced off the shelves. I offset this straightedge to make up for the fact that I'm registering the base of the biscuit joiner, not its adjustable fence, against the straightedge. Here's how I figure out the offset: I measure the distance from the bottom face to the bottom of a V-shelf slot (see the top left photo on the facing page). On my biscuit joiner, I measure the distance between the bottom of the blade (I use a raker tooth) to the base. I subtract the first number from the second; that's the offset, which I lay out on the side (see the top right photo on the facing page). I use two clamps each time I reposition the straightedge, and then I cut all the slots.

Template Routing the Cutouts and Shaping the Edges

I made up a template for the cutouts in the sides using a piece of $\frac{1}{4}$-in. hardboard. It's easy to work with, and if you don't like the look of a template you've just shaped, it's cheaper and faster to make another template than another bookcase side. If you add a router with a guide bushing, a template also makes quick work of cleaning out the cutouts. When I made my template, I used a compass to draw the curve of the handle and a French curve to draw the whale tail. I faired out the curves by sanding and filing.

I mark the cutouts on both ends and remove the waste with a jigsaw, staying at

ASSEMBLE THE BOOKCASE ON END. Cauls, a squaring jig, and backer boards ensure that the case is clamped tightly and won't be marred.

least ¹⁄₁₆ in. off the line. Then I clamp the template over a cutout and go over the area again using a router fitted with a ⁵⁄₁₆-in. guide bushing and a ¼-in. straight bit. The bookcase's handles get one more run past the router. After removing the templates and guide bushing, I chuck a ¼-in. roundover bit in the router and ease the edges of the cutouts.

The final shaping of the sides is accomplished using hand tools. Using a file and chisel, I shape the corners of the handles and the sharp junctures where the curves of the whale tails meet.

Assembly, Cleanup, and Finish

Before final assembly, I dry-fit the case to make sure that everything lines up. To avoid marring the piece and to make sure I get even clamping pressure, I use cauls and backer boards. The backer boards are two pieces of scrap plywood slightly larger than each side. To these, I attach a pair of cauls with double-faced tape.

I also use a shopmade squaring jig that's nothing more than a right-angled triangle made of scrap. I clamp this jig to the bottom shelf and one side to keep the case properly aligned during glue-up.

When I assemble the case, I stand it on its side. After clamping it, I check whether all the shelves fit flat against the sides (see the photo on p. 59). I mark any that don't and after unclamping the case, plane them to fit.

Prior to finishing, I sand all the pieces through 180 grit. Then I wipe everything down with a damp rag to raise the grain. When the pieces are dry, I continue sanding up to 320 grit. When I sand the edges, I'm careful not to lose their definition.

I lied earlier when I said that selecting and matching the stock was my favorite part of building furniture. I forgot about applying the first coat of oil. It's nice to see the grain and figure pop out when oil is rubbed into the wood.

I use three coats of Kaldet finish oil, which is made by Livos®, a German company. It is a linseed oil-based product that contains citrus solvents. I prefer Livos products because of their low toxicity, nice satin sheen, and pleasant lemony scent.

PETER TURNER builds custom furniture in Portland, Maine.

A Choice of
Three Bookcases

BY PHILIP C. LOWE

THE RIGHT BOOKCASE IS A MATTER OF CIRCUMSTANCE. The author regularly makes decisions about how much time and materials to put into a piece.

When customers arrive at my shop inquiring about having a piece of furniture made, it's part of my job to ascertain what quality of furniture they're looking for and to translate their desires into a dollar amount that will equal the time and materials needed to complete the piece. We all know that more time spent equals more dollars. The quicker the joinery and construction and the cheaper the materials, the less expensive the piece, and vice versa. The woodworker working in his or her home shop faces this same dilemma. Regardless of your skill level, you must decide how much time and materials are worth putting into a piece.

Imagine three scenarios. In scenario one, your floors are piled high with books, you need a handful of bookcases, and you need them in a hurry. It's pretty hard to justify building bookcases that are going to take two weeks a piece to complete. But in a day, you can knock together a sturdy bookcase with premilled pine from the lumber yard and simple dado construction.

In scenario two, you want something more substantial than a pine case, but you don't have the time or the money for a solid hardwood piece. In this instance, a bookcase made from hardwood plywood with solid wood facings is the ticket.

In scenario three, you have only a few books to house, no time constraints, and a pile of mahogany left over from another project. In this instance, it makes sense to build a fine, hardwood bookcase with adjustable shelves, dovetail joinery, a face frame, and curvaceous ogee bracket feet.

I'll show you how to make all three bookcases, and I'll leave it up to you to decide which case is the right one for your time, budget, and circumstance.

A Quick Case

If you have a tablesaw with a dado blade, a quick bookcase is as close as your local lumberyard and a day's work. At the yard, purchase 1-in. by 12-in. D select pine, which is the most expensive but has the fewest knots. Make sure the boards are relatively free of cup, bow, twist, and crook and that the thickness of the boards is consistent. When you mill the boards back at the shop, cut the shelf pieces ¼ in. narrower than the sides to accommodate the back.

Locating the shelves on each side piece is crucial. To make sure the dadoes line up properly, stack the side pieces on top of each other and mark each shelf location on the edge of both boards. At the tablesaw, install a dado blade of a width corresponding to the thickness of the shelves. Add paperboard shims (or even playing cards) to the dado set if its width needs to be increased just slightly. A sample cut will help ensure the fit. Cut the dadoes ¼ in. deep or one-third the thickness of the board (see the photo on the facing page).

Change to a ⁵⁄₁₆-in. dado blade and rabbet the rear edge of each side to accept the back. I like to draw the decorative shapes at the top and bottom of the side pieces with a compass or by grabbing a can, cup, or anything round that will form the shapes. Cut the shapes with a jigsaw and clean them up with a file or drum sander. Sand all of the parts before joining them.

To assemble the case, run a bead of glue in each dado, set the shelves in place, drill pilot holes with countersinks and drive in 1⅝-in. coarse-threaded drywall screws. Screwing the back into position will square the case as the glue dries.

Finally, glue and screw a rabbeted backsplash above the back (see the drawing on the facing page). After a final sanding and the easing of all the sharp edges, the case is ready for a coat of paint.

A Better Bookcase in a Weekend

If you can spare a weekend to build a hardwood plywood bookcase with adjustable shelves, then you'll end up with a piece that's more gratifying and versatile than a bookcase made of simple 1x pine. Preparing a scale drawing—with full-size details of the dadoes, rabbets, facings, and moldings—and selecting the right materials will help the process move along smoothly and efficiently.

A good-quality sheet of hardwood plywood won't be cheap—the curly maple sheet I used cost about $200—but you'll only need one sheet. To determine the overall size of the bookcase, divide the 4-ft. by 8-ft. sheet of plywood lengthwise four times, taking into account the saw kerf. That means the case can be 10 in. deep, plus the thickness of the facings. To figure the height and width of the case, determine the number of parts you can get from the four 96-in. lengths. You'll need only a couple of pieces of solid wood, for the facings and the base.

A tablesaw with a fine combination blade works well for cutting the parts from the sheet of plywood, leaving edges with

ONE-DAY BOOKCASE

Books piling up on the floor? Build this bookcase from 1x pine in a day using a tablesaw and jigsaw.

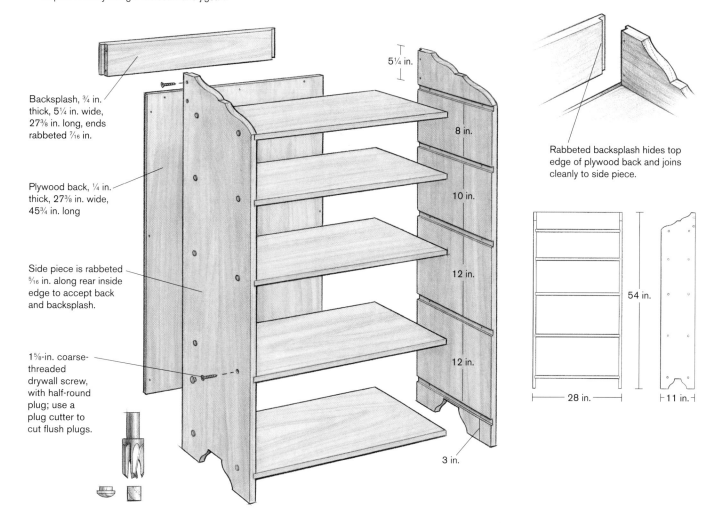

Backsplash, ¾ in. thick, 5¼ in. wide, 27⅜ in. long, ends rabbeted 7⁄16 in.

Plywood back, ¼ in. thick, 27⅝ in. wide, 45¾ in. long

Side piece is rabbeted 5⁄16 in. along rear inside edge to accept back and backsplash.

1⅝-in. coarse-threaded drywall screw, with half-round plug; use a plug cutter to cut flush plugs.

5¼ in.

8 in.

10 in.

12 in.

12 in.

3 in.

Rabbeted backsplash hides top edge of plywood back and joins cleanly to side piece.

54 in.

28 in.

11 in.

very few saw marks. Rough-cut the solid lumber to length and joint the pieces on one surface. The parts for the base should be planed to their finished thicknesses, but the parts that will become the facings should be planed only to within 1⁄16 in. of their finished thicknesses. The facings are left thicker than the plywood so they can be scraped to the same thickness after they are glued to the edges. When gluing the facings to the front edges of the sides and shelves, bar clamps and a large batten will help you apply even pressure along the length. Once the glue has cured, cut away any extra length to even the facings up with the ends of the plywood pieces. Note that the wider facings applied to the top have mitered front corners.

DADOED SHELVES To avoid having too much of the side pieces overhanging the table-saw top when cross-dadoing, work from each end toward the center.

TWO-DAY BOOKCASE

If you have a weekend, build this case from a single sheet of plywood, and dress it up with solid wood moldings, facings, and base.

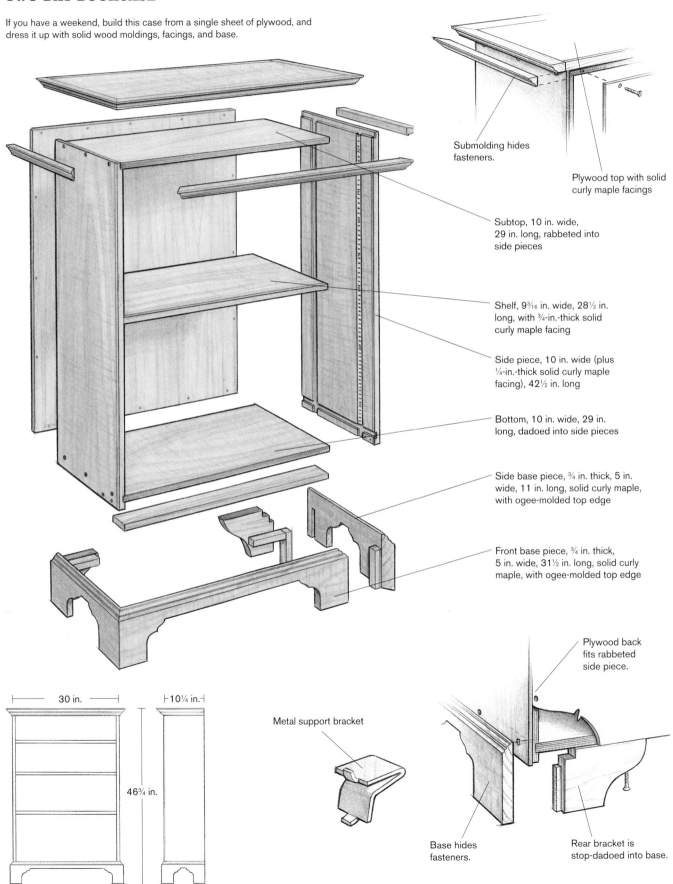

Submolding hides fasteners.

Plywood top with solid curly maple facings

Subtop, 10 in. wide, 29 in. long, rabbeted into side pieces

Shelf, 9³⁄₁₆ in. wide, 28½ in. long, with ¾-in.-thick solid curly maple facing

Side piece, 10 in. wide (plus ¼-in.-thick solid curly maple facing), 42½ in. long

Bottom, 10 in. wide, 29 in. long, dadoed into side pieces

Side base piece, ¾ in. thick, 5 in. wide, 11 in. long, solid curly maple, with ogee-molded top edge

Front base piece, ¾ in. thick, 5 in. wide, 31½ in. long, solid curly maple, with ogee-molded top edge

30 in.

10¼ in.

46¾ in.

Metal support bracket

Plywood back fits rabbeted side piece.

Base hides fasteners.

Rear bracket is stop-dadoed into base.

With a marking gauge set to the thickness of the plywood, scribe lines across the side pieces to locate the rabbets for the carcase top. Scribe with a heavy hand so that the gauge will cut through the face veneer and help prevent chipout as the rabbets are cut. Also, scribe lines across the side panels to locate the dado for the bottom piece of the carcase. Because plywood doesn't measure exactly ¾ in., add an auxiliary fence and cut into its face or shim the dado set to match the actual thickness of the panels. Once you've cut rabbets and dadoes across the side panels for the top and bottom pieces, cut dadoes from top to bottom for the metal shelf standards and then rabbets along the rear inside edges for the back.

The construction of the carcase, prior to adding the molded top and base, is similar to that of the one-day case, in that dado and screw construction is used, as well as a rabbeted back. Before the top and bottom are glued and screwed to the ends, sand the visual surfaces to their finished state. Now the assembly can take place. Use 1⅝-in. coarse-threaded drywall screws, countersunk to keep the heads of the screws below the surface. The screws will be covered by the moldings.

For the base, mold one long blank before cutting the pieces to length, which makes for fewer passes across the router. Cut the molded blank into three pieces, miter the ends and test-fit the joints at the front corners. Then lay out the curves of the bracket feet. I made a plunge cut on the tablesaw for the straight section of the front base piece and cut out the curves on the bandsaw (see the photos on p. 66). Because the rear of the base has such short grain (see the drawing on the facing page), cut a stop dado and install a bracket to help prevent the foot from breaking off if kicked. Glue the base to the bottom of the carcase and then rub glue blocks into the inside corner of the joints to add strength.

Using a router, shape the molding around the top piece into the extra-wide facings that have been applied. The narrow submolding, which will be applied just below the molded top piece, should be shaped onto a wider board from which a narrow strip can be sawed off. I shaped the edge molding on the base and the top submolding with the same ogee bit (when applied, the submolding is turned upside down). The molded edge on the top piece itself is a cove and quarter round, run with the quarter round to the top.

When molding a top with solid facings, it's best to make the first cut across the left side, beginning at the front corner and working toward the rear. Make the second cut across the front, beginning at the right corner, and then the third cut across the right side, working from the rear to the front. This progression of cuts helps eliminate tearout at the corners.

METAL SHELF STANDARDS **Numbers on the standards help align slots for the brackets.**

Two-Day Bookcase: Base Construction

A plunge cut is the surest way to cut a straight line between the curves at either end. First raise the tablesaw blade and mark the fence at the blade's farthest point. Retract the blade and position the base piece to the mark. Clamp a stop to the fence to avoid kickback. Now, carefully raise the blade through the base piece (below left), then push the base piece across the blade. Finish by cutting out the curves at the bandsaw (below right). Glue and clamp the front and side base pieces to the carcase at the same time (right). Add brackets at the rear and glue blocks to the inside corners.

Take Your Time for a Real Fine Bookcase

Building an heirloom bookcase requires greater effort than building one that's dadoed and screwed together, but the result is, well, an heirloom. Making a drawing of this bookcase is crucial. A scaled layout with full-size details and a stock list will eliminate guesswork.

Dovetail joints are solid, and a face frame adds substance–Locking the carcase together with dovetail joints makes for a solid foundation onto which to attach the top, back, shelves, and ogee bracket feet. I chose to use lapped dovetails at the top of the carcase and housed, tapered half dovetails at the bottom.

The lapped dovetails leave a smooth surface onto which to glue the top molding; a through-dovetail, by contrast, has end grain that can interfere when you glue on the moldings. Using two narrower pieces at the top rather than one full-width piece saves stock and requires fewer dovetails.

Housed, tapered dovetails make sense at the bottom because a piece with lapped dovetails would have to be 1½ in. thick to enable the base to be applied—a waste of expensive stock. The taper allows the half dovetail to fit easily into its housing, without weakening the joint. By selecting both types of dovetail joints, you can make the length of the tails the same; thus, each of the three top and bottom pieces can be cut to the same length.

To make a housed, tapered half dovetail, start by cutting the housing itself into the side pieces. Two steps are required (see the top photos on p. 69): First, router-cut a full dovetail dado, then taper one side of the dado with a tablesaw.

Cut the tails onto the bottom piece back at the router. With the bit remaining at the same height as it was for cutting the housing, reposition the fence to cut a half dovetail onto one edge of the bottom piece. You'll need to run the bottom piece vertically against the fence.

Use a rabbet plane to taper the half dovetail on the bottom piece to fit the tapered housing on the side piece. Secure a fence across the flat side of the bottom piece, in line with the shoulder of the dovetail. With the rabbet plane against the fence, carefully plane a taper, starting at zero at one end and working down to 1/8 in. at the other end. Keep testing the dovetail in position until it fits snug in the housing. Before gluing up the frame, drill holes in the side pieces for brass shelf pins; space the holes using a predrilled board as a jig.

The face frame is of simple mortise-and-tenon construction. The top rail should be wider than the other pieces because a portion of it will be covered by the submolding below the top. A face frame gives the bookcase front a substantial appearance. The drawback is that books can get trapped behind the frame.

Ogee bracket feet add style–With the case glued and the face frame applied, add filler pieces to make up the thickness of the bottom. Now you can assemble a spline-jointed frame, onto which ogee bracket feet will be attached. Cut and fit the miters first. Next, cut grooves for the splines, using a 1/2-in. dado set on your tablesaw. Use a bandsaw to fashion pointed splines to fit the grooves formed where the four pieces come together.

The ogee bracket feet added to this case certainly elevate its design. The feet are made from six pieces that start out as one long blank. These feet all stem from the detail that is drawn at the very beginning of the project. Transfer the outside curve of the foot from your drawing to thin, plywood pattern stock by stippling through the drawing onto the plywood with a stippling tool. The plywood pattern can be cut out with a jigsaw. Use this pattern to transfer the ogee profile onto the two ends of the long blank. Now this shape needs to be cut into the surface. I like to do this with a series of cuts on the tablesaw, followed by a final shaping with a handplane and a scraper (see the photos on p. 70).

Begin by cutting the concave portion of the ogee shape. I achieve this by raising the sawblade to the height of the concave curve and then positioning the blank diagonally until the tablesaw blade fills the curve. Clamp a straightedge to the table, parallel to the piece. Now lower the blade until it projects just 1/16 in. above the table and pass the blank across the blade. Here, there is a safety issue. Angle the fence from the front left to the rear right of the saw table. As you push the piece across the sawblade, the rotation of the blade naturally pushes it against the fence. This will prevent any kickback from occurring. Raise the blade only 1/16 in. with each subsequent pass. A telltale sign of an aggressive cut is the sound of the blade cutting. If it starts to sing wildly, the cut is too deep or the pass across the blade is too rapid. Altering one or the other will solve the problem.

Once you've completed this series of cuts, remove the temporary fence and replace it with the regular fence. Angle the blade to 45° and set the fence so that the square corner at the top of the foot can be cut away by running the blank on its top edge. Then adjust the blade angle to 22½° and cut a second bevel, taking away the sharp corner of the angle you've already cut. Cut at this angle two more times, once with the blank lying flat on the table, profile down, and a

MULTIDAY BOOKCASE

If you have the time to make a truly fine bookcase, you can build this one from solid mahogany or another premium hardwood. Ogee bracket feet add complexity to the project but give the piece elegance and character.

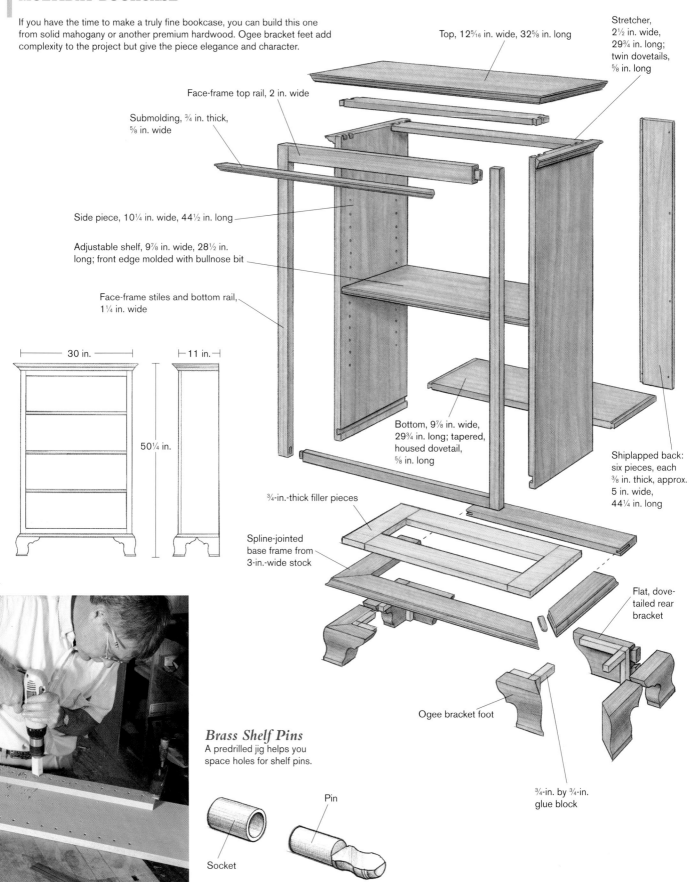

Top, 12⁵⁄₁₆ in. wide, 32⁵⁄₈ in. long

Stretcher, 2½ in. wide, 29¾ in. long; twin dovetails, ⁵⁄₈ in. long

Face-frame top rail, 2 in. wide

Submolding, ¾ in. thick, ⁵⁄₈ in. wide

Side piece, 10¼ in. wide, 44½ in. long

Adjustable shelf, 9⁷⁄₈ in. wide, 28½ in. long; front edge molded with bullnose bit

Face-frame stiles and bottom rail, 1¼ in. wide

30 in.

11 in.

50¼ in.

Bottom, 9⁷⁄₈ in. wide, 29¾ in. long; tapered, housed dovetail, ⁵⁄₈ in. long

¾-in.-thick filler pieces

Shiplapped back: six pieces, each ⅜ in. thick, approx. 5 in. wide, 44¼ in. long

Spline-jointed base frame from 3-in.-wide stock

Flat, dovetailed rear bracket

Ogee bracket foot

Brass Shelf Pins
A predrilled jig helps you space holes for shelf pins.

Pin

Socket

¾-in. by ¾-in. glue block

Tapering a Housed Half Dovetail

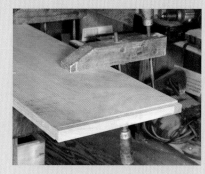

First router-cut a ⅝-in. dovetail dado across the side piece, then taper the dado. A ⅛-in.-thick, ⅜-in.-wide spacer taped to the end of the side piece allows you to taper one wall of the dovetail dado by running it across a tablesaw blade. Wax the tabletop and fence to avoid kickback.

Cut a half dovetail into the bottom face of the shelf piece, then taper the top face. With a board clamped to the bottom piece as a guide, plane a taper from zero at one end to ⅛ in. at the other.

A tapered, housed half dovetail is easier to fit than a straight one. Properly sized, the tapered half dovetail will still lock tightly in its housing.

second time with the fence moved to the left side of the blade and the blank run between the fence and the blade. For this final cut, raise the blade to remove the hard angle where the cove meets the round.

At the bench, plane the roundness of the ogee into the blank and scrape it free of saw marks and facets left by the plane. Follow with a progression of sandings to achieve the final shape and smoothness.

Now that the blank has its finished shape, you can cut it into three lengths, each long enough for two halves of an ogee bracket foot. Each front foot is formed from two halves mitered together; the back feet each require a shaped half to be dovetailed to a flat rear bracket that has been shaped with a simple curve. Miter-cut four ends of the lengths for the front feet and leave two ends straight for the rear feet. Use a plywood pattern to draw the inside curve onto the lengths and cut out the shape on the bandsaw. Clean up the curves by rasping, filing, and sanding. Gluing the feet together

SHIPLAPPING ALLOWS SOLID BOARDS TO MOVE. A single screw placed near one edge of each board (at top and bottom) will enable each rabbeted board to hold down the board next to it, while allowing each board to move with seasonal changes.

Cutting Ogee Bracket Feet

Multifaceted ogee bracket feet begin as one long blank. First mark the outside curve of the foot onto the end of the blank.

1. To shape the concave curve, pass the blank diagonally across a tablesaw blade, cutting just 1/16 in. with each pass.

2. To shape the convex curve, set the blade at an angle and make successive rip cuts. At the bench, shape and smooth the curves, first with a plane, then with a scraper, and finally with sandpaper. Now cut the long blank into short lengths.

3. Miter-cut the ends as necessary and cut the inside curve of the ogee feet at the bandsaw.

4. Glue up each foot from two pieces and then glue the feet to the base.

requires nothing more than a rub joint, if the miters are planed and fit correctly. Rub glue blocks into the inside corner of each ogee bracket foot to provide additional strength. You can then glue the feet to the mitered base frame.

Shiplapped back allows for wood movement–Shiplapping is an excellent means of attaching solid boards to the back while allowing each board to move with seasonal changes in the weather. Determine the width of the boards for the back by dividing the width of the opening by the number of pieces you feel is suitable without having to glue up any pieces. It's best to do a full-size layout to determine the sizes of the boards, keeping in mind that

the rabbets will overlap. I settled on six boards for my bookcase. The theory is that each rabbeted board will hold down the board next to it, if you position two screws (one at the top and one at the bottom) near the edge (look closely at the bottom photo on p. 69). Two screws will leave each board free to move. And if you've had books piled on the floor, the bookcase itself will provide you the same freedom.

PHILIP C. LOWE designs, builds, and restores fine furniture and teaches carving and woodworking at his waterfront shop in Beverly, Mass.

A Bookcase That Breaks the Rules

I remember the first bookcase I ever built. I didn't want to spend too much money on material, so I used AC fir plywood and had to sand the stuff until my hands hurt. I wanted the case to last forever, so I dadoed all the shelves into the sides—a time-consuming job, especially when my ¾-in. router bit was a little too wide for the ¾-in. plywood shelves.

I attached the face frame one piece at a time, which meant the joints weren't fastened together tightly, which was okay. But I made the shelves the same depth as the sides, so when I installed the nosing on the shelves, the face frame spread apart. Then, after all that, I had to finish the thing.

Since that first attempt and during my 30-plus years of finish carpentry, I've built a lot of bookcases—not just for clients, but for myself as well. Over that time I have learned a lot of valuable lessons about bookcase design and construction. I have some tips and methods as well as some misconceptions (see "Challenging Bookcase Myths" on p. 72) about building a better bookcase faster and easier (see the drawing on p. 73.)

BY GARY M. KATZ

Challenging Bookcase Myths

- Shelves don't have to be 12 in. deep; 9½ in. is deep enough for most books.

- Dadoes aren't necessary for shelf support; screws are strong enough for bookshelves.

- Adjustable shelves aren't necessary; no one changes shelf heights, so make them permanent.

- Rabbeting the back into the sides is unnecessary and time-consuming.

Cutting List

One sheet of plywood yields all the parts for the main case plus optional outer sides.

Use Readily Available Materials

I've built bookcases from many different materials, from ¾-in. fir plywood to 2x12s. On occasion I've also used ¾-in. veneered MDF-core (medium-density fiberboard) sheet goods, but I've found that plywood is stronger, spans farther, and holds screws better than MDF. So I usually choose ¾-in. hardwood-veneer plywood for stain-grade work or ¾-in. birch-veneer plywood for paint-grade work.

I make stiles, rails, and nosings from solid stock to hide the edge grain of the plywood sides and shelves. I prefer poplar for paint-grade bookcases, and for stain-grade work, I use hardwood that matches the plywood veneer, in this case Honduras mahogany.

The bookcase back can be made from any ¼-in. sheet stock, but I opted for mahogany-veneer plywood to match the rest of the material. By the way, MDF core is fine for the bookcase back.

I keep costs to a minimum by using plywood for the shelves and sides and solid stock for the stiles and rails. The materials for this 32-in.-wide bookcase in Honduras mahogany (with the face-frame end panel) cost about $230★ (see "Shopping List" at right).

Paint-grade materials would cost about half that amount. Considering that the bookcase took me less than a day, I figure it could be built, finished, and installed for around $500★.

Getting the Most From Material

I can get the shelves and sides for a single 32-in. unit easily out of a single sheet of plywood (see "Cutting List" at left). I start by ripping the two finished outer sides (if both sides are exposed), and then the two narrower inner sides (see the photos on p. 74). (The outer sides are ¼ in. wider to cover the edges of the back.) I make the height of the bookcase around 60 in. so that the cut-off pieces from each of the sides can be used for shelves. Enough material should be left over for the top or for shelves on additional bookcases.

I cut the material for the back with the grain running horizontally. That way, I get the backs for two bookcases out of one sheet of material. When all the bookcase

Shopping List

One sheet: ¾-in. plywood (shelves, sides, and top)

Half-sheet: ¼-in. plywood (back)

Four: ¾-in. by 2-in. by 60-in. stiles (face frames)

Two: ¾-in. by 4 ½-in. by 36-in. rails (face frames)

Five: ¾-in. by 1-in. by 48-in. nosings

One: 1-in. by 1 ¾-in. by 48-in. crown molding

Join Several Sections for a Modular Library

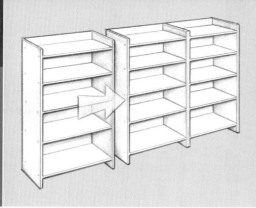

Lightweight and easy to carry, 32-in.-wide units can be fastened together on site for larger capacity bookcases.

QUICK BOOKSHELVES

Main case

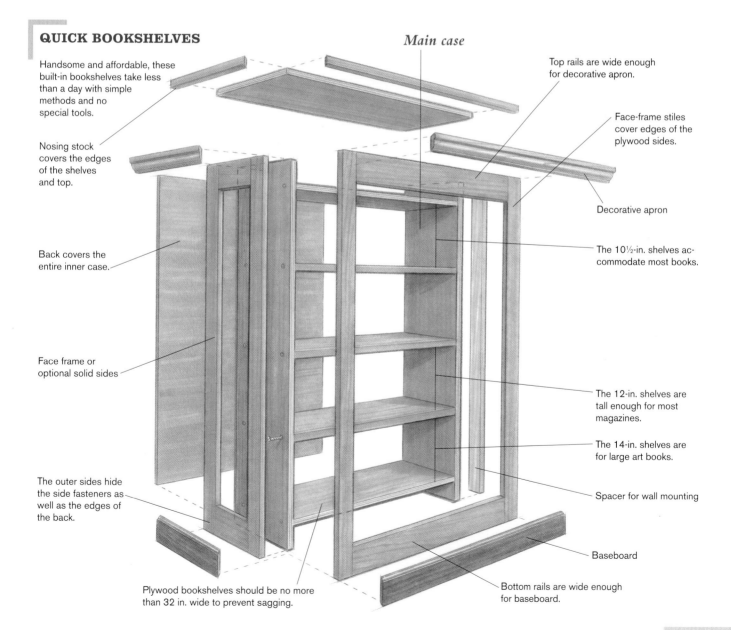

Handsome and affordable, these built-in bookshelves take less than a day with simple methods and no special tools.

Nosing stock covers the edges of the shelves and top.

Back covers the entire inner case.

Face frame or optional solid sides

The outer sides hide the side fasteners as well as the edges of the back.

Plywood bookshelves should be no more than 32 in. wide to prevent sagging.

Top rails are wide enough for decorative apron.

Face-frame stiles cover edges of the plywood sides.

Decorative apron

The 10½-in. shelves accommodate most books.

The 12-in. shelves are tall enough for most magazines.

The 14-in. shelves are for large art books.

Spacer for wall mounting

Baseboard

Bottom rails are wide enough for baseboard.

TURNING THE PLYWOOD INTO BOOKCASE PARTS

First, rip the sheet of plywood into lengthwise strips. A tablesaw makes these cuts straight and even (left). Next, a chopsaw makes quick work of cutting the strips to length for the shelves, sides and top (above).

pieces have been cut, I put nosing on the shelf stock, and I prefinish everything with a couple coats of polyurethane.

Assembly Requires No Special Tools

Story sticks can be helpful in just about every phase of home construction. They usually are made from a length of 1x material, and they're used to lay out and record all the pertinent measurements for a particular project. For a bookcase story stick, I mark the location of each shelf as well as the width of the top and bottom face-frame rails based on the trim details I plan to use.

I use the story stick to lay out temporary spacers that I cut to set the shelf positions exactly on both sides of the bookcase (see the top photo on p. 76). The story stick and spacers also can be used to make additional bookcases identical to the first if necessary.

I attach the shelves to the sides with 1⅝-in. drywall screws driven through the predrilled holes. To avoid "shiners" (screws or nails that miss their mark), I trace a pencil line with a square at each shelf location before driving any fasteners. Before drilling and driving the screws, it helps to tack the shelves in place with 18-ga. brads.

Back Squares the Bookcase

I secure the back to the assembled case with glue and staples (see the sidebar on p. 77), although small nails or screws work, too. Once the glue is spread, the back must be set carefully to keep the glue from oozing. If glue does squeeze out, it's easily cleaned off the prefinished pieces with a wet cloth.

I first attach the back along just one side. Although I cut the back square, I double-check by racking the case until the diagonal measurements are exactly the same. Again to avoid shiners, I use a straightedge to draw shelf locations across the back before stapling it home.

Hidden Fasteners Hold Bookcase to the Wall

If the bookcase is going in a corner, I install a 1x spacer block on the end panel to keep the stile overhangs similar (see the top photos on p. 78). Then I set the unit in position and shim it plumb.

One of the advantages of this bookcase system is that all the fasteners are hidden. The ¼-in. plywood sides have plenty of strength, so I drive a screw through the side that abuts the wall and into a wall-framing member. However, the ¼-in. plywood back isn't strong enough by itself to fasten to the wall. So I drive screws through angled holes in the top shelf. Another option would be to add a reinforcing cleat across the back of

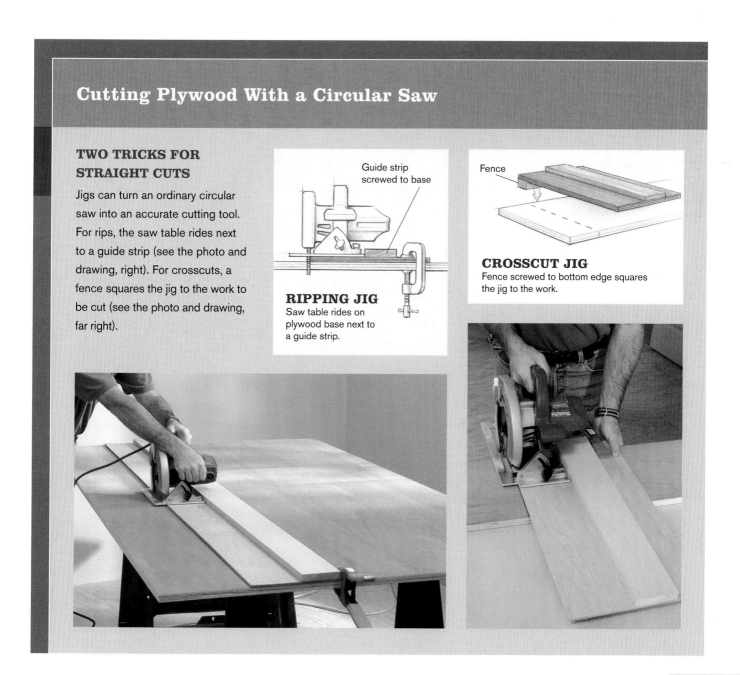

Cutting Plywood With a Circular Saw

TWO TRICKS FOR STRAIGHT CUTS

Jigs can turn an ordinary circular saw into an accurate cutting tool. For rips, the saw table rides next to a guide strip (see the photo and drawing, right). For crosscuts, a fence squares the jig to the work to be cut (see the photo and drawing, far right).

Guide strip screwed to base

RIPPING JIG
Saw table rides on plywood base next to a guide strip.

Fence

CROSSCUT JIG
Fence screwed to bottom edge squares the jig to the work.

Site-Built Tools Ensure Accurate Assembly

A story stick records the vertical layout of the bookcase to minimize mea surement errors and to keep the layout consistent with multiple cases.

Measured from the story stick, 1x8 spacer blocks clamp to the sides and keep the shelves properly space and positioned during assembly.

PINPOINT THE SCREWS. Once shelves are positioned, a line is drawn to center the fasteners (left). Shelf is held against spacer while screws are driven through predrilled holes (right).

Back Adds Strength and Squares the Bookcase

PLYWOOD BACK COMPLETES THE MAIN CASE

After glue is spread on the back edges of the shelves and sides, the back is carefully set in place (left), and one edge is attached. Diagonal measurements confirm that the bookcase is square (lower left), and the rest of the back is nailed off after guidelines are drawn (below).

the top space. A third attachment point is through the side with a screw into either a stud or the bottom sill plate.

Face Frame Covers Raw Edges

The end panels go on next to hide all the fasteners in that side (see the bottom photos on p. 78). The next step is installing the face frame, which covers the unfinished edges of the plywood. The face frame can be installed one piece at a time on the case, but I prefer to assemble the face frame using pocket screws (Kreg®; 800-447-8638; www.kregtool.com). Pocket screws ensure

tight-fitting and flush joinery. Then glue and a few 18-ga. brad nails are all that's necessary to secure the face frame to the carcase.

Next, I apply nosing to a piece of ¾-in. plywood for the top, and I glue and nail it in place. I like to put an apron under the edge of the top. A simple piece of 1x2 works well, but other moldings that are either made in a factory or made in my shop can be used to gussy up the design.

*Note—Prices are from 2003.

GARY M. KATZ is a carpenter and writer living in Reseda, Calif. He is the author of *The Doorhanger's Handbook* (The Taunton Press, 1998).

Concealed Screws Attach Bookcase

SPACER KEEPS TRIM CONSISTENT. A 1x spacer is screwed to the side that goes against the wall (above left), and shims make the bookcase level and plumb (above right).

Three Places to Hide Screws

Drive screws through the sides into the wall.

Drive angled screws through the top shelf into the wall studs.

Drive angled screws through the side and into studs or sill plates.

Trim Hides the Rough Edges

FANCY FINISH. To give the bookcase an Arts and Crafts look, a stile-and-rail frame covers the shelf screws (above). Screws secure it from the inside and another preassembled frame hides its edges as well as the edges of the plywood (right).

A BASEBOARD COMPLETES THE BUILT-IN LOOK. A nosing strip on the top hides the edge of factory-made crown molding, and a matching baseboard finishes the bottom (above).

Simpler Sides for a Contemporary Look

PLYWOOD PANELS KEEP COSTS DOWN

Minimal and clean-looking, side panels cut from the same sheet of plywood hide the screws that hold the shelves (left). The preassembled face frame goes on in one piece to cover the edges of the plywood (center). A square-edge apron under the top adds a sleek, simple touch (right).

A Classic Bookcase in the Craftsman Style

BY GARY ROGOWSKI

Of the many qualities that help define the Arts and Crafts style, perhaps the most apparent is straightforward and honest joinery. Wedged joints and through-tenons show the world how a piece was made. Open-grained woods like white oak give a piece an unabashed look, perhaps even a rustic quality that says, "Here's what I am—sturdy, well-made furniture." No abstractions get in the way, no conceptualizing need be done. This frank simplicity is just the style the progenitors of the Arts and Crafts movement in England hoped for—a style in direct counterpoint to the machines and machined look of the Industrial Age and its products—and it's just the style for the bookcase I made to fit in my bungalow.

The bookcase is just 50 in. high and 31 in. wide. Quartersawn white oak, the quintessential Arts and Crafts material, was clearly the wood of choice. For the sides and shelves, I glued two boards together, then scraped and sanded them. Wedges made of the same oak secure the through-tenons to the mortised sides and give the bookcase its strength and honest face.

Mortise-and-tenon joinery usually requires precise fitting; however, these long through-tenons need to be a bit loose to fit easily through the mortises. The wedges provide holding power at three locations. The back of the wedge pushes against the outside face of the side. This does nothing until the angled front of the wedge starts to press against the angled slot cut into the tenon. Then the wedge pulls the tenon through the joint until the tenon shoulders lock against the inside face of the case side.

Cut Mortises With a Plunge Router and Template

I cut the mortises using a plunge router, a ⅝-in. straight bit, a ¾-in. template guide, and a mortising template (see the sidebar on p. 83). The template, made of ½-in. medium-density fiberboard (MDF), is milled as wide as my case side and with perfectly square ends. First mark the centerline of the template. On this centerline, lay out the mortises. Cut the mortises with a ¾-in. straight bit on the router table, using a fence with stops clamped onto it. Cut the two outer mortises using the same stops and fence setting; flip the board over to cut the second one. For the center mortise, simply move the stops over to the proper position. If the template is square, the mortises will locate properly and be the same size. Finally, glue and screw a fence onto one end of the template.

Only the centerlines of the mortises need to be laid out on the case sides. Clamp

Wedged Tenons and Clean Lines Dignify This Oak Original

PROFILES

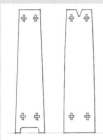

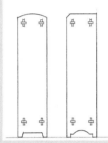

The way the bookcase is shaped on its sides and rails strongly influences the appearance of the piece. Try drawing out a few shapes on cardboard to see them full scale. Flat or beveled bottom edges, simple indents, shallow arcs, or other combinations of shapes all lend a certain feel to a piece. My advice is to keep the shaping details consistent throughout. So a negative shape cut out of the bottom of the sides can be nicely recalled at the top, in the toe kick or in the backsplash.

TOEKICKS

Don't overlook the toe kick as a design element. It greatly influences how the bookcase "stands" and can also help tie all of the pieces in the case together. A toe kick can be of a simple design, but you may find a complex pattern more suitable. The toe kick on this case echoes the shallow arc of the top rail; arcs also appear in the sides, at both top and bottom. The motif is a unifying element.

WEDGES

The material of the wedges and their shape and placement can really make a difference in the look and feel of the bookcase. Using a contrasting species, like darker rosewood, gives the wedges a visual punch. But be sure the wedge material

is as tough as the white oak. Oak wedges can be colored to provide contrast. An ebonizing solution of vinegar and rusty nails or steel wool will give oak a color anywhere from a dusky gray to black, depending on the solution and the amount of tannin in the oak. Wedges can be shaped any number of ways. Double wedges allow you to mortise straight through the tenon at no

angle. The angle of the wedges themselves creates the necessary force. The number of wedges can be varied to suit your taste; for instance, you can put three wedges at the bottom and two at the top.

HONEST LINES, SOLID WOOD, SUPERIOR CRAFTSMANSHIP

Wedged through-tenons are key to both the visual design and structural integrity of this Arts and Crafts bookcase. All parts are made of ¾-in.-thick quartersawn white oak.

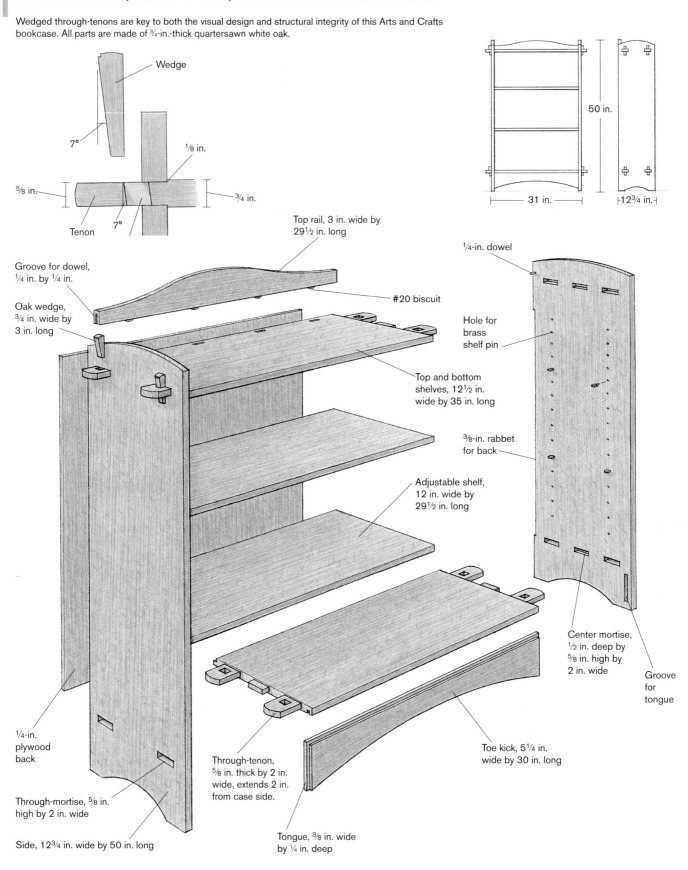

Wedge

7°

⅛ in.

⅝ in.

¾ in.

Tenon

7°

50 in.

31 in.

12¾ in.

Top rail, 3 in. wide by 29½ in. long

Groove for dowel, ¼ in. by ¼ in.

Oak wedge, ¾ in. wide by 3 in. long

#20 biscuit

¼-in. dowel

Hole for brass shelf pin

Top and bottom shelves, 12½ in. wide by 35 in. long

⅜-in. rabbet for back

Adjustable shelf, 12 in. wide by 29½ in. long

Center mortise, ½ in. deep by ⅝ in. high by 2 in. wide

Groove for tongue

¼-in. plywood back

Through-mortise, ⅝ in. high by 2 in. wide

Through-tenon, ⅝ in. thick by 2 in. wide, extends 2 in. from case side.

Toe kick, 5¼ in. wide by 30 in. long

Side, 12¾ in. wide by 50 in. long

Tongue, ⅜ in. wide by ¼ in. deep

a side to the bench, align the centerlines on the template with the centerlines on the side and clamp the template in place. Next, set the bit depth. Put a folded index card on the benchtop and rest your router on the edge of the case. Then zero the bit down to the card and set the turret stop on the router to its lowest depth. This setting will allow you to rout almost through the case side but without blowing out the mortise or marring your benchtop. Then set another turret stop for the center mortises, which aren't through-mortises.

After routing, chop the mortise corners square with a chisel. I found that the standard 25° angle on my chisels really took a beating in this oak; they looked like I had been prying nails with them. To get through the job, I adjusted each chisel's edge about 5° with a secondary bevel. When chopping mortises, remember to pull the chisel back hard to the mortise wall to keep it lined up. You want these corners to be cut square and neat. I use a block of wood as wide as my mortises to check each for consistency. I also bevel the edges of the mortise with my chisel to give a nice shadow line and to prevent tearout when fitting the tenons.

Cut Tenons and Wedges to Fit Easily

Cut the cheeks and shoulders of the tenons with a plunge router and a straight fence (see the sidebar on p. 84). The fence rides tightly against the end of the board to locate the tenon shoulder. Cut one face of all of the boards about $\frac{1}{16}$ in. deep and back to the tenon depth, then cut the second face so that the tenons will fit easily into the mortises. Next, on the bandsaw, rough out the waste between each of the tenons. Then reset your router bit to the full depth of the board and, in several passes, cut the shoulders between the tenons.

I set up the router table with a fence to finish-cut the roughed-out edges of the tenons so that they slide easily through the

Simple Mortising Jig

ROUTER-CUT MORTISES ROUGH OUT QUICKLY

With this template (left), you don't have to mark mortises on the case sides, just the centerlines. Use a folded index card (right) to set your router depth so that the bit will not break through the sides when cutting mortises. Pop out the thin waste with a chisel.

mortises. Use a rabbeting plane to pare the tenons down on both their faces and edges. The fit should be smooth; you shouldn't have to fight the joint home, nor should you be able to see Paris through the gaps. Work one tenon at a time until you can push all of the joints home by hand.

Dry-assemble the case, then mark the outside face of the case side onto each tenon. Be sure to locate the end of the slot for the wedges $\frac{1}{8}$ in. in from this line so that part of the slot lies inside the face of the case side. If you cut the slot flush with the case side, the inside face of the slot will push against the wedge, preventing it from providing a totally snug fit.

Next, make a mortising template to router-cut the wedge slots in the tenons. The slot needs to be angled on its front edge, so glue a 7° angled block to the bottom of the template. Your plunge router will then rout at that angle. Rout each wedge slot with a $\frac{1}{4}$-in. straight bit and a $\frac{5}{16}$-in. o.d. template guide, and chop its corners square with a chisel.

To make all of the wedges the same size and angle, you'll need to make a simple tapering jig for the bandsaw. Cutting out the triangular shape of the wedges on a 3-in. by 5-in. piece of ¼-in.-thick scrap ply gives you a place in which to hold your wedge stock as you pass it by the blade. Move the fence over to the proper spot and cut all of the wedges. Next, plane each wedge edge until the wedge fits easily through the mortise. Then clean up the angled face until it just starts to snug up when it's about 1 in. above the top face of the tenon.

Have a Plan Before Assembly and Glue-Up

Once the through-tenons on the shelves fit easily into the mortises on the case sides, it's time to add a top rail, or backsplash, above and a toe kick below. The toe kick needs to be strong, just in case it gets used as it was so aptly named, so rout stopped grooves into the case sides and a through-groove into the bottom shelf, referencing off each board's back edge. Then rout a tongue into the toe kick so that it can slide home after the case is glued together.

The top rail doesn't need the strength of a tongue-and-groove joint, so after the case is together, glue the rail onto the top with biscuits. To keep it from twisting, add two dowels to the case sides. These dowels fit slots cut into the ends of the top rail. For easy assembly, use the offcuts from the top rail and toe kick as clamping blocks when gluing up these two curved rails.

Shape the bottom of the case sides on the bandsaw and finish with a template router. Rabbet the case sides for the back on a router table. For a long-grain cut like this, a climb cut—one made with the rotation of the router bit—can help avoid tearout. File the shaped edges slightly round, then scrape and sand the entire case with 180-grit paper. Raise the grain with a damp rag and resand to get rid of any puffed fibers.

Nothing will save you more from heart palpitations and profuse sweating than planning out a strategy for glue-up. Dry-fitting your case and laying out your clamps, glue, hammer, and wedges will help make this assembly an occasion for whistling.

Glue up one side at a time. With one side in place but unglued, apply glue to the tenons of the other side, gluing only the long grain. Don't over-glue these joints or you'll have a mess to clean up. Clamps pull everything in tight, with maybe a wallop or two from a dead-blow hammer.

After clamping, place the wedges and bang them home. I use a metal hammer for this because the sound it makes will change when the wedge is in far enough. Do not bang the wedge past this point. You'll bust out the short-grain end of the tenon. This is why I left the tenon ends poking through the case sides at a relatively long 2 in. This much wood provides enough room to put in the wedges safely.

GARY ROGOWSKI, a contributing editor to *Fine Woodworking*, teaches a class on building this bookcase at The Northwest Woodworking Studio.

Router-Cut Tenons

A ROUTER WITH A FENCE cuts clean shoulders between tenons, and an angled block sets the bevel. First, bandsaw the waste between the tenons (below left). Then, with the template tipped 7°, your router will automatically bevel the slot in the through-tenon to accept a tapered wedge (below right).

Knockdown Bookshelves in a Day

BY STEVE LATTA

I get the most pure enjoyment from reproducing 18th-century furniture, but every now and then it's nice to break out of that mode and dive into a project that I can knock out in a day or two. This set of bookshelves is just such a beast, and it will cover a lot of wall in the little amount of time required to build it. I've made three versions of this design since I built the first one about 10 years ago. The first has lived in three separate homes, but now it fits the dining room in our new home.

There are some nice features about this design. When you combine the simplicity of the joinery with the absence of hardware, you have a bookcase that can be taken apart and reassembled in minutes. The angle on the bottom of each vertical makes the case lean toward the wall, so the more weight that you put on it, the more secure it is. In most cases, there is no need to tie it to the wall. Although, if you have kids, you may want to add a few fasteners as a precaution. A couple of corner braces attached under the bottom shelf and along the top shelf should do the trick.

Choose Your Wood and Size the Joints

This is a great project for using up old scraps. For these units, I used some less than

perfectly clear leftovers of walnut for the verticals and dimensioned #2 white pine 1x12s for the shelves. If you don't have boards wide enough to make the verticals (mine are 10 in. wide at the bottom), you can glue them up from smaller boards, but make sure the front piece is wide enough that you won't expose a glueline when you cut the taper on the front edge. For the pine shelves, I bought more width than I needed so that I could cut around knots and defects to end up with clear front edges on all of them.

The shelves and the verticals lock together with what I call a housed lap joint (see the drawing on p. 88). The shelves are notched wherever they meet a vertical, and the verticals are notched and dadoed on both sides so that the shelves sit firmly on the shoulders of the dadoes. I cut the dadoes slightly wider ($\frac{1}{32}$ in. or so) than the shelf material is thick. That way, the pieces slide together fairly easily, even after a finish has been applied to them. Don't be obsessive about getting a microfine fit. The joy of this design is lost if you end up having to put together the unit by beating it with a block of wood and a hammer.

In figuring sizes and spacing for the shelves, I kept it simple. The bottom shelf sits high enough off the floor (7 in.) to clear the tallest baseboard in an old house where we used to live. The spacing between shelves decreases in 1-in. increments from the bottom to the top.

Cut the Dadoes Before Tapering the Verticals

Shoot for a thickness on the verticals of around $1\frac{1}{8}$ in. to $1\frac{1}{4}$ in. (Make sure you leave some extra scrap pieces to use in setting up the joinery cuts.) You can cut the joinery using a router, a radial-arm saw or a tablesaw with a carriage jig like the one I used (see the photos on p. 88–89). If you use a tablesaw, you'll need a long auxiliary fence to keep the stock steady. You'll also need to support the weight of the stock that hangs out over the end of the saw table.

Before cutting the joints in the verticals, make a practice cut halfway through a scrap piece of shelf stock. Use this sample to set the depth of the dadoes in the verticals. To be sure all of the verticals are dadoed correctly, first cut them all to length and then use a story stick to mark the locations of the dadoes on the front edges of the verticals. A pencil line provides a reference to cut to, and a blue chalkline indicates on which side of the line to cut.

To set the depth of the dadoes, take a scrap from one of the verticals and set it against a stop block on the carriage. Raise the dado blades, make a cut, flip over the

scrap and make another cut opposite the first. Adjust the height of the dado blades until the notched shelf sample slides easily onto the dadoed sample without excessive play. Now begin making the dadoes on only one side of each vertical. Then use a small square and a sharp pencil to mark the dado cuts across the front edges of all the verticals. Flip over the verticals and, lining up the pencil lines with the kerf in the carriage, cut the dadoes on the other sides of the verticals. Hold-down clamps keep the boards from sliding out of position.

After cutting the dadoes, lay out the taper on one of the verticals and mark each dado for where a chunk of waste needs to be taken out to receive the shelf. Use a sabersaw to cut away most of the waste. Stay about 1/16 in. from the edges of the dado and clean up using a router with a bearing-guided, flush-trimming bit.

Cut the taper on one vertical using the bandsaw and then, with a jointer or a handplane, clean up that edge. Use the first vertical as a pattern to mark and cut the others. The radius on the top front corners of the verticals (and on the ends of the shelves) can be cut a number of ways. If I'm doing lots of shelves and supports, I make a template out of medium-density fiberboard (MDF) and flush-cut the pieces using a router. Once the verticals have been cut to

shape, soften the outside edges with a 1/8-in. roundover bit. Finally, notch the bottom back edge of each of the verticals to clear any baseboard on the wall where they will live. Now use a sliding compound-miter saw to make a 5° angled cut on the back edge of the bottom of each vertical, leaving a 2-in.-wide flat at the front.

Notch the Shelves to Fit

After ripping the shelves to width, mark out the notches from the back edge. Cut the notches for the shelves using the same dado setup you used for the verticals, and set up the carriage with a stop block. Use the hold-down clamps on blocks to grip the shelves firmly. Raise the dado blades as high as possible to get the flattest cut on the downward arc. Setting the dado blades at full height is dangerous, so keep your hands completely away from the cut. After cutting all of the shelves at one setting, reset the stop block and repeat the process until all of the notches have been cut. Make any necessary adjustments in the length of the notches so that the shelves line up with the back edge of the verticals. When you are done notching, radius the ends of the shelves and round over the front top and bottom edges. If your layout and machining have been accurate, all of the pieces should slide together easily. At this point they're ready for a final sanding and finish.

You can assemble this bookcase by yourself, but it never hurts to have a second pair of hands to help out. Lean the verticals against the wall and slide the bottom shelf into place. One by one, work your way up to the top. This process should take only a few minutes. Use small shims with double-sided carpet tape to level the case. If the unit is installed on a slippery wood or tile floor, you can mount a few small metal corner braces beneath the bottom shelf.

STEVE LATTA teaches woodworking at the Thaddeus Stevens College of Technology in Lancaster, Pa.

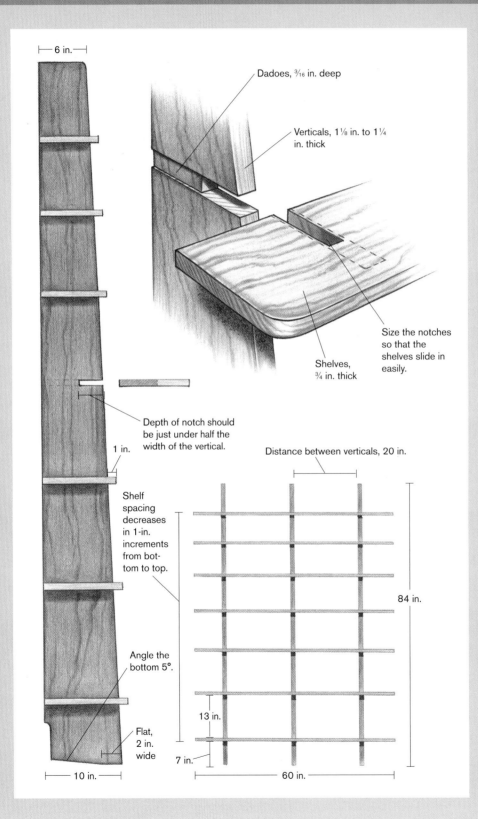

6 in.

Dadoes, ³⁄₁₆ in. deep

Verticals, 1¹⁄₈ in. to 1¼ in. thick

Size the notches so that the shelves slide in easily.

Shelves, ¾ in. thick

Depth of notch should be just under half the width of the vertical.

1 in.

Shelf spacing decreases in 1-in. increments from bottom to top.

Distance between verticals, 20 in.

84 in.

13 in.

Angle the bottom 5°.

Flat, 2 in. wide

7 in.

10 in.

60 in.

DADO ONE SIDE AT A TIME. After setting the blades to the right height, make all of the dado cuts on one side of the verticals. Transfer the cut lines for the dadoes on the second side with a square and a sharp pencil.

Latta chose this joint for its ease of construction and its strength. Shoulders created by the dadoes in the verticals give full support at the intersection with each shelf. The interlocking shelves and verticals fit together without the need for hardware.

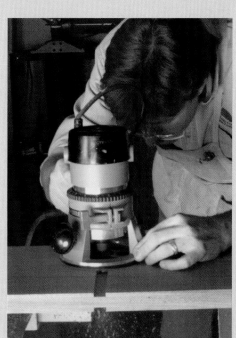

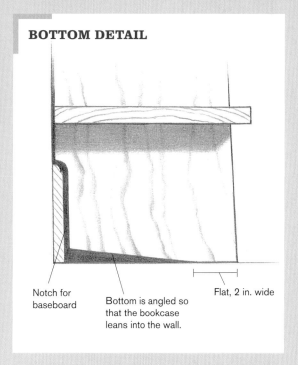

CLEAN UP THE SABERSAW CUT. Use a router equipped with a bearing-guided, flush-trimming bit.

CUT AWAY THE WOOD YOU DON'T NEED. Housed lap joints require you to remove some wood from all of the pieces being joined. In the verticals, remove most of the waste with a sabersaw (above).

NOTCH CUTS REQUIRE CLAMPS. While plowing out the notches for all of the shelves, Latta clamps the workpiece in place for each cut, being careful to keep his hands well clear of the exposed dado blades.

BOTTOM DETAIL

Notch for baseboard

Bottom is angled so that the bookcase leans into the wall.

Flat, 2 in. wide

Updated Arts and Crafts Bookcase

BY GREGORY PAOLINI

Anyone familiar with American furniture would immediately identify this bookcase as an Arts and Crafts design. However, it differs from traditional pieces in two important ways. Arts and Crafts furniture usually is made from quartersawn white oak, but I built this bookcase from curly cherry. Traditional Arts and Crafts pieces are joined with mortises and tenons, while I use a modern variation—the floating tenon.

In floating-tenon joinery, a wooden spline (the floating tenon) joins mortises routed in both pieces (see the photo on the facing page). I find floating-tenon joinery to be much faster than traditional mortise-and-tenon, and plenty strong.

I spent time choosing highly figured boards for the front rails and the side panels, which will be most visible. The back is of shiplapped cherry, resawn (sliced in half to produce two thinner boards) from 4/4 stock. Shiplapping is a method of slightly overlapping boards by rabbeting the opposite edge of each side. Shiplapped boards rarely end up sitting exactly flush with each other. Those who don't like that look might substitute plywood or tongue-and-groove boards for the back.

BOOKCASE ANATOMY

Built from cherry and joined with floating tenons, this case is a modern take on an Arts and Crafts classic. The tenons provide rigidity so that the sides and back can float within the rails and stretchers. The side panels are book-matched and the back is shiplapped.

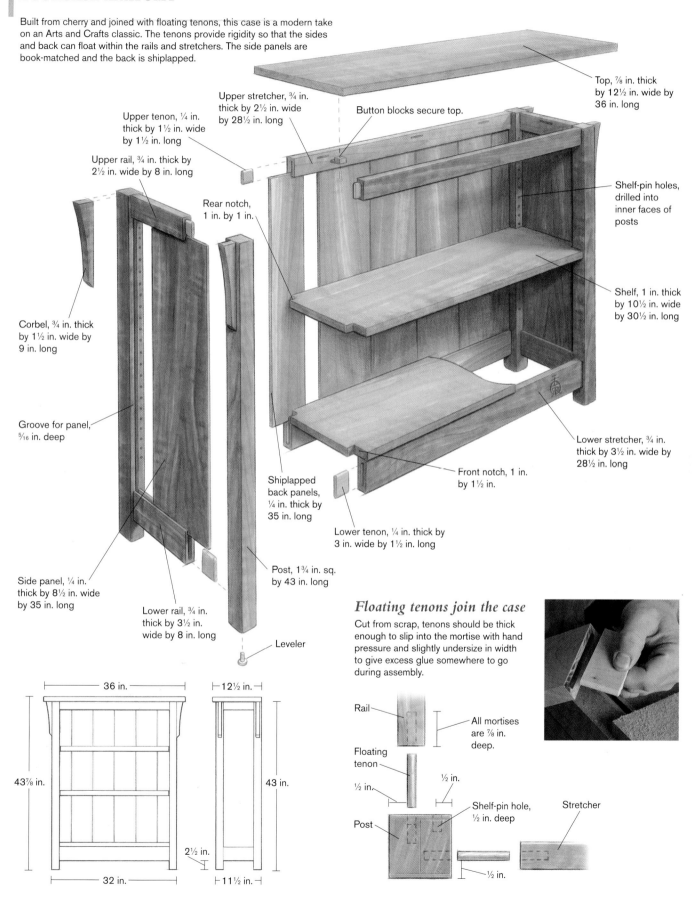

Upper stretcher, ¾ in. thick by 2½ in. wide by 28½ in. long

Button blocks secure top.

Top, ⅞ in. thick by 12½ in. wide by 36 in. long

Upper tenon, ¼ in. thick by 1½ in. wide by 1½ in. long

Upper rail, ¾ in. thick by 2½ in. wide by 8 in. long

Rear notch, 1 in. by 1 in.

Shelf-pin holes, drilled into inner faces of posts

Corbel, ¾ in. thick by 1½ in. wide by 9 in. long

Shelf, 1 in. thick by 10½ in. wide by 30½ in. long

Groove for panel, 5/16 in. deep

Lower stretcher, ¾ in. thick by 3½ in. wide by 28½ in. long

Shiplapped back panels, ¼ in. thick by 35 in. long

Front notch, 1 in. by 1½ in.

Lower tenon, ¼ in. thick by 3 in. wide by 1½ in. long

Side panel, ¼ in. thick by 8½ in. wide by 35 in. long

Post, 1¾ in. sq. by 43 in. long

Lower rail, ¾ in. thick by 3½ in. wide by 8 in. long

Leveler

36 in.

12½ in.

43⅞ in.

43 in.

2½ in.

32 in.

11½ in.

Floating tenons join the case

Cut from scrap, tenons should be thick enough to slip into the mortise with hand pressure and slightly undersize in width to give excess glue somewhere to go during assembly.

Rail

All mortises are ⅞ in. deep.

Floating tenon

½ in.

½ in.

½ in.

Post

Shelf-pin hole, ½ in. deep

Stretcher

½ in.

Routing the Rail Mortises

A SIMPLE MORTISING JIG

Fitted with a guide bushing the same diameter as the slot, a plunge router easily mortises the ends of the rails and stretchers.

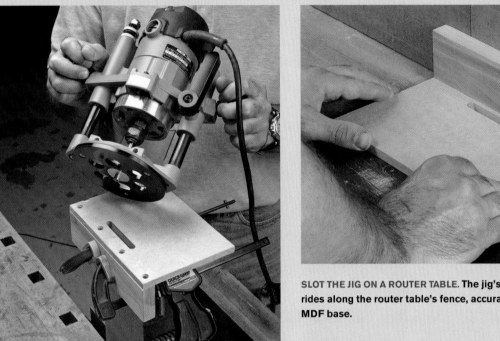

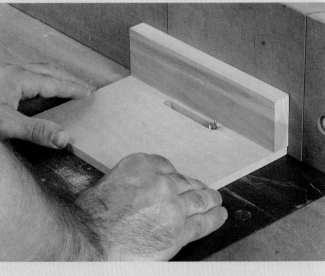

SLOT THE JIG ON A ROUTER TABLE. The jig's hardwood fence rides along the router table's fence, accurately slotting the jig's MDF base.

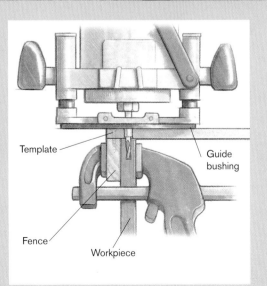

Template

Fence

Workpiece

Guide bushing

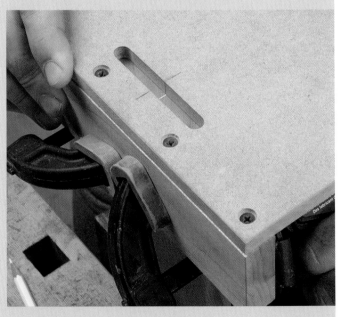

MARK CENTERLINES ON BOTH THE JIG'S SLOT AND THE WORKPIECE. Line up the centerlines and clamp the stock in the jig.

Prepare the Stock Before You Begin

As with all projects, I make sure the lumber is dried properly, and acclimate it to my shop for a couple of weeks. After that, I rough-cut all of the boards slightly oversize, and let them sit for an extra day or two in case the wood still wants to shift a bit.

Face-jointing is a critical, but often overlooked, step in dressing lumber. Jointing one face flattens the board, removing flaws such as cupping or mild twisting. To keep track of it as a reference surface, I mark the jointed face with chalk. After face-jointing, I square one edge of each board, being sure to feed it through the jointer with the flattened face against the fence. When I plane the stock to thickness, the jointed face rides across the bed of the planer, ensuring a flat board.

Like the shiplapped back, the side panels are resawn from 4/4 stock. I leave the stock destined for resawing as thick as possible, planing it only to remove the rough face.

My bandsaw is a basic 14-in. model with a 6-in. riser block to add capacity. It's not terribly powerful, so to help it out while resawing wide stock, I start by kerfing both edges of the boards on the tablesaw. This leaves less wood in the center of the board to bandsaw, and the kerfs help guide the bandsaw blade to ensure a straighter cut.

The boards resawn for the back are planed to finished thickness, and then weighted down in a stack to keep them flat. These boards can vary in width, which adds a little character to the bookcase, and should be left a little oversize for fitting to the back of the case.

The side panels are book-matched (resawn panels are glued edge to edge so that the grain of each mirrors the other). When the glue has cured, scrape away the excess, and plane the sides to their final thickness. As with the back, I leave the side panels oversize and fit them to the case later.

I couldn't find any 8/4 stock for the posts, so I glued each one from two pieces of 4/4 stock planed to ⅞ in. To give the illusion that these posts came from one piece of wood, I ripped some cherry to about ⅛ in. thick, and used it as a thick veneer on the sides of the posts that showed the glueline. Although this technique also results in gluelines, they're so close to the corners of the posts that they're barely noticeable.

Floating Tenons Speed Construction

As with traditional mortise-and-tenon joints, floating tenons should be about one-third the thickness of the stock. In this case, the finished thickness of the bookcase rails is ¾ in.; the tenons are ¼ in. thick. Accordingly, I cut the mortises with a ¼-in. spiral upcutting bit on a plunge router using a simple jig (see the sidebar on the facing page).

I make the tenons by ripping and planing lengths of stock to fit the mortises. The tenon edges are bullnosed on a router table. The tenons should be thick enough to slip into the mortises with hand pressure, and a little undersize in width to give air and excess glue somewhere to go. The mortises are just over ¾ in. deep; I cut the tenon stock into 1½-in.-long pieces.

Mortise and Groove the Frame

I mortise the posts using a plunge router and a fence. The bit is the same ¼-in. spiral upcutting bit used to mortise the rails and stretchers. I have to set up the router and fence anyway to groove the posts for the side panels and shiplapped back, and the panels are the same thickness as the tenons. So, cutting the mortises at the same time is only a matter of deepening the groove at the top and bottom of the post. To provide additional support for the router, I place a second post alongside the one being routed (see the drawing, on p. 94). So as not to strain the router bit, it's important

Routing the Post Mortises

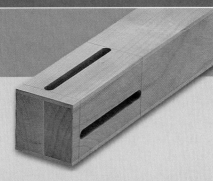

SUPPORT THE ROUTER

When mortising the posts, there's not much surface area to support the router. A second post laid beside the workpiece adds support.

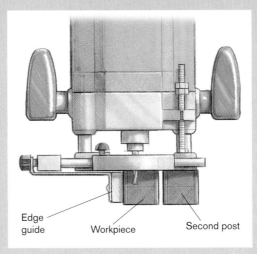

Edge guide   Workpiece   Second post

to make several light passes instead of one heavy pass. When a router bit spinning at 20,000 rpm breaks, bad things happen. Before putting the router away, I cut small grooves in the upper rails and stretchers. Later on, I will use them to secure the top with button blocks (see the drawing on p. 91).

Bookcases get loaded with hundreds of pounds of books, and it's tough on the joints if the piece is not level. I like to add adjustable levelers to the bottoms of the posts. I use common metal pad levelers available at most hardware stores, and screw them into threaded inserts that I install in the base of each post.

The next operation on the posts is to drill an array of holes for the adjustable shelf pins. To keep them out of view, I locate the bores for these pins on the inner faces of the posts. I use a jig that I made, with holes drilled at the cabinetmaker's standard 32-mm spacing. These holes are drilled to accept a ⅜-in. router bushing. With my plunge router so equipped, I "drill" the holes with a ¼-in. spiral upcutting bit.

Finally, I ease the bottoms of the posts by holding them at an angle and spinning the bottoms against a sander.

Dry-Assemble to Check Final Dimensions

With all the joints cut, I dry-assemble the bookcase and measure for the back and side panels. Both the side panels and the back will expand and contract due to seasonal humidity—about ⅛ in. per foot of width. How you size the panels depends on the season. For example, if it's humid, the panels should fit snugly because they'll dry and

Grooves for the Back and Side Panels

MILL THE GROOVES IN THE RAILS AND STRETCHERS ON THE TABLESAW. **This method is a safer, easier alternative to routing the thin edges of these pieces.**

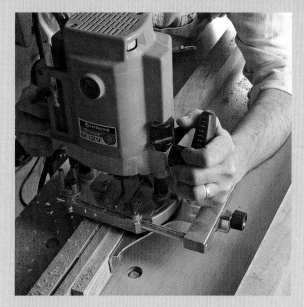

A PLUNGE ROUTER FITTED WITH A FENCE MILLS THE GROOVES IN THE POSTS. **Use the same router setup used to cut the mortises in the posts.**

PREFINISHING SAVES HOURS OF TIME CLEANING GLUE SQUEEZE-OUT. **Shop towels shoved into the mortises keep them finish free to ensure glue adhesion. Glue-up starts with the sides (right). Allow them to dry overnight before removing the clamps.**

shrink when the season changes. If your shop is very dry, keep the fit looser (to allow some expansion).

Now is also the time to measure the final length and depth of the shelves, and lay out the notches at the corners where the shelves will fit around the posts. I cut these notches on a bandsaw, but you could just as well use a handsaw or jigsaw. Leave a 1/16-in. space between each post and its corresponding notch to accommodate seasonal movement.

After I have sized the side panels, back, and shelves, I do one last dry-fit and make any required adjustments. When I know everything will fit together, I sand all the pieces to 220 grit.

Making and attaching the corbels is the final step before finishing. I bandsaw them, then smooth the sawn surfaces with a spokeshave and a little sanding. Because the corbels are only ornamental, they can be attached with brads and glue.

Finished—but Not Done

To minimize the problems glue squeeze-out can cause, I finish all the parts before assembly. Prefinishing takes discipline; after all this time, you just want to see the bookcase take shape. But finishing the parts first means you won't have to spend tedious hours trying to clean up glue squeeze-out later.

I apply a coat of Zinsser® Bulls Eye® SealCoat™ sanding sealer over the raw wood to minimize grain raising. The sealer also adds a nice amber hue typical of traditional oil-based finishes, but lacking in the water-based ones I use. I let it dry over-

NEXT COME THE STRETCHERS AND THE BACK. You may want to enlist a helper when putting together the shiplapped back.

TOP OFF THE ASSEMBLY WITH THE FINAL SIDE. Use pine blocks on each side of the corbels to transfer clamping pressure to the posts.

night, then apply several coats of Minwax® Polycrylic. Be sure to apply the same number of coats to all sides of the pieces to minimize the chance of the wood warping.

Putting It All Together

I assemble the bookcase in stages, starting with the sides. The best way I've found to glue the mortises and tenons together is to apply a thin bead of glue along the top of the mortise, and let gravity pull it down. As soon as I've clamped the assembly, I check it with a carpenter's framing square.

After the sides have cured, I move on to assembling the front and the back (see photos above). You might want to use polyurethane glue for assembling the back; it has a longer open time than yellow glue.

While clamping the bottom is straightforward, the top with its corbels causes a problem. The solution is to use small pine blocks on each side of the corbels to transmit clamping pressure to the posts. Once the glue has cured, I can easily remove any squeeze-out, which doesn't bond to the top coat very well. Then I attach the top with button blocks to allow for wood movement, and install the shelves. I finish up with a quick coat of wax for its tactile benefit.

GREGORY PAOLINI is a Roycroft Renaissance Artisan who builds furniture part time in his Depew, N.Y., basement shop.

Outfitting a Clothes Closet

BY GARY M. KATZ

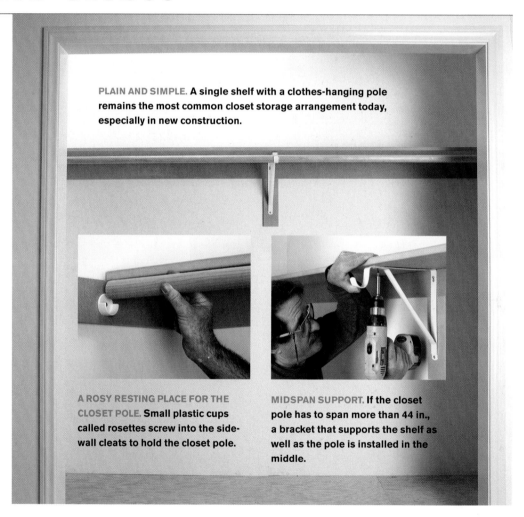

PLAIN AND SIMPLE. A single shelf with a clothes-hanging pole remains the most common closet storage arrangement today, especially in new construction.

A ROSY RESTING PLACE FOR THE CLOSET POLE. Small plastic cups called rosettes screw into the side-wall cleats to hold the closet pole.

MIDSPAN SUPPORT. If the closet pole has to span more than 44 in., a bracket that supports the shelf as well as the pole is installed in the middle.

lothes closets used to be really simple. A single shelf with a pole high enough to keep long dresses off the floor seemed to be all anyone ever needed. Maybe people didn't have as many clothes then, or maybe space wasn't at such a premium. These days, though, people are demanding much more from their closets (see the photo on the facing page).

That Good Old Shelf and Pole Might Be All You Need

The most common closet-shelf arrangement in American households is probably still a single shelf and pole (see the photos above). With this system, the shelf is installed at 68 in. with the pole at about 66 in. from the floor, which is high enough to

Sizing Up Clothes Storage

A well-organized closet makes the most out of available space with single-pole as well as double-pole hanging areas and different-size shelves for a variety of purposes.

Minimum distance between shelf and pole: 1¼ in.

40 in. to 42 in.

Single pole for long items

Double pole for shirts, jackets, and pants

Maximum unsupported width of pole: 44 in.

Sweater shelves: 12 in. high

Shelf sections should be 30 in. to 44 in. wide.

Shoe shelves: 7 in. high

Bottom shelf: 16 in. off floor for boot storage

42 in.

66 in.

Hanging clothes need 24 in. to any adjacent walls or shelving.

keep even the longest hanging clothes, such as coats and dresses, off the carpet.

I make most single-shelf arrangements out of medium-density fiberboard (MDF), and the layout is simple. First, I mark the shelf height of 68 in. and draw a level line on the back wall of the closet. Then I measure and cut the cleat for the back wall. The side-wall cleats have to hold the closet pole, so I cut them long enough to catch a stud for solid support. I make the cleats out of 1x4 so that they are wide enough to attach the rosettes that I install to hold the closet pole.

Back in the closet, I hold the back-wall cleat to the level line, and I attach the cleat with two 8d finish nails at each stud. Next, I level the side cleats with a torpedo level and then shoot them into place. The closet shelf is now ready to be dropped into place on top of the cleats.

For any span greater than 44 in., I install a shelf-and-pole bracket midspan, using a 10-in. piece of cleat stock as a backer block to hold the bracket away from the wall. If there is no stud for securing the backer block, I use screws driven into drywall fasteners that will be hidden by the bracket. The bracket is then screwed to the cleat, to the backer block, and to the shelf.

On the side cleats, I center the pole rosettes the same distance from the back cleat as the hook on the support bracket, usually 11½ in. to 12 in., depending on the bracket. Next, I measure and cut a wooden dowel for the closet pole and drop it into place. A screw driven into the pole through the support bracket completes the installation. I always predrill so that the screw doesn't split the pole.

Planning Lets You Maximize Storage and Production

These days, most homeowners want to make the most of clothes storage in their closets, so the old shelf-and-pole system won't do. Besides the single shelf and pole, which is needed for long, hanging items such as dresses and coats, other closet-storage arrangements include a double pole for shorter hanging items, such as pants and shirts, and banks of shelves for shoes and sweaters.

I try to incorporate a section of each type of storage in every closet. In general, I keep each section to between 30 in. and 44 in. Anything shorter is too narrow to be of much use, and anything longer requires additional support.

One of the first things I look at is the type of closet being outfitted. With a reach-in closet (usually 22 in. to 36 in. deep), the storage sections all have to fit on the back wall of the closet. In these cases, I try to divide the closet into three equal spaces. For example, an 8-ft.-wide closet can be split into three 32-in. sections. If a reach-in closet is less than 7 ft. wide, I often leave out one section, depending on the client's needs.

Walk-in closets, on the other hand, are bigger and deeper and have storage on more than one wall. Shelving options in these closets are less restricted. Walk-in closets come in many shapes and sizes, from large rooms that double as dressing rooms to deep, narrow spaces with L-shaped shelving. Most walk-in closets I work on are 5 ft. to 6 ft. deep. If a closet is to have storage on both side walls, it should be at least 6 ft. wide.

The homeowner's needs also play a part in determining the width of each storage section. For example, if a client has only a few long dresses or coats, I may opt to keep the single pole smaller to maximize the space for other sections.

Finally, I keep layouts as simple as possible, and I try to standardize the sizes of the various sections for all the closets throughout the home. Keeping section sizes the same from closet to closet allows me to set repetitive stops on my chopsaw and to cut shelving kits (dividers, cleats, shelves, and poles) for several closets at once.

MDF Shelf System

MDF SHELVING HAS TO BE LAID OUT ON THE WALL. Because MDF shelving is supported on permanently mounted cleats, the entire layout is done on the unfinished closet walls.

DIVIDERS ARE NAILED TO THE CLEATS. Vertical dividers with the bottoms angled for minimal flooring interference are nailed to the ends of the cleats to hold them in place until they can be locked in by the top shelf.

SHELVES STABILIZE THE DIVIDERS. Each shelf is nailed to the cleats permanently to help hold the dividers straight and square to the wall.

WOODEN BISCUIT CONNECTS THE CORNER. A dry-fit wooden biscuit is inserted to keep the top shelf at the same level where two legs join in a corner (inset above).

READY FOR THE PAINTER. With the top shelf nailed in to lock all the dividers in place (left), the last items to be installed are the rosettes and closet poles. The shelves will be painted at the same time as the closet walls.

PREFINISHED DIVIDERS ARE SET ON A LEDGER. A 1x4 ledger, 16 in. from the floor, is attached to the closet wall to keep prefinished dividers off the floor.

THE DIVIDER SETS THE HEIGHT OF THE CLEAT. With a level ledger and dividers cut to the same length, the cleat for the top shelf is set flush to the top of the divider.

THE ONLY MEASUREMENT IN THE CLOSET. Other than the initial measurement for the ledger, the only measurement that needs to be taken is for the width of the remaining space. All other measurements are predetermined.

MDF Shelves Are Not Adjustable

For new construction or for unfinished closet walls, I usually go with MDF shelving, and the first step is always careful layout (see the top left photo on p. 101). (MDF shelving and closet walls are usually painted at the same time, covering any pencil marks I might leave.)

I begin by drawing a plumb line for each vertical divider that separates areas of shelving and hanging clothes. I put an X on the side of the line where the ¾-in.-thick divider will land. Then I draw level lines for each shelf. The disadvantage to this system is that the cleats are permanently installed, so spaces between shelves must be predetermined.

I cut the cleats, dividers, and shelves for the entire closet. Again, any cleat that carries a closet pole is made of 1x4, but I use 1x2 for cleats that support only shelves. I make my dividers 14 in. to 16 in. wide and cut the top corners at a slight radius for a

nicer look. I usually cut the bottom of the MDF dividers at a 45° angle, leaving only 1 in. of the divider on the floor. This 1-in. bearing surface gives ample support without making a hassle for the flooring contractor, and it gives me a place to end the baseboard at each divider. A laminate trimmer fitted with a ⅛-in. roundover bit eases the sharp edges on the dividers.

Start in a Corner

After cutting, I stack all the cleats and dividers in the closet under the spot where they will be installed. Then I begin in one corner, installing the cleats on the lines that I drew.

When the first set of cleats is secured, I nail the first divider into the ends of the cleat and install the next set of cleats. This process is continued until all the dividers and wall cleats have been installed (see the top center photo on p. 101). Next, I glue and nail cleats onto the dividers for each shelf. I cut these cleats so that they end

GADGETS FOR PREFINISHED SHELVING. Special pieces sold by shelving manufacturers help with installation. Shelf-attachment brackets (above left) eliminate weak end-grain fastening. When screws are used, decorative end caps cover the heads (above center). Oval-shaped steel closet poles hang on brackets that slip into predrilled holes (above right).

about ½ in. short of the front edge of the divider for a neat, clean look.

Once all the cleats and dividers are in, I cut and install the shelving. At this point, the dividers are still fairly flimsy, but the shelves help to hold them in place and keep them square to the wall. I install the shelves nearest to the floor first, nailing through the ends and the back edge into the cleats below. I then work my way up each section, nailing the shelves to the cleats as I go (see the top right photo on p. 101). Because the spacing of MDF shelves is determined ahead of time and because the shelves get caulked in and painted after the installation, I nail every shelf in place permanently.

I leave the top shelf for last. In most closets, the top shelf will turn a corner. You can buy aluminum H-clips that join the shelves at the corner, but these clips are unsightly even after everything on the interior of the closet is painted. Instead, I use a dry-fit wooden biscuit to join the inside corner (see the inset photo at the bottom of p. 101).

TOPPING OFF A WELL-FITTED CLOSET. The top shelf goes in last and is attached to the cleat in the back and to the dividers in the front to tie the shelving system together.

With the shelf in place, I shoot a nail every foot or so along the back edge as well as a single nail into each divider along the front edge.

The last things to go in are the closet poles. I locate and install the rosettes and then cut each pole long enough so that it fits snugly into the rosettes, but not enough to push the dividers out of line (see the photo on p. 101).

No Detailed Layout for Prefinished Shelving

When I'm asked to put a shelving system into an existing closet that has been painted, I opt for prefinished shelving, usually melamine. Heavy layout lines can't be drawn on the finished walls, so to avoid unsightly marks and blemishes, I let cleat and shelf sizes determine where the dividers are located. Also, because the shelving is prefinished, any cut edges that will be seen have to be edge-banded. With careful planning, I can minimize or eliminate edgebanding.

Most prefinished dividers have predrilled holes that accept shelf supports, eliminating the need for divider cleats. Unless the client requests dividers run all the way to the floor, I support the dividers on a 1x4 ledger along the wall 16 in. off the floor.

I cut all the dividers the same, and I cut extra dividers to hold shelves and poles on the side walls. I cut the shelves for all but the last section to the predetermined lengths. I also cut lengths of cleat for each section to hold the tops of the dividers and the top shelf.

I begin by setting the side-wall dividers on the ledger and nailing them to the wall (see the left photo on p. 102). Next, I nail the first top cleat to the wall. A divider is placed on the ledger and held against the cleat to set its height (see the center photo on p. 102). After the cleat is secured, the top-rear corner of the divider is nailed to the end of the cleat. The next top cleats and dividers are now nailed into place until I'm

left with the last section. Up to this point, I have not made a single measurement or pencil mark in the closet except for the height and length of the ledger.

I measure and cut the top cleat and shelves for the last section and nail the cleat into place (see the right photo on p. 102). The bottom shelf in each section squares and stabilizes the dividers, so it is attached permanently with special fasteners sold with the shelving material (see the top left photo on p. 103). The back edge of the shelf is nailed to the ledger.

Near midheight of the divider, I set shelf-support brackets and lay in a single shelf. I predrill and drive a 1⅝-in. screw through the divider and into this shelf to stabilize the middle of the divider. Small decorative caps cover the screws (see the top center photo on p. 103). With the shelf holding the divider straight, I install corner brackets that secure the dividers to the back wall. Corner brackets also join the dividers to the top cleats.

After the dividers are secured and stabilized, I can space the rest of the shelves on the adjustable supports according to my client's wishes. Next come the poles. With prefinished shelving systems, I use brackets that hold oval-shaped chrome-plated steel poles (see the top right photo on p. 103). The brackets pop into the predrilled holes, and the pole stock is cut to length with a hacksaw. If I don't think that the dividers have been stabilized adequately, I can run a cleat and shelf at every pole to keep the dividers from bulging and weakening. The final step is putting in the top shelf, which I nail or screw along the back edge as well as into the front corners of each divider (see the bottom photo on p. 103).

GARY M. KATZ, is a carpenter and writer living in Reseda, Calif. He is the author of *The Doorhanger's Handbook* (The Taunton Press, 1998).

Wire Shelving: A Do-It-Yourself Alternative

One type of closet shelving gaining popularity today is wire shelving, especially among homeowners who like to do their own work. This product is prefinished and simple to install with few tools. Also, the open nature of wire shelving lets air circulate around clothes. Many building-supply outlets sell wire-shelving kits for standard-size closets, and many of these kits don't require cutting.

Admittedly, I haven't installed a whole lot of wire shelving, but when I have, I found that the instructions were always vague and misleading, so here's how I approach a wire-shelving installation.

In place of cleats, wire shelving is attached to the wall with plastic clips. Instead of solid dividers, the front edge of wire shelving is supported by poles also equipped with plastic clips. After screwing clips to the pole at whatever height I want the shelves, I use the poles to transfer shelf heights to the wall (photo 1).

I then rest the back edge of the shelf against the wall and mark between the wires where I want the clips to fall. I put clips every 8 in. to 10 in., enough to support most clothing. With a level at the height mark, I now mark the exact location of all the clips. The clips are screwed into the framing wherever possible, and the rest go in with drywall anchors.

The shelving is prepared by first cutting it to length (if necessary) with either a hacksaw or with bolt cutters. Tiny flexible plastic caps slip over all the cut wire ends. The back edges of the shelves can now be snapped onto the clips, leaving the shelves hanging in place (photo 2).

Wherever a shelf meets an adjacent wall, I install a special bracket that holds the front edge of the shelf. With the magnet of my torpedo level stuck to the shelf, I rotate the shelf into place and install the bracket. Next, I snap the shelves into the pole clips (photo 3) and work on the shelving for any adjacent walls. Angled support brackets hold shelves level where they meet a shelf on an adjacent wall (photo 4). Closet poles can be hung from any shelf with factory-made pole brackets, but special shelving with heavy wire on the outer edge is designed specifically for hanging clothes.

–G.M.K.

POLES TAKE THE PLACE OF DIVIDERS. Metal poles with plastic clips support the front edge of wire shelving. Here, shelf heights are taken from the pole.

SHELVES SNAP ONTO THE WALL FIRST. After clips are screwed to the wall, the shelving is snapped in and left hanging.

CLIPS ON THE POLES HOLD THE FRONTS OF THE SHELVES. While clipped to the wall, the shelves pivot up and snap to the poles.

ANGLE BRACES SUPPORT THE SHELVES. Braces that snap into the wire shelving and screw to the wall reinforce long spans and support the shelves' ends where they meet in a corner.

Built-in Basics

TONY O'MALLEY

When designing and building the more utilitarian pieces for your home—entertainment centers, bookcases, corner hutches—you'll inevitably consider the question: Should I make it free-standing or built-in? The answer involves both aesthetics (which will look better?) and economics (do you want to spend all of that time and effort on a project you'll have to leave behind if you move?). Sooner or later, you're likely to tackle a built-in.

Over the last few years I've earned an increasing portion of my income from woodworking, and the majority of it has been from built-in projects. Built-ins are popular with homeowners for two important reasons: First, they add value, becoming a permanent, handcrafted part of a home. Second, you can buy a piece of furniture at a store, but you can't buy a built-in.

Continued on p. 111

ANATOMY OF A TYPICAL BUILT-IN

For this home office, separate cabinets made of hardwood plywood were screwed together on a level base. Then solid face-frame pieces were nailed to the cases with the two outside stiles scribed to fit the walls. Crest and base moldings went on next. Shelves (on adjustable pins) and doors (on cup hinges) were installed, and last, the thick desktop slab was slid into place.

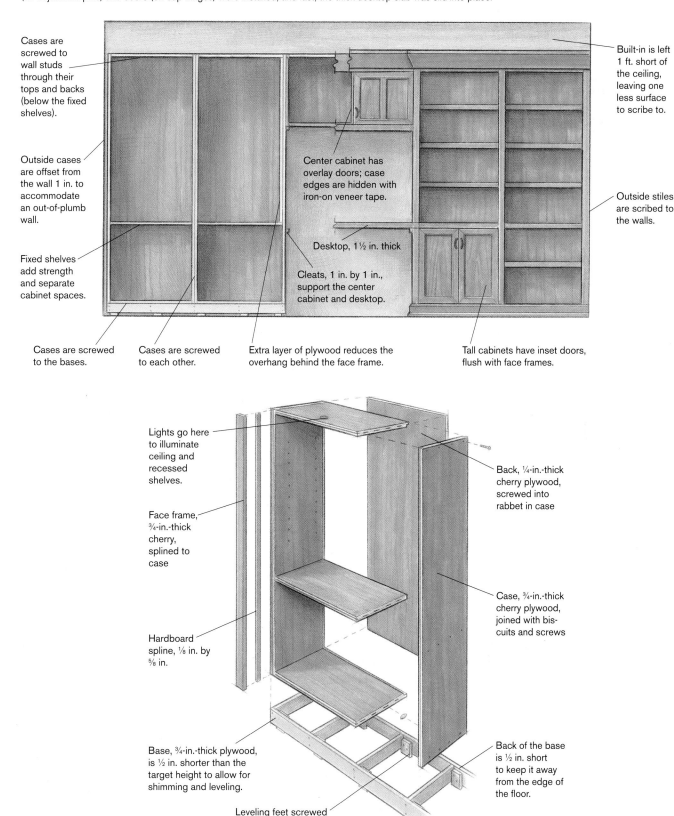

Cases are screwed to wall studs through their tops and backs (below the fixed shelves).

Outside cases are offset from the wall 1 in. to accommodate an out-of-plumb wall.

Fixed shelves add strength and separate cabinet spaces.

Cases are screwed to the bases.

Cases are screwed to each other.

Center cabinet has overlay doors; case edges are hidden with iron-on veneer tape.

Desktop, 1½ in. thick

Cleats, 1 in. by 1 in., support the center cabinet and desktop.

Extra layer of plywood reduces the overhang behind the face frame.

Built-in is left 1 ft. short of the ceiling, leaving one less surface to scribe to.

Outside stiles are scribed to the walls.

Tall cabinets have inset doors, flush with face frames.

Lights go here to illuminate ceiling and recessed shelves.

Face frame, ¾-in.-thick cherry, splined to case

Hardboard spline, ⅛ in. by ⅝ in.

Back, ¼-in.-thick cherry plywood, screwed into rabbet in case

Case, ¾-in.-thick cherry plywood, joined with biscuits and screws

Base, ¾-in.-thick plywood, is ½ in. shorter than the target height to allow for shimming and leveling.

Leveling feet screwed to inside of base

Back of the base is ½ in. short to keep it away from the edge of the floor.

Bases and Cases

START WITH LEVEL BASES

SHIM ONE BASE LEVEL. Check it along its length and width. While leveling it, raise it to the target base height.

USE SMALL SQUARES OF PLYWOOD AS LEVELING FEET. Screw these to the base, which will remain level even when shifted slightly during later stages.

RAISE AND LEVEL THE SECOND BASE. Use a level and a tight mason's cord to bring the second base up to the same level as the first one.

PLACE TWO CASES ON EACH LEVEL BASE. These cases should be sanded and finished before installation.

SCREW THE CASES TOGETHER. Drive the screws just below where an adjustable shelf might go.

SCREW THE CASES TO THE BASE. Make sure the cases are flush with the front and inside edges of the base so that the face frame and base molding go on straight. Note that the base ends up ½ in. short of the wall, avoiding inconsistencies at the edge of the floor.

CONNECT THE SIDES. Set the center cabinet on its cleats to set the distance between the tall cases. Clamp in the desktop slab to plumb the cabinets, and screw through the cabinet backs to attach them to the wall studs. Shim where there are gaps.

Splines add strength and ease assembly

All of the frame pieces receive ⅛-in. splines, which serve a number of functions: They locate the pieces precisely on the cases, hold them in place during dry-fitting, and add some strength to the glued-and-nailed joints.

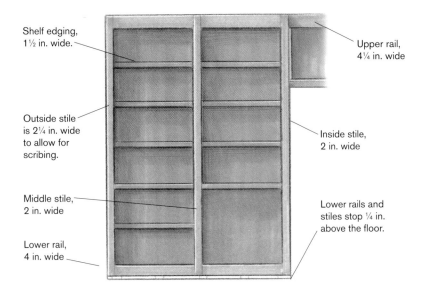

Shelf edging, 1½ in. wide.

Outside stile is 2¼ in. wide to allow for scribing.

Middle stile, 2 in. wide

Lower rail, 4 in. wide

Upper rail, 4¼ in. wide

Inside stile, 2 in. wide

Lower rails and stiles stop ¼ in. above the floor.

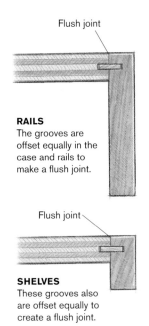

Flush joint

RAILS
The grooves are offset equally in the case and rails to make a flush joint.

Flush joint

SHELVES
These grooves also are offset equally to create a flush joint.

OUTSIDE STILES
The groove in the stile is offset an extra ¼ in. to create a ¼-in. overlap inside the case.

Wall

Groove for scribing (see below)

¼-in. overlap

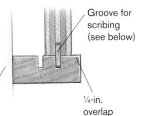

MIDDLE STILES
The groove in the stile is offset ¼ in. to create a ¼-in. overlap in the case. Only one spline is necessary.

¼-in. overlap

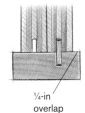

INSIDE STILES
The grooves are offset equally to make a flush joint outside the case. Plywood filler reduces the overhang inside the case.

Outside of case

Flush joint

Filler sheet

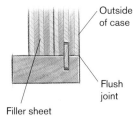

A two-groove sequence makes scribing a cinch. First, make the outside stiles ¼ in. wider to accommodate walls that are slightly bowed. Cut the first groove for final positioning, and cut a second one for scribing.

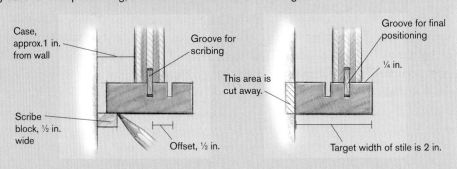

Case, approx. 1 in. from wall

Groove for scribing

Scribe block, ½ in. wide

Offset, ½ in.

This area is cut away.

Groove for final positioning

¼ in.

Target width of stile is 2 in.

1. Position the stile on the scribing groove and use the scribe block to mark the area to be removed.

2. Cut to the scribe line with a jigsaw or bandsaw. Use the other groove to install the stile.

Continued from p.106

Built-ins are a unique form of woodworking, sharing elements of furniture, cabinetry, and finish carpentry. Because the built-in is permanently attached to one or more of the walls, the floor, or the ceiling of a room, the design goal must be to make the built-in appear as an integral part of the room. That means matching and integrating the room's features, especially moldings, into the design. But a built-in also can stand out as a bold counterpoint to the design features of a room. Either way, a successful built-in requires careful planning for its installation. Ideally, all of the finishing is done prior to installation. That, in turn, leads to a number of construction techniques specific to built-ins, including modular cases, scribed edges, and reveals or V-grooves to conceal seams and joints where the cases or face frames come together.

This article follows the making of a built-in wall unit for a home office and includes many of the typical challenges that built-ins present, especially those that involve bookcases and cabinets.

Start With the Room

No two rooms are exactly alike, so no two built-ins are alike either. It's rare to find room surfaces that are dead straight, let alone level and plumb. Yet a built-in must stand level and plumb if it's to look right and if the doors and drawers on the unit are to work properly.

Every built-in starts with a careful assessment of the room conditions, in addition to the obvious measuring of the space it will be built into. The key to success is to scribe parts accurately where they meet the walls, floor, or ceiling, which requires cutting those parts oversize.

Then Work Out the Design

Built-ins run the stylistic gamut from traditional to modern. A painted built-in generally is less expensive than a natural or stained-wood version. In my painted built-ins, I use birch plywood for most case construction and solid poplar for the trim. Painted built-ins are more forgiving because the joints can be caulked and painted over.

The built-in here was planned for in the home's original design and construction. It fills the entire length of a 14-ft. wall but stops a foot short of the 8-ft. ceiling. It also calls for lights on top of the cabinets behind the crown molding and inside the top of each bookcase.

The design is contemporary and straightforward but with some subtle refinements worth mentioning. The wood is cherry, straight-grained in the face and door frames. For contrast, the door panels are plainsawn with custom walnut pulls. The four tall cabinets are in the same plane at 16 in. deep, with the upper shelves set back a few inches to allow the interior lighting to reach them. The open shelves are deep enough for oversize books and magazines, while the closed cabinets are deep enough for storage. The desktop extends to 25 in., and its flared shoulders lie neatly over the vertical face frame, visually connecting the desktop to the fixed shelves in the bookcases. The center cabinet above the desktop is recessed from the main cabinets, creating a visual counterpoint and making the crown molding more eye-catching.

Build the Cases

The cases were built from ¾-in.-thick cherry plywood, and the backs from ¼-in.-thick cherry plywood. Hardwood plywood usually has an "A" side and a mediocre side, so orient it for best appearance.

I use biscuit joinery for almost all case construction because it's versatile, simple, and reliable. On this project, most of the joints could have been screwed together as well because the rows of screws are concealed by moldings, the desktop, or adjacent case sides. Screwing together the cases strengthens the joinery and makes assembly easier because it eliminates clamping.

1. Dry Fit the Face Frames

AFTER SCRIBING THE OUTSIDE STILE TO THE WALL, PUT THE REMAINING
STILES IN PLACE. Their long splines should secure them during the dry-fit.

FIT THE RAILS. Starting at the outside cabinets,
mark and fit the upper and lower rails and the
edging for the fixed shelf. Then move to the
inside cabinets.

PREPARE THE FACE-FRAME PIECES FOR INSTAL-
LATION. Chamfered edges hide inconsistencies at
the joints, allowing you to prefinish the parts in
the shop and nail them on one at a time.

Before assembling the cases, I ran a ⅛-in.-wide groove in the front edge of all the case parts. These grooves will receive splines to position the face-frame parts. I also cut rabbets into the case parts for the back panels.

Before installation, I finished all of the parts with Waterlox®, which is a tung-oil-based finish that can be wiped, brushed, or sprayed on, and builds like a varnish. I applied three coats, sanding in between with 320-grit paper.

Install Level Bases

The bases for built-ins always should be separate from the cases. That way, you can level the bases independently of the larger, more cumbersome cases. There are lots of simple ways to make structural bases for built-ins. Stud lumber can work in many situations; just mill it straight beforehand. But I generally screw together simple boxes from the scrap ¾-in.-thick plywood that's left over from the cases.

Start with a target height—in this project it was the floor of the cases—and work from there. Whatever the target height, the rough base should be built ½ in. shorter to allow for dips in the floor and for shimming up to the target height.

If the base molding is going to touch the floor, it should be milled ½ in. wider than the finished dimension to scribe it to an uneven floor. In this project, I tacked a small shoe molding onto the base molding, which eliminated having to scribe the base molding to the floor.

For this unit, I started by shimming one of the two bases level (see the photos on p. 108). If possible, determine which side of the room is highest overall, and start on that side. To level the second base to the first, I stretched a length of mason's cord from the outside corner of the first base to the outside corner of the second (a laser level also will work), then raised the second one up to the stringline. Once leveled, a base can be screwed to the floor or the

2. Install the Face Frames

START WITH THE INNERMOST STILE. This joint must be flush. Adjust the alignment as you nail on the piece. Shoot through a thin piece of cardboard if your gun has a tendency to dent the surface (inset). Later, fill the nail holes with colored wax.

Crown Molding

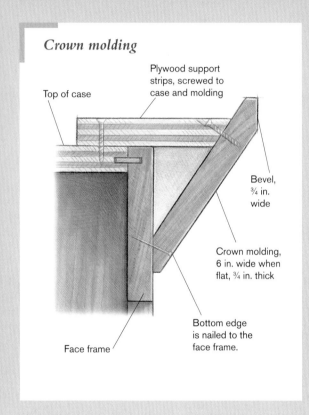

Crown molding

Top of case

Plywood support strips, screwed to case and molding

Bevel, ¾ in. wide

Crown molding, 6 in. wide when flat, ¾ in. thick

Bottom edge is nailed to the face frame.

Face frame

WORK FROM THE CENTER OUT. Clamp blocks to the face frame to ensure an even reveal. On the return pieces, fit the miters first, then dry-fit the pieces and mark their lengths. The front pieces will be trickier. You must nibble away at each end to creep up on a good fit.

wall studs. But in this project, because the bases needed to be shifted slightly when the entire row of cabinets was brought together, I let them float. Once the bases are in place, it's a good time to locate and mark the wall studs.

Install the cases–Set the cases on their leveled bases, and screw them together. Attach the cleats that will support the center cabinet and the desktop. Position the center cabinet and clamp it to the side cabinets. Screw through the walls of the center cabinet to attach it to the side cabinets. Next, set the main desktop slab on its cleats and snug a clamp across the two cases to true up the entire assembly.

Now the entire unit can be attached to the wall. Because I had access to the top of the cabinets, I drilled through the tops at an angle into the studs. I also screwed through the case backs underneath the fixed shelves.

Install the lighting next–Before the face-frame parts, moldings, doors, and desktop are in the way, install any lighting or power strips that you desire.

For the set of cabinets in this project, I used small, surface-mounted halogen lights, which are shaped like hockey pucks and available in home centers. I mounted one underneath the top of each open case, hidden behind the top face-frame rail. These throw some light onto the recessed shelves below. I also mounted one atop each cabinet to throw soft light into the 1-ft. space above the cabinets. The lights are hidden by the crown molding, as is the four-way outlet that was installed above the cabinets by an electrician.

Mill and Dry-Fit the Face-Frame Pieces

With the cabinets installed, I proceeded to dry-fit the face-frame pieces to the cases. Traditional kitchen-cabinet face frames are built as independent frames, held together either with mortise-and-tenon joints or pocket-hole screws, then applied to the cases. With some built-ins, this is a sensible approach. But building large face frames is awkward and unnecessary.

Instead of having flush, glued joints at the intersections of the face-frame panels, I chamfered the edges of all the parts and the ends of the horizontal pieces, leaving a small V-groove wherever parts come together, to hide any minor inconsistencies. As a result, I was able to cut and dry-fit all of the face-frame pieces to the installed cabinets but finish them in the shop on my bench.

With all of the face-frame pieces in place—dry-fitted at this point—you can record the exact openings for the mitered frame doors. The idea is to avoid trimming the doors to fit, as mitered doors must be trimmed equally on all four sides to maintain their symmetry. If you make the doors before at least dry-fitting the face frame, you may end up with uneven miters or uneven gaps around the doors.

Finish and Install the Face Frame

Sand and finish all of the face-frame stock, along with the base- and crown-molding stock. The face-frame parts on most large built-ins are nailed to the cases because it is difficult to clamp and glue face frames to installed cases. I filled the nail holes with wax colored to match the wood tone. I removed the excess wax by rubbing hard with a clean rag.

Working from the stile nearest the center—with its flush joint—I reinstalled the precut, prefinished face-frame parts using a pneumatic nail gun for speed. If you don't have a nailer, you can predrill and nail on the parts with #6 finish nails. I also ran a quick bead of glue into the spline grooves.

A Trick for Mitering Crown Molding

 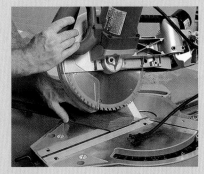 

USE A SAMPLE BLOCK TO BREAK DOWN THE ANGLE. The 6-in.-wide molding won't fit in the miter saw when tilted into its 35° position. But you can fit a smaller version of the molding in the miter saw, tilted against the fence. Set the fence to 45°, and make a cut (left). Then lay the molding flat on the saw (center) to find the proper fence and blade angles for cutting the real thing, which must lie flat.

MAKE TEST CUTS TO FINE-TUNE THE FIT. You will have to reverse the saw fence to cut the opposite angle.

Base Molding

Base molding

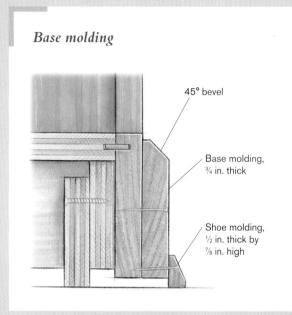

45° bevel

Base molding,
¾ in. thick

Shoe molding,
½ in. thick by
⅞ in. high

INSTALL THE BASE MOLDING. Starting with the return piece, shim the molding up to its proper height and mark the miter (above). Cut the return, and mark and cut the front piece, then nail the moldings in place. A small shoe molding will hide the gap below (see the drawing at left).

Fit and Install the Moldings

Base molding seems like it should slap on easily and quickly, but that's rarely the case with built-ins. Miter any outside corners first; here I started with the return pieces under the desk. Then cut the end that meets the wall, scribing it to fit if necessary. Last, cut or scribe the bottom edge of the piece to bring the top edge of the base molding to the target height.

Installing crown molding is trickier–

The crown molding is a flat piece of 6-in.-wide stock with chamfers cut at the bottom and top edges (see the drawing on p. 114). The chamfer at the bottom determines the angle at which the crown projects from the case; I chose 35°. Pieces of plywood attached to the top of the cases support the upper half of the molding. Basically, I nailed the bottom of the molding in place, then screwed the support pieces to the back of the molding and to the tops of the cases.

I added some glue to the outside miters when everything was ready for final nailing. The squeeze-out cleaned up easily from the finished wood. I nailed the miters together, then went back and added nails along the rest of the molding to secure it to the cases. I finished by screwing on the support blocks behind the top edge.

Make and Install the Doors

The doors on this project are mitered frames around a ¼-in.-thick plywood panel. The mitered look suits this project's contemporary, angular demeanor, and the walnut splines added after assembly will ensure the joints stay tightly closed.

You can use off-the-shelf plywood for the panel, but the back side of the wood is likely to be pretty shabby. To get clean faces in and out, I veneered both sides of a plywood panel, making a nice book-match from sequential leaves of veneer.

I used biscuits to align the faces of the miters during assembly. The biscuits add some strength to the joint but would not be sufficient without the splines.

Make a simple jig for the tablesaw and cut slots through the mitered corners. Clamp a tall auxiliary fence to the tablesaw fence to keep the jig from tipping. Then plane stock for the splines.

Hang the doors–I chose cup hinges for their versatility and ease of installation, though traditional butt hinges would work just as nicely. Cup hinges are classified according to the relationship between the door and the case part they are hung from—inset, full overlay, or half-overlay. The doors on the center cabinet are full overlay, while the bottom doors are inset—with a twist. Because the cabinet side is set back from the edge of the face frame, I had to block out behind the face frames to create a flush surface for an inset hinge.

Make and Fit the Desktop

The desktop is a solid slab of 8/4 cherry planed to 1½ in. thick. It rests on cleats screwed to the case sides. I wanted the extended portion of the desktop to overlap the face frame, angling outward to meet the inside edge of each stile and connecting the desktop visually to the fixed shelf. But cutting clean, precise notches in a single slab would have been impractical.

Instead, I glued up one slab for the entire desktop, then ripped off the front, overlapping section. I crosscut the back section to the same length as the top cabinet and dry-fitted it on its cleat to mark the location of the front of the cabinets. After ripping the back flush with the front of the cabinets, I glued on the longer front extension piece and did another dry-fit to lay out the angled ends. Last, I slid the desktop into place and screwed through the cleats to attach it.

TONY O'MALLEY makes furniture and built-in cabinetry in Emmaus, Pa.

Engineering an Entertainment Center

BY BROOKS TANNER

Entertainment centers have been around since the days of the Victrola®, but with the advent of enormous televisions and sound systems that would astonish Thomas Edison, entertainment centers too need to evolve. A modern cabinet not only needs to house the television but also sound and video media, satellite receivers, DVD players, CD players, audio amplifiers, and the center-channel speaker.

Most designs today are large boxes that differ little from bookshelves or display cabinets, their only concession to electronics being that they have holes for wires. But a good design for an entertainment center takes a little more planning. It starts by examining the requirements of each component and then integrating everything seamlessly.

Television Is the Focal Point of the Cabinet

Television placement is of primary importance. The center of the screen should be at eye level—approximately 43 in. from the floor, assuming an 18-in.-high seat and 25 in. to eye level from the seat.

Any cabinet built today should be made to house a high-definition television (HDTV). A screen that was once 24 in. high now has a width of 32 in. Under the new format, that same 24-in.-high screen will be approximately 43 in. wide. A cabinet that is made for a present television without extra room on the sides will only fit a future television of shorter height.

The new HDTVs allow for six audio channels, so the entertainment center requires a place for center-channel audio. Because this is where most of the dialog comes out, it is important that the sound seem to emanate from the screen, requiring the speaker to be in the middle of the cabinet, directly above or below the television. If it must be placed away from the television, the speaker should be angled toward the listener; otherwise, information from that speaker will sound as if it's above the listener's head or coming from the floor, depending on the height of the speaker.

Drawers for media storage are almost always located in the bottom of the cabinet, convenient for both children and adults. CDs, DVDs, and videotapes fit in a drawer that has an external height of a little over 6 in. To separate media and keep them in neat rows, I usually attach a ⅜-in.-high wood spline to the drawer bottom with double-faced tape. The spline can be removed if the drawer function changes. If small children will use the drawers, plastic media holders usually

DESIGN AROUND THE COMPONENTS

A number of features distinguish a dedicated entertainment center from an ordinary cabinet that happens to house a television.

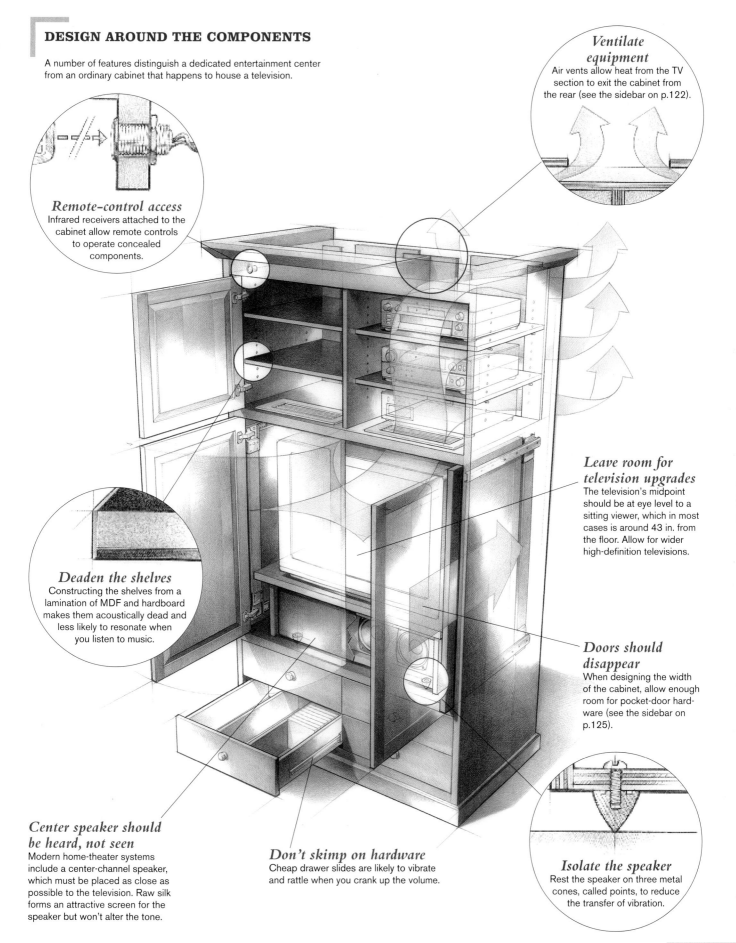

Remote-control access
Infrared receivers attached to the cabinet allow remote controls to operate concealed components.

Ventilate equipment
Air vents allow heat from the TV section to exit the cabinet from the rear (see the sidebar on p.122).

Deaden the shelves
Constructing the shelves from a lamination of MDF and hardboard makes them acoustically dead and less likely to resonate when you listen to music.

Leave room for television upgrades
The television's midpoint should be at eye level to a sitting viewer, which in most cases is around 43 in. from the floor. Allow for wider high-definition televisions.

Doors should disappear
When designing the width of the cabinet, allow enough room for pocket-door hardware (see the sidebar on p.125).

Center speaker should be heard, not seen
Modern home-theater systems include a center-channel speaker, which must be placed as close as possible to the television. Raw silk forms an attractive screen for the speaker but won't alter the tone.

Don't skimp on hardware
Cheap drawer slides are likely to vibrate and rattle when you crank up the volume.

Isolate the speaker
Rest the speaker on three metal cones, called points, to reduce the transfer of vibration.

DIMENSIONS TO CONSIDER

The needs of the components determine the dimensions more than aesthetic considerations do.

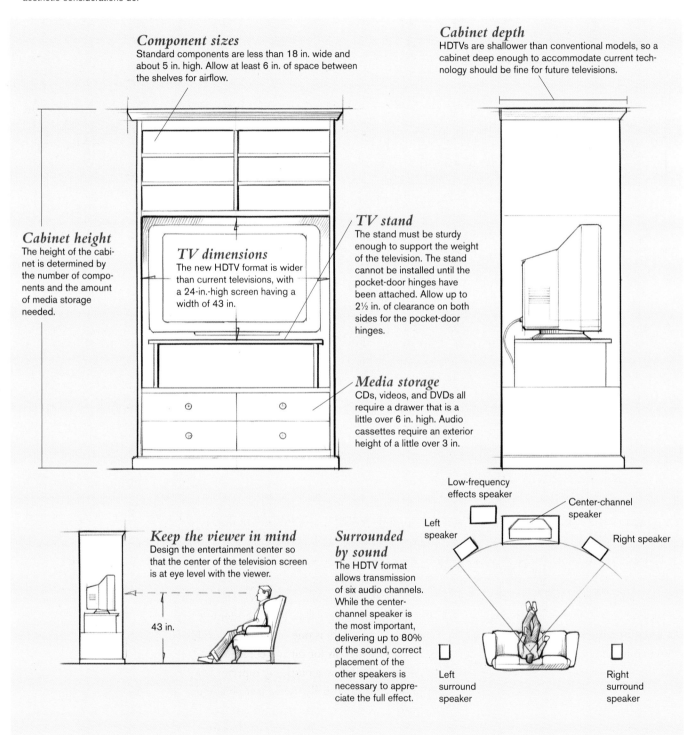

Component sizes
Standard components are less than 18 in. wide and about 5 in. high. Allow at least 6 in. of space between the shelves for airflow.

Cabinet depth
HDTVs are shallower than conventional models, so a cabinet deep enough to accommodate current technology should be fine for future televisions.

Cabinet height
The height of the cabinet is determined by the number of components and the amount of media storage needed.

TV dimensions
The new HDTV format is wider than current televisions, with a 24-in.-high screen having a width of 43 in.

TV stand
The stand must be sturdy enough to support the weight of the television. The stand cannot be installed until the pocket-door hinges have been attached. Allow up to 2½ in. of clearance on both sides for the pocket-door hinges.

Media storage
CDs, videos, and DVDs all require a drawer that is a little over 6 in. high. Audio cassettes require an exterior height of a little over 3 in.

Keep the viewer in mind
Design the entertainment center so that the center of the television screen is at eye level with the viewer.

43 in.

Surrounded by sound
The HDTV format allows transmission of six audio channels. While the center-channel speaker is the most important, delivering up to 80% of the sound, correct placement of the other speakers is necessary to appreciate the full effect.

Low-frequency effects speaker

Center-channel speaker

Left speaker

Right speaker

Left surround speaker

Right surround speaker

Rattle-Free Panels

HOT-MELT GLUE MAKES A CUSHION. To reduce vibration, shim the rear panels down into their grooves and then apply hot-melt glue in a few areas. Remove the shims after the glue has set.

MORE PANELS MAKE LESS NOISE. Small rear panels are less likely to resonate than one large sheet (left).

work better at keeping the contents in order.

The space above the television is reserved for the other electronic components, such as VCRs and CD or DVD players. Mounted on adjustable shelves, the equipment is at eye level for adults and out of reach of young children.

A Solid Structure Minimizes Vibration

In addition to eating prime cabinet space, the center-channel speaker may introduce vibration into the cabinet, if played at a high volume. Vibration can cause both visual and audio distortion. Another effect is the rattling of doors and other cabinet components. For this reason, antivibration solutions should be employed in cabinet construction as well as in speaker mounting.

Cabinets should be as acoustically dead as possible. This is done by keeping the structure rigid and eliminating as many large, thin, flat areas as possible. Medium-density fiberboard (MDF) is one of the better readily available materials for carcase construction. Although MDF is acoustically superior to plywood, I still usually use veneer plywood for the primary carcase. It is stronger and lighter, and by designing a rigid structure, I believe I minimize the acoustical difference between the two materials.

The main sections of the center are glued and dadoed, reinforced with angled nails from a nail gun. I also use multiple rear stress panels, not just one over the entire

Wire Chase and Ventilation

A LABYRINTH OF OVERLAP-PING PANELS PROVIDES AIRFLOW AND ACCESS FOR WIRES. Attach a piece of ½-in.-thick hardwood to the back of the top vertical divider.

INSTALL THE SIDE PANELS. Use pocket screws or biscuits to attach similar hardwood panels to the sides of the cabinet.

TWO PLYWOOD PANELS COME LAST. Attach 2-in.-thick battens across the top and bottom of the opening. Then screw on two ¼-in.-thick panels so that they overlap the center and side panels.

cabinet back. Hot-melt glue applied around each rear panel eliminates any chance of a rattle and also allows some flexing during seasonal changes. Pocket doors have tight closure hardware, with thick felt padding between the door and the face frame. Use good, tight slides for drawers. Most important, use your head when constructing the cabinet—look and listen for anything that may rattle or resonate.

The transmission of vibration from the center-channel speaker to the cabinet also should be minimized by mounting the speaker on three points—which are sharp metal cones available from audio suppliers. By minimizing contact between the speaker and the cabinet, the points reduce the transmission of vibration energy. An easier and cheaper method is to place foam rubber between the speaker and the cabinet.

Designing Airflow Into the Cabinet Keeps Components Cool

The television and the other electrical components all produce heat and require constant airflow to prevent overheating. The easiest solution is not to use doors, allowing the components to sit in free air. A typical cabinet, however, has doors in front of the components, and with the doors closed, there is no airflow. Many commercial units have air slots in the rear panel that allow heat to escape and also serve as a wire chase. The problem with these slots is that the shelves block the slots and reduce or eliminate airflow.

My solution to the airflow problem is twofold: First, I make a labyrinth in back of the shelves consisting of two panels attached to the cabinet sides and a third panel screwed to the rear of the center divider. A 2-in.-thick batten is then attached to the top and bottom of these three panels, and two panels of ¼-in.-thick plywood are screwed to the battens. These panels overlap the side and center panels and disguise the opening. The

Shopmade Air Grille

MAKING THE GRILLE. To make a grille for ventilating the TV cabinet, first build a mitered frame with a rabbet on the inside and outside edges. Then glue in strips of wood with smaller pieces acting as spacers.

labyrinth creates two wire chases for each side of shelves, allowing separation of AC power and signal. This design also creates a rear outlet for airflow.

By itself this labyrinth is insufficient to cool the electronics because air must flow across the components. For better cooling I set the shelves a couple of inches back from the door. An air grille is then inset in the front of the shelf above the television to allow air to flow from the compartment below. With this method, cool air is drawn into the TV area and flows up through the grille, across the components and out the back. If additional cooling is necessary, fans may be located in the grille area for forced ventilation.

Considerable Importance Rests on the Shelves

After time has been spent designing a center that is rigid and rattle free, many woodworkers put in shelving without thought. A shelf is just a shelf, right? Well, not really.

A shelf should be acoustically dead: One of the worst shelves I see in many cabinets is glass. It's beautiful, and it saves space. But from an acoustical standpoint, it is one of the poorest-performing shelves you could use. The rigidity of glass makes it highly resonant at audio frequencies. Just think of how well a fine wine glass resonates when you tap it.

Composite shelves work well and look good–Shelves for the serious audiophile are available at specialty stores, starting at $100★ per shelf and increasing to more than $1,000★. These prices indicate the importance placed on shelving, but inexpensive, shopmade alternatives are available. From a cost and availability standpoint, MDF is a good choice. But a better choice is to use a lamination of dissimilar materials, such as MDF and hardboard. Together, dissimilar materials acoustically dampen each other, a process called constrained layer dampening.

SHELVES THAT DAMPEN NOISE.
Use contact cement to laminate sheets of ½-in.-thick MDF and ⅛-in.-thick hardboard.

I join ½-in.-thick MDF on one side to ⅛-in.-thick hardboard with contact cement. To give an exotic look to this laminated shelving, I apply a black dye to both surfaces. After the dye has dried, I apply wood edgebanding to the edges. When clear coated and rubbed with steel wool and wax, the surface has the luster of polished slate.

Give thought to how the shelves are attached—In a typical installation, I use basic L-type hangers that fit into ¼-in.-dia. holes. Shelves simply placed on the hangers may rattle at particular frequencies. Attaching the shelf to the hanger with a screw stops the rattle but transfers the vibration from the carcase to the shelf, which in turn will vibrate the component. To stop the rattle you can add a rubber pad that is typically used for mounting glass, but doing so may actually increase the vibration to the shelf at specific frequencies, due to the high rebound (bounce) of the rubber. The best solution I have found is simply to apply a thick felt pad to the surface of the hanger.

CLOTH-COVERED FRAME HIDES SPEAKER. A raw-silk screen conceals the center-channel speaker but doesn't distort the sound.

Felt has a low rebound and allows the carcase and the shelf to move independently of one another, decoupling the vibration.

Cosmetic Touches Add Class

Unlike Victorian children, the center speaker should be heard and not seen, which is why the speaker is hidden behind a cloth-covered frame. Many commercial cloths are available as covers, but according to speaker designers, raw silk adds the least acoustical distortion of any fabric. Raw silk does not have the tight, fine weave as the silk used for clothing and scarves. Instead, its texture and appearance are similar to burlap. Usually available through large fabric stores, raw silk is a strong fabric that stretches. When stapling or tacking the fabric to the frame, place thin cardboard tack strips (used in upholstery) over the fabric edge (see the bottom photo on the facing page). The strips keep the pressure even and minimize tearing from the staples.

Attach the cover to the cabinet with hook-and-loop fasteners, but be sure to leave a pull-tag so that you can access the speaker for maintenance. Doors in front of electronic components can create problems with remote controls. Several solutions exist: The easiest is to use a glass panel in the door, allowing direct access with the remote. If solid-wood doors are used, a remote repeater may be used. A repeater typically has a receiver that is attached to the outside of the cabinet and has stick-on elements that are placed on the remote-receiver area of the component.

Adding these touches to a cabinet designed around the components distinguishes an entertainment center from a cabinet that just happens to house the television.

*Note—Prices are from 2002.

BROOKS TANNER builds custom, high-end entertainment centers in Manchester, N.H.

Pocket Doors

PLACE THE HINGES. Although the manufacturer recommends that the hinges be installed on the rails of the door, Tanner prefers to locate them on the top and bottom of the stiles to avoid drilling the 35-mm holes just above the tenons.

DO A DRY RUN FIRST. A wood follower connects the upper and lower slides. Tanner finds it easier to measure the cabinet and then test-fit the follower to the slides before installation.

INSTALL THE LOWER SLIDE. To make sure the door closes flush with the front of the cabinet, place shims behind, below, and in front of the slide to account for the face-frame overhang and the location of the hinge.

Entertainment Center in Quartersawn Maple

BY PETER TURNER

As my 2-year-old daughter, Morrigan, grew and became more mobile and curious, so did the urgency to design and build an entertainment center. My aim was to keep the unit looking more like a piece of furniture than a refrigerator while efficiently housing the television, VCR, and other audio components out of sight and temptation's way.

In an effort to move away from the large, heavy look of a typical entertainment center, my first design ended up as a horizontal case on a skinny, four-legged frame. I eventually scrapped this design because I realized the weight of components, especially a television, would overwhelm such a delicate piece. Instead, the cabinet evolved into a more conventional two-piece structure, with a lower section housing three drawers for storage of CDs and tapes and a slightly narrower but taller upper section enclosed by a pair of doors. I did what I could to keep the piece from getting bulky by maximizing the usable internal space and adding soft curves to the exterior, which help mask its rather hefty dimensions.

I chose cranked door hinges that allow a door to be opened a full 270° instead of pocket door hardware, which would have added several inches to the width of the piece. The curved legs lift the case off the floor and help reduce its visual weight. And to blend the lower case with the upper, I applied cove moldings at the waist and at the crown. I really like the swoop of a cove, which lends vitality to a piece.

To ensure that components such as an amplifier, tuner, CD player, and a television would fit inside the upper cabinet, I took a tape measure to my electronic gear. I also checked the dimensions of stereo and TV components at an electronics store. New electronic components are fairly standardized, being about 17 in. wide or less and just a few inches tall. Older components vary more in size. I settled on four 18-in.-wide adjustable shelves that are shallower than the interior of the case, which allows room for routing wires and for air circulation. The cabinet will easily hold half a dozen components plus a 27-in. television. The back of the upper case has a panelless frame, which makes for easy access to wires and lets the heat produced by a television escape.

With the help of a friend, Sam Robinson, I built the cabinet within a narrow time frame—one month—because I wanted to exhibit the piece at the Philadelphia Furniture Show. Sam was assigned the upper case, and I took on the lower box. We kept our fingers crossed and hoped that the bridge would eventually meet in the middle.

Quartersawn maple is the predominant wood used in the piece. The wood was chosen for its light color and subtle grain. Soft maple was used for the drawer sides and one internal frame. The drawer bottoms are made of plywood.

My local hardwood supplier, Dennis Day of Day Hardwoods in Scarborough, Maine, has a knack for finding high-quality wood at fair prices. He supplied me with 200 bd. ft. of quartersawn maple with several pieces close to 8 in. wide, unusually wide for quartersawn stock. The widest planks were used for visible panels and drawer fronts. The narrower stock was used for frames, internal panels, and shelves.

We were unable to locate thicker quartersawn stock, so we used plainsawn 16/4 material when needed, sawing it to best show off the grain.

The Stoutest Timbers Are Used in the Lower Case

I rough-cut the 16/4 stock and let it sit a few days to stabilize. It seemed as if this big plank was custom-made for my purposes. I was able to get quartersawn boards for the side frames and coves. The rest of the plank had diagonal end grain, which was used for the legs. Diagonal end grain is ideal for legs because you can orient the stock to show rift-sawn figure on the two exposed faces.

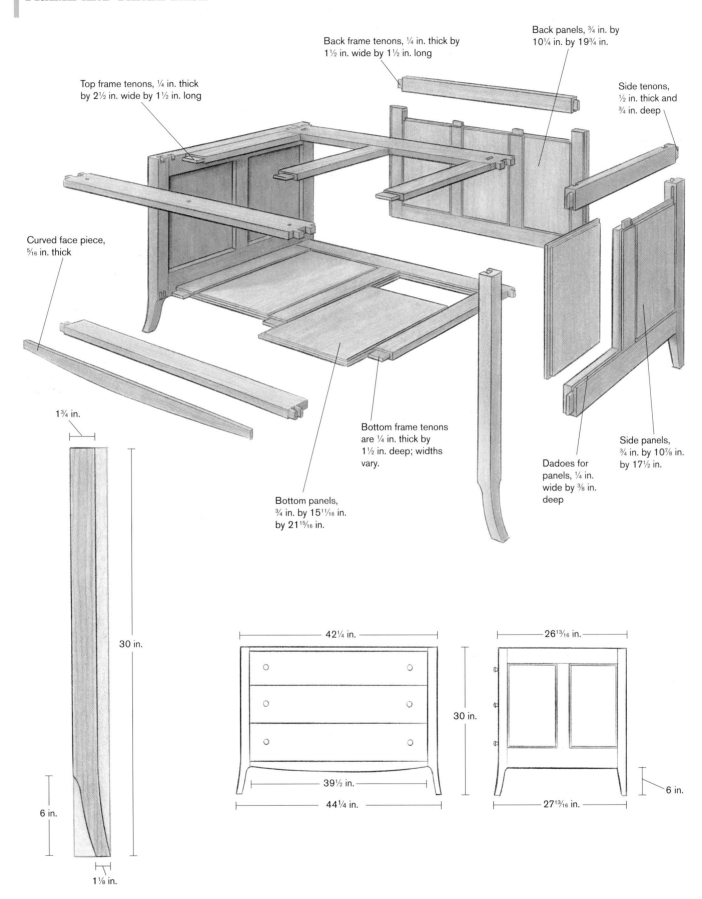

Top frame tenons, ¼ in. thick by 2½ in. wide by 1½ in. long

Back frame tenons, ¼ in. thick by 1½ in. wide by 1½ in. long

Back panels, ¾ in. by 10¼ in. by 19¾ in.

Side tenons, ½ in. thick and ¾ in. deep

Curved face piece, ⁵⁄₁₆ in. thick

Bottom frame tenons are ¼ in. thick by 1½ in. deep; widths vary.

Bottom panels, ¾ in. by 15¹¹⁄₁₆ in. by 21¹⁵⁄₁₆ in.

Dadoes for panels, ¼ in. wide by ⅜ in. deep

Side panels, ¾ in. by 10⅞ in. by 17½ in.

1¾ in.

30 in.

6 in.

1⅛ in.

42¼ in.

30 in.

39½ in.

44¼ in.

26¹³⁄₁₆ in.

27¹³⁄₁₆ in.

6 in.

I rough-cut the front legs about 3 in. square; the rear legs were roughed in at 2 in. by 3 in. The flat, inside faces of the legs were mortised to receive the side rails. I used a Multirouter to cut all of my lower case joinery. Dadoes were routed into the legs for the panels. I cut the feet on the bandsaw and cleaned them up with a cabinet scraper (see the top photo at right).

The back, top, and bottom frames are of mortise-and-tenon construction with routed stopped dadoes for all panels. Double dovetail joints were used to join the top frame to the rest of the lower case (see the center photo at right). I used double tenons on the front corners of the bottom frame to reinforce these joints (see the bottom photo at right). Single tenons are adequate at the rear of the case because the back provides additional strength.

The panels were rabbeted along all four exterior edges. The reveal between the panel and frame is slight, about 1/16 in. at the top and bottom and a hair more along the sides. To simplify production, I rabbeted all panels using the same setting. Next, I machined the dadoes in the frames, making them all 1/4 in. wide and 3/8 in. deep. Then I placed slivers of neoprene in the lower rails, which lift the panels to the correct height. Neoprene is available from window-repair companies.

The dry assembly of the lower case was my first opportunity to appreciate the real scale of the piece. I clamped a temporary spacer across the front between the upper corners of the sides to hold them in place. I then placed the completed top frame on top of the case and knifed the dovetail socket placement into the leg tops and upper rails.

After knocking the sides apart, I finished cutting the joinery. Then I glued it together. The back is handplaned to fit. It is glued in place.

A waist molding, built as an open framework, separates the top from the bottom half of the case. Three sides are shaped; the back is square. I cut the cove molding on

AFTER CUTTING THE MORTISES, SHAPE THE FEET. The feet are cut out on the bandsaw, then cleaned up with a scraper.

DOUBLE TENONS JOIN THE BOTTOM TO THE FRONT OF THE LOWER CASE. A single tenon is sufficient for the rear because the glued-in back panel will add strength.

THE TOP OF THE LOWER CASE IS A SIMPLE FRAME WITHOUT PANELS. Double dovetail joints are used at each corner to ensure the case won't bow.

the tablesaw with the blade at 90°, using a 25° angle of approach and ending up with a final blade height of 1½ in. I ran the stock facedown to provide a stable riding surface. Small, successive cuts with a grazing final pass are the keys to producing a clean cove safely. No matter how carefully you cut, there's still a bit of cleanup required. I made a custom scraper by grinding a stock scraper to the same radius as the cove. The front corners of the cove were mitered, and the rear corners were butt-joined. I used double #20 biscuits to reinforce all of the corner joints. The completed framework was glued directly to the top of the lower case. Biscuits are not needed here because there is plenty of face grain between parts.

Hidden, Full-Extension Drawer Slides Are Used

The three drawer boxes are all the same size and were built using a Leigh® dovetail jig. The drawer fronts were screwed in place from the inside. For visual balance, I graduated the height of the false fronts, with the

A SPACING GUIDE SIMPLIFIES THE INSTALLATION OF SLIDES. The guide positions each pair of slides at the correct height for attachment to the inside of the case. Cut the guide down to attach the next pair of slides.

REMOVABLE DIVIDERS MAKE THE DRAWERS VERSATILE. Whether you need to store CDs, tapes, or video-cassettes, the drawers can accommodate all.

DOVETAILED UPPER CASE

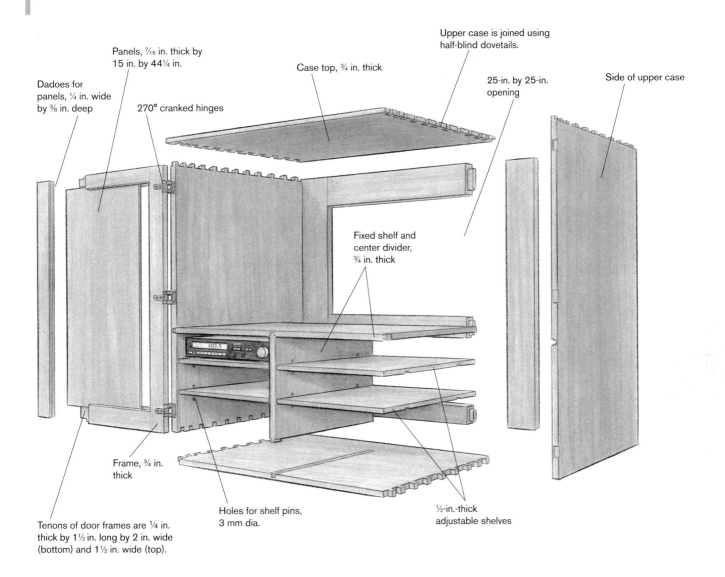

Panels, ⁷⁄₁₆ in. thick by 15 in. by 44¼ in.

Dadoes for panels, ¼ in. wide by ⅜ in. deep

270° cranked hinges

Case top, ¾ in. thick

Upper case is joined using half-blind dovetails.

25-in. by 25-in. opening

Side of upper case

Fixed shelf and center divider, ¾ in. thick

Frame, ¾ in. thick

Tenons of door frames are ¼ in. thick by 1½ in. long by 2 in. wide (bottom) and 1½ in. wide (top).

Holes for shelf pins, 3 mm dia.

½-in.-thick adjustable shelves

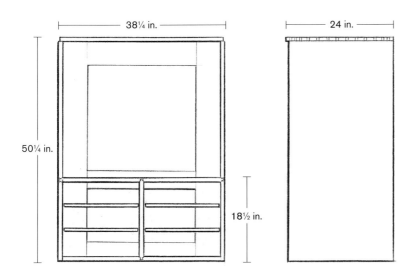

38¼ in.

50¼ in.

18½ in.

24 in.

lower drawer front being the deepest. After cutting all of the dovetail joints, I machined dadoes in the fronts and sides of each drawer for the plywood bottom panel, which is rabbeted along three edges. Then I ripped the bottom inch from each drawer back to allow the bottom panels to extend past the rear edge of the drawer. The bottoms were screwed in place to the rear drawer wall.

I also cut grooves in the front and rear of the upper drawer to hold removable partitions, good for CDs or tapes. The partitions are ¼ in. thick by 4 in. high, and they divide the drawer into six equal channels. I cut these after cutting the dovetails and dadoes. I clamped matching fronts and backs flat on my bench, butting their top edges together. Then, starting in the dado, I routed rounded, ⅛-in.-deep dadoes across both pieces using a ¼-in. core-box bit. After a little trial and error, I cut the partitions to length and rounded over the ends to match the round-bottomed dadoes. I carried the same profile along the top edge. Round dadoes are time-consuming, but I much prefer their softer look. Depending on the size of your CD or tape collection, other drawers could also be partitioned.

I chose Hettich® Quadro 30 V6 full-extension slides for their ease of installation, smooth operation, and clean look. Each drawer gets a pair of slides, which are screwed to the inside of the case. Two plastic clips, which engage the slides, are screwed to the underside of each drawer near the front. Drawers must be constructed so that their sides project ½ in. deeper than the drawer bottom. The slides are completely hidden by the drawer sides. With this type of hardware, I don't have to worry about whether my drawers will bind in the humid summer heat or get sloppy in the dry air of winter. I particularly like the self-closing action, which kicks in when a drawer is open an inch or less. Blum® also makes a hidden drawer slide called the Tandem®.

To locate each pair of drawer slides uniformly within the case, I made a spacing guide out of scrap plywood (see the top photo on p. 130). Here's how it works: Lay out the location of the slides. Then trim the guide so that when placed inside the case, the slide, when laid on top of the guide, is in position for attachment to the case. The guide ensures that the opposite slide will be at the same level and parallel to the first. Start with the top drawer and cut the guide down for each subsequent pair of slides.

If you use Hettich slides, order their screws, too, which cost extra. I didn't and discovered that standard round-head screws interfered with the action of the slides. To finish off the lower case, I drilled ½-in.-deep mortises for the pulls, then attached the drawer fronts to the drawers with countersunk screws.

I added a curved face piece to the outside edge of the bottom of the case, below the last drawer, which helps tie the case to the curve of the legs. This face piece is glued in place. The pulls are classic Shaker design and made of ebony. The pulls for the upper case have soft tips to prevent dinging the case (see the sidebar on p. 137).

Meanwhile, the Upper Case Is Taking Shape

While I was busy cutting mortises and tenons, Sam was working away at the long

Sources of Supply

Blum Inc.
7733 Old Plank Road
Stanley, NC 28164
800-438-6788
Drawer slides

Häfele America Co.
3901 Cheyenne Drive
Archdale, NC 27263
800-423-3531
Hinges

Hettich America
6225 Shiloh Road
Alpharetta, GA 30202
800-438-8424
Drawer slides

Sugatsune® America, Inc.
221 E. Selandia Lane
Carson, CA 90746
800-562-5267
Hinges

Upper and lower cases are joined
using bolts and threaded inserts.

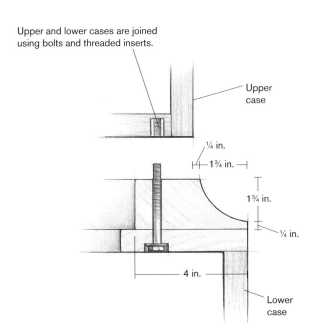

Upper
case

¼ in.

1¾ in.

1¾ in.

¼ in.

4 in.

Lower
case

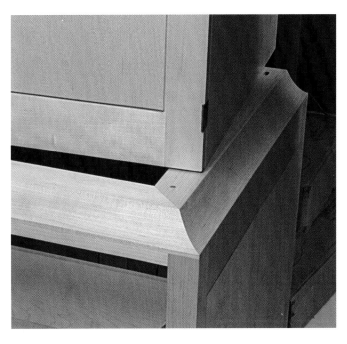

UPPER AND LOWER CASES CAN BE SEPARATED FOR EASE IN MOVING.
Threaded inserts and bolts are hidden from view but make a strong
connection.

Waist Molding

Pairs of biscuits are used to join parts.
The assembly is glued directly to the
lower case.

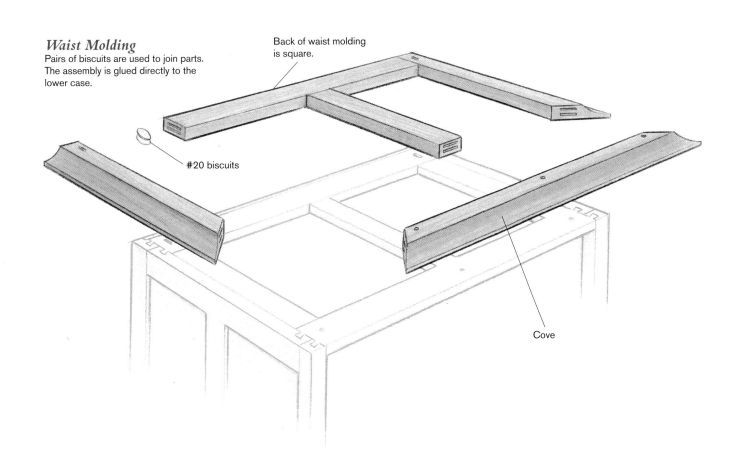

Back of waist molding
is square.

#20 biscuits

Cove

CROWN MOLDING

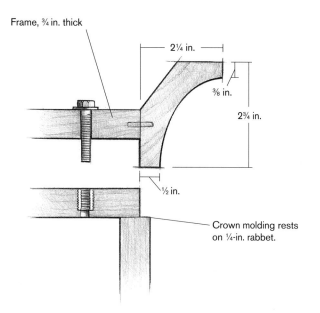

Frame, ¾ in. thick

2¼ in.

⅜ in.

2¾ in.

½ in.

Crown molding rests on ¼-in. rabbet.

REMOVABLE MOLDING. It's much easier to protect the molding if it can be wrapped separately when transporting the case.

Crown Molding
Sections are joined to a frame using biscuits.
The assembly bolts to the upper case.

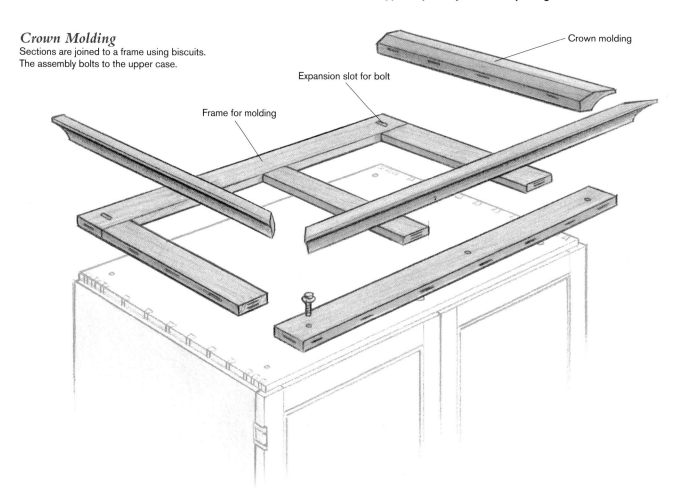

Crown molding

Expansion slot for bolt

Frame for molding

rows of half-blind dovetails that join the upper case. Once he finished the dovetails, he loaded the stock into his van and came to my shop for a dry assembly and test fit. We knocked his case together and placed it on top of my lower unit. Amazingly enough, it sat nice and flat with appropriate reveals on all sides.

The upper case has a fixed shelf, which fits into a ⅛-in.-deep stopped dado. The front of the fixed shelf has two ½-in.-deep ears, which are dovetailed into the front edge of the cabinet. The dovetails prevent the case from bowing. A center divider was attached to the case in a similar fashion, using dadoes and dovetailed ears. To place the sockets for the dovetailed ears accurately, it's best to dry-fit the case with the shelf and divider and mark out their locations with a knife (see the bottom photo on p. 136).

Back at his shop, Sam chopped out the sockets. He also attached threaded inserts into the case. The inserts, in conjunction with bolts, allow the upper and lower cases to be joined. The crown molding was also attached in this way.

Don't Come Unhinged Because of Hardware

Sam built the door frames using haunched mortise-and-tenon joints. Panels were constructed using the same methods employed in the lower case. The hinge mortises were marked using a knife, then most of the waste was removed by routing freehand. A chisel and gouge finished the mortises.

We used Häfele hinges (No. 307.04.806) and ran into a few bumps along the way. Because I wanted the doors to be flush to the sides of the case, we mortised the hinges into the outside edges of the doors. As designed, the hinges require that a door be inset from the side of the case by half the thickness of the hinge. When we hung the doors, they didn't swing open all of the way.

First we thought it was because we had modified the hardware installation. But as it turned out, the problem was with the thickness of the doors. For these hinges to work properly, the doors need to be a hair under ¾ in. thick, or $^{47}/_{64}$ in. thick, to be exact. We also discovered that the hinges didn't close properly through no fault of our own. We removed them after a trial fit and found that the hinges were not manufactured perfectly square. We fixed them with a hammer and vise.

After the doors were planed to fit, Sam drilled the mortises for the knobs, which are located at the level of the interior fixed shelf. He also drilled the 3-mm-dia. holes in the sides of the case and center divider for Häfele shelf pins (No. 282.06. 500). I like these brass pins, which are round and stepped from 3 mm dia. to 5 mm dia. Typical shelf pins require larger-diameter holes, 5 mm or ¼ in., and it's surprising how discreet the 3-mm holes are. Finally, Sam routed short recesses into the shelf bottoms to house the pins and keep the shelves from sliding.

The Crown Molding Is Bolted in Place

We designed the crown molding as a frame and made it detachable, which comes in handy when the case has to be moved. Sam cut the molding on his tablesaw in two steps.

The lower section of the molding has a bigger radius than the upper sweep. The lower radius was done with a 33° angle of approach with a final blade height of ½ in. The upper radius was done with a 21° angle of approach with a ⁹⁄₁₆-in. final blade height. Then Sam blended the transition between the two radii by moving the fence and blade and setting it by trial and error. A scraper was used to clean up the saw marks.

The crown was mitered at the front corners, and butt joints were used elsewhere. Pairs of #20 biscuits were used at all of the joints. The entire frame slips down over the

A FIXED SHELF AND CENTER DIVIDER STRENGTHEN THE UPPER CASE. Both the shelf and divider fit into ⅛-in.-deep stopped dadoes. The protruding ears at the front of the shelf and divider are dovetailed.

MARK THE SOCKET OF THE DOVETAILED EARS DURING DRY FITTING. Clamp the case flat and use a sharp marking knife.

case and rests on a rabbet cut into the sides. This rabbet was cut with a router after the upper case was assembled. Bolts and threaded inserts hold the molding in place.

To finish this cabinet, we sanded up to 220 grit, then wiped everything down with a damp cloth to raise the grain. Once the piece was dry, we finish-sanded to 320 grit.

Most of the case was finished with three coats of Bartley gel varnish. We chose this finish because it can be applied by hand, has good durability and does not yellow maple unlike many oil finishes do. The insides of the lower case and the drawers were finished using extra blond shellac. Last, we attached the knobs, and before the epoxy had set, the entertainment center was inside my van, on its way to the Philadelphia Furniture Show.

PETER TURNER builds custom furniture in Portland, Maine.

Pulls That Won't Ding the Case

A door that swings on a 270° cranked hinge is great for access but can be hard on the case. That's because the pulls will smack into the side of the cabinet. To prevent dings I added nearly invisible neoprene bumpers to the upper pulls.

After turning a pull, I drilled a shallow hole in the tip. Using a leather punch the same diameter as the hole, I punched out a disc of black neoprene. The disc was pressed in place. I added a drop of cyanoacrylate glue to help keep it there. The protruding neoprene was trimmed flush using a sharp chisel. Because the pulls contact the sides in a direct line, not at an angle, the neoprene won't leave scuff marks.

CRANKED HINGES ALLOW DOORS TO OPEN WIDE. Mortises must be cut in the doors and the front edge of the case.

DRILL A SHALLOW HOLE IN THE TIP OF THE PULL. The author uses a ¼-in. brad-point drill bit fitted to a chuck in the lathe's tailstock.

PUNCH OUT A NEOPRENE PLUG. Use a leather punch the same diameter as the hole in the pull.

PRESS THE NEOPRENE INTO THE TIP OF THE PULL. Use cyanoacrylate glue and then trim off the excess using a sharp chisel.

An Inside Look at Kitchen Cabinets

BY SCOTT GIBSON

At the giant KraftMaid® cabinet factory just outside Cleveland, workers stand by with glue guns and pneumatic nailers as parts for a complete set of kitchen cabinets approach on a conveyor. Drawers, face frames, prefinished panels, shelves, and moldings arrive from all corners of the million-square-foot plant. Although the customer who ordered this kitchen may have taken months to plan its every detail, KraftMaid assemblers will put it together in 15 minutes. Cabinets are shipped about a week after the order has arrived.

Did you think your new kitchen cabinets would be hand-built by fussy artisans? Guess again. Cabinets are a $6 billion industry, and they pour off assembly lines like hubcaps or lawn chairs. If that prospect unsettles you, consider a smaller company, one like Rutt® Custom Cabinetry of Goodville, Pa. Here, door panels are matched for color and figure, one board at a time. A specialist is standing by to custom-blend a paint color. The catch? Rutt charges more than twice as much, and you can count on waiting 40 or 50 days to get your order.

KraftMaid and Rutt are only two among hundreds of cabinet manufacturers. Yet they help to illustrate the many choices buyers will face before plunking down thousands of dollars for a new kitchen.

Manufactured Kitchens Fall Into Three General Categories

To help make sense of what's available, the industry has traditionally divided cabinets into three grades: stock, semicustom, and custom. The labels don't mean as much as they once did, but they are still a good starting point.

Stock cabinets are at the low end of the market. Available in limited styles and finishes and with fewer options, stock cabinets are built in standard sizes in increments of 3 in. in width. They are manufactured and then stockpiled, without regard to who will buy them.

Semicustom cabinets are built to order, also on a 3-in. grid, and offer more choices when it comes to styles, accessories, and finishes. Materials may be of higher quality. Custom cabinets, such as those from Rutt, are built to fit the available floor space exactly with just about any option the customer is willing to pay for. They are the most expensive of all.

And then there are the small shops, the local cabinetmakers found in virtually every corner of the country. Working on one job at a time, these shops turn out cabinets designed for just one client. Detailing, construction,

and wood selection may range from ordinary to exquisite. Yet these cabinets are not manufactured in the same sense as factory-built, mass-produced goods.

Any cabinet is a sum of its parts, and the choices can seem overwhelmingly complicated. Assessing quality is not always easy. Many manufacturers submit their cabinets to the Kitchen Cabinet Manufacturers Association[SM] for voluntary testing and certification. Although the process is wide ranging and rigorous (roughly half of those seeking certification for the first time will flunk), it's not useful for comparing individual components such as drawers, doors, and cabinet boxes. And makers of high-end cabinetry may skip the test altogether.

Whatever the cabinet industry's tests show, it pays to buy cabinets that are carefully built from good-quality materials and hardware. To me, that means avoiding cabinets made from paper-coated panels or ones with thin shelves that bend under pressure. Drawers should open smoothly, without wobbling. A finish should be silky to the touch, without any visible sanding marks. In short, buyers should seek cabinets that look and feel as if they are solidly made.

Prices vary as widely as quality. Bottom-of-the-line stock cabinets for a kitchen of roughly 120 sq. ft. are available for less than $2,500★, not including countertops and installation. According to estimates provided by both KraftMaid and Merillat®, one of the country's largest cabinet manufacturers, a better-quality kitchen might range from just over $5,000★ to $12,800★, depending on materials and accessories. A custom-manufactured kitchen can approach $20,000★.

The following pages look in detail at four manufactured base cabinets that are typical of what's on the market. More expensive often means more quality and a longer life. But getting the best value also should include a careful look at the many differences in construction, hardware, finish, and materials.

Cabinet Boxes: Your Kitchen's Foundation

A salesman may call the cabinet French provincial, Shaker, or Arts and Crafts, but from a construction standpoint, manufactured cabinets are one of two types: traditional face frame or frameless. In a face-frame cabinet, a rigid frame made of ¾-in. solid wood is attached to the front of a plywood or particleboard box. Face frames create square door and drawer openings while adding strength to the cabinet and helping to keep it square during construction, shipping, and installation. Depending on the type of hinge used, some or all of the frame is visible when doors and drawers are installed. In a frameless cabinet, overlay doors and drawer fronts hide the cabinet box. Often made from melamine, which is particleboard covered by a thin layer of plastic laminate, these cabinet boxes are usually held together with dowels and glue.

The days of solid-wood construction are long gone, mainly because panel products such as plywood, particleboard, or medium-density fiberboard make a stronger, more stable cabinet at a lower cost. Upper and lower cabinet boxes are now typically constructed of particleboard topped with wood veneer, vinyl paper, melamine, or the same kind of high-pressure laminate used on countertops. Boxes of veneer-core plywood, lighter and stronger than particleboard, also are available but often cost more. Whether plywood or particleboard, more expensive cabinets tend to use thicker material for cabinet boxes and shelves.

A solvent-based varnish is a common choice for kitchen cabinets. It's tough and durable. In cheaper cabinets, the top coat may look glossy and rough, with some sanding marks still visible. Many companies, however, offer sophisticated, layered finishes in many colors or wood tones.

($115)*

Frameless melamine is inexpensive, easy to clean–Frameless cabinets, such as this melamine base unit from LesCare Kitchens of Waterbury, Conn., use a full-overlay door and drawer front that span the width of the carcase. Upgrading the door and drawer front to a more durable high-pressure laminate raises the price of this cabinet to $180★.

1., 2. Carcase: Cabinet sides are ¾-in. melamine-faced particleboard with a ¼-in. back and a ¾-in. floor. Parts are assembled with glued dowel joints and are reinforced with full-width stretchers.

3. Shelf: Held in place by adjustable plastic clips, the ¾-in. melamine shelf is 12 in. deep, about half the depth of the cabinet itself.

4. Drawer: Sides of ⅝-in. melamine are doweled and glued together with a ¼-in. bottom and a thermofoil drawer front (medium-density fiberboard wrapped in plastic).

5. Door: A full-overlay thermofoil door is hung on adjustable hinges that can be removed without any tools, making it easy to pop off the door for a thorough cleaning.

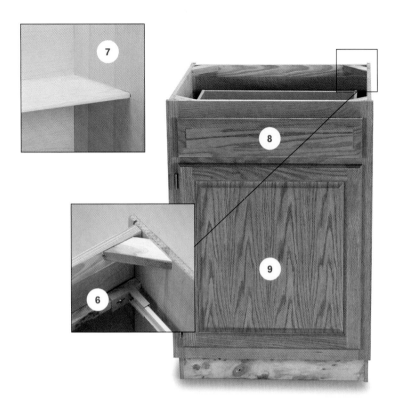

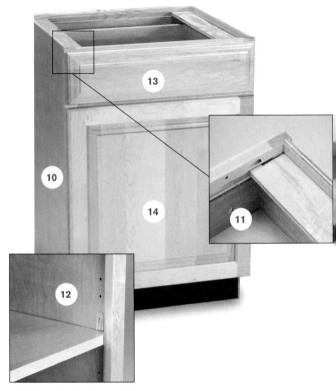

($125)*

Stock face-frame cabinet made with lighter materials–This cabinet, made by Kitchen Kompact of Jeffersonville, Ind., uses a traditional face frame to reinforce the front of the carcase. In this price range, some materials are likely to be relatively thin with a simulated wood-grain finish.

6. Carcase: Materials include sides of ½-in. wood-veneer particleboard, and a back of ⅛-in. vinyl-covered hardboard. The cabinet floor is ¼-in. vinyl-covered hardboard that flexes under a load. Corner blocks that reinforce the cabinet are stapled in place, but not all of the staples hit their target.

7. Shelf: Not adjustable and only ½ in. thick, the 11-in. wide shelf is made of vinyl-covered particleboard.

8. Drawer: Sides are ⅜-in. fiberboard faced in a wood-grain vinyl with a solid drawer front of red oak.

9. Door: A wood-veneer panel is set in a frame of solid oak. Hinges cannot be adjusted.

($300)*

For more money, a sturdier cabinet–This semicustom KraftMaid cabinet has several advantages over lower-priced alternatives, including heavier materials and more durable construction.

10., 11. Carcase: This cabinet box is made from ½-in. veneer-core plywood with a ⅜-in. plywood back and a fully finished interior. Two ⁷⁄₁₆-in. plywood stretchers reinforce the top of the cabinet.

12. Shelf: A ¾-in. plywood shelf runs the full depth of the cabinet. Held in place by plastic clips, the shelf is fully adjustable.

13. Drawer: A dovetailed hardwood drawer box is made with ¾-in. sides with a ¼-in. bottom and a ¾-in. hardwood drawer front.

14. Door: The solid door frame of ¾-in. maple has a solid-wood panel on adjustable hinges.

($700)*

Top of the line, with a price tag to match–
This Rutt Custom Cabinetry base unit has
a sophisticated painted finish and an inset
door, making it look more like traditional
furniture-grade cabinetry. Good-quality
hardware operates smoothly.

15., 16. Carcase: The cabinet box is
made from ⅝-in. veneer-core plywood
with a ¼-in. veneered back of medium-
density fiberboard. A full dust panel rein-
forces the top of the cabinet.

17. Shelf: Although the retaining clip
on the shelf is plastic, the weight is actually
carried by a concealed metal pin, which is
stronger. Adjustable and 18 in. deep, the shelf
is made from ¾-in. veneer-core plywood.

18. Drawer: The drawer is made from
⅝-in. hardwood joined with glue and
dowels at the corners with top-quality
undermount drawer slides. The drawer has
a ¼-in. bottom.

19. Door: A traditionally mortised and
tenoned door frame has a beaded detail on
the inside edge and is hung with decorative
butt hinges, which are not adjustable.

Drawers: A Sturdy Box Can Take a Lot of Abuse

Few kitchen components get as much wear
and tear as a drawer. Before the introduc-
tion of modern drawer slides, a wood drawer
box ran on wooden runners fastened to the
inside of the cabinet. Often overloaded and
yanked on unmercifully in sticky summer
weather, drawers had a hard life. Good drawer
slides incorporating plastic or metal rollers
have eliminated much of that stress, making
drawer construction less of an issue than it
used to be. Even so, a drawer made of undersize material and running on cheap slides
will be a never-ending source of irritation.

Solid hardwood traditionally has been the
material of choice for good-quality drawer
boxes. One big advantage is that the material
does not dictate the joint that will be used to
join the corners of the box. Solid wood can
be dovetailed, doweled, biscuited, or dadoed,
and a raw edge will never show. Many drawers also are made from engineered wood:
veneered plywood, particleboard, melamine,
or medium-density fiberboard. These drawers,

DOWELED HARDWOOD DRAWER BOX. Light and strong, this ⅝-in. box of yellow poplar is joined with dowels at the corners and comes with a ½-in. plywood drawer bottom. That may be overkill in a narrow drawer, but a bottom this thick won't sag. Self-closing Blum undermount drawer slides are completely hidden and perform flawlessly.

DOVETAILED HARDWOOD. Always the darling of the cabinet trade, a dovetailed drawer should last a long time. This one has sides of ¾-in. hardwood and a ³⁄₁₆-in. plywood bottom (a heavier drawer bottom would be better in a wider drawer intended for heavy objects). Undermount slides are out of the way, but they do not operate as smoothly or seem as sturdy as those made by Blum.

MARGINAL MATERIALS AND CONSTRUCTION. Drawers like these are unlikely to give you a lifetime of dependable service. Faced with a drawer front of red oak, the drawer box is ⅝-in. medium-density fiberboard faced in wood-grain vinyl and joined with nails and glue. The ³⁄₁₆-in. drawer bottom flexes easily under pressure. Even when new, the three-quarter drawer slide did not operate smoothly.

DOWELED MELAMINE. Typical for a frameless cabinet, this drawer box is made of ⅝-in. melamine, doweled at the corners, with a ¼-in. bottom. The three-quarter extension epoxy-coated slide (this one made by Blum) operates smoothly. The gap between the applied drawer front and the front of this box should not be there.

common in frameless cabinetry, are often glued and doweled together. Raw edges must be banded. Plywood or melamine drawers certainly can be durable, but the material should be at least ½ in. thick. Avoid drawers made from thin, vinyl-covered particleboard and nailed at the corners. They feel flimsy, and they are more likely to come apart over time.

A standard drawer slide is an epoxy-coated, three-quarter extension unit rated at 75 lb. But full-extension slides, rated to 100 lb. and allowing access to even the back of the drawer, may be available as an upgrade. Undermount slides stay out of sight and, like other hardware, come in various levels of quality. The best are made from heavy-duty materials and quiet, smoothly operating rollers or ball bearings, such as the Tandem slide by Blum, used on Rutt cabinets.

Drawers made from wood parts are by far the most common, but metal drawers also are available. One variety found in some frameless cabinetry has epoxy-coated metal sides attached to a standard melamine drawer front. The drawer side incorporates part of the slide mechanism.

Cabinet Doors Are a Visual Focal Point

Manufacturers devote a lot of attention to the doors on their cabinets for good reason: Along with drawer fronts, these parts are dominant visual elements in any kitchen. A single company may offer dozens of door styles. Many cabinet manufacturers do not build their own doors, buying them instead from vendors such as Conestoga® Wood Specialties Inc. in East Earl, Pa., which makes some 5.5 million doors a year.

On frame-and-panel doors, virtually everyone now uses what's called a cope-and-stick joint in which the interlocking edges of the frame parts form the glue joint. Although this joint might horrify traditionalists, it is by now time-tested and strong

Where to Buy a Kitchen

Manufacturers sell their cabinets through a retail network that includes building-supply stores, lumberyards, and stores specializing in kitchen and bathroom cabinetry. Larger cabinet retailers offer more variety, and those located near big home-improvement centers such as Home Depot® may offer everyone the prices that once were reserved for builders. If you have a particular cabinet brand in mind, the company can provide the name of a nearby retailer.

Driving from store to store is a time-honored way to shop, but doing some homework on the Internet first can help. Many manufacturers maintain their own Web sites where you can browse product offerings, learn more about how their cabinets are built, and find out where to buy them. One place to start is with a search engine such as www.dogpile.com or www.askjeeves.com (or whatever your favorite might be), where a search for "kitchen cabinets" will turn up companies all over the country. Content can range from specific information on construction techniques and materials to collections of glossy photos. Some cabinet-manufacturing companies offer interactive sites that will help you to design a kitchen layout and to choose various accessories.

For lists of manufacturers, try www.buildingonline.com or www.kitchen-bath.com. Lists are organized so that you can search for a smaller company in your region. Another good resource is www.nkba.org, the home page of the National Kitchen and Bath Association (NKBA℠), an industry trade group. You'll find design tips, budgeting information, and industry links for cabinets and other products. The Kitchen Cabinet Manufacturers Association's site (www.kcma.org) details the association's certification process for kitchen cabinets, valuable information for anyone in the market for a new kitchen.

A STEP UP IN A WOOD DESIGN. This maple KraftMaid door has a solid wood raised panel and a smoother, less brassy finish than the door on a budget cabinet. The cope-and-stick joinery is essentially the same. The color and figure of the maple pieces used in both the panel and the frame of this door are not perfectly matched.

A STOCK FRAME-AND-PANEL DOOR. A solid red oak frame surrounds a veneered panel in a door typical for a budget cabinet. Frame pieces are joined at the corners in a cope-and-stick pattern, a standard door joint. The panel is a very thin wood veneer over particleboard, not solid wood. Some sanding marks are evident on the inside of the door.

THERMOFOIL DOORS HAVE A CORE OF ENGINEERED WOOD. A traditional frame-and-panel look-alike, this door is actually a vinyl-like plastic formed around a core of medium-density fiberboard milled by a computer-controlled router. Unlike other kinds of laminated doors, this one has only a single seam. MDF is heavy and stable.

enough. Be wary of any door showing gaps in the joinery. Raised door panels may be either solid wood with a profile milled into the outside edge or engineered wood faced in a thin wood veneer. Profiles will be crisper, and panels more durable, when of solid wood. Thermofoil doors mimic frame-and-panel styles but are made of engineered wood covered in plastic.

Some doors have mitered corners, like a picture frame, which are doweled together. Seasonal wood movement makes this type of joint more likely to open up than other designs, just like mitered door and window casings.

Most kitchen cabinets have overlay doors, meaning the doors overlap the door opening. A full-overlay door covers the front of the cabinet completely. Because the doors are slightly bigger than their openings, overlay doors don't require any fitting. Less common are inset doors, which are housed in the door opening. When closed, inset doors are flush with the face of the cabinet, making the cabinet look more like a piece of furniture.

Overlay doors are usually hung with cup hinges, which are hidden when the door is closed. Cup hinges allow the door to be adjusted in several directions, making alignment easy for manufacturer and buyer alike. Better hinges have more adjusting points, and some allow the door to be popped off the cabinet without using tools.

Door hinges can be a trouble spot for cabinets. According to the Kitchen Cabinet Manufacturers Association, failing hinges are one of the most common reasons that cabinets flunk certification tests. So it pays to check them carefully when looking for cabinets. Avoid hinges that have too much play or feel flimsy.

Note—prices are from 1999.

SCOTT GIBSON is a freelance editor who works from his home in Maine.

EASY ON AND OFF This cup hinge design allows door to be popped off without tools.

NO ADJUSTMENTS This economy hinge offers no door adjustments, and it flexes under a load.

ADJUSTABLE CUP HINGE This cup hinge allows door to be adjusted in two directions.

TRADITIONAL BUTT HINGE A furniture-like hinge on this door is set into a mortise in the frame.

OLD-STYLE DETAILING IN A PAINTED DOOR. This pine door uses more traditional joinery. Its sand-through finish relies on layers of color and paint, plus sanding, to mimic the effects of years of hard use. The satin finish is silky to the touch.

Installing Kitchen Cabinets

BY TOM LAW

Well, there you are, just walking into a new kitchen with freshly painted drywall. Or maybe you're remodeling, and you've spent the last few days gutting the kitchen. But now you've got a clean slate to work with. The kitchen cabinets are in cardboard boxes, and all you have to do is unpack them and fasten them to the wall, right? Easy, tiger.

Kitchen cabinets are like carryout food: A lot can go wrong with the order, and you don't want to be five miles down the road when you discover that something's missing. Before you begin installing cabinets, check all the boxes. Make sure you have everything you need and that the cabinets are what the customer ordered.

Take a close look at the walls and the floor—they're probably not as flat as they appear. You'll have to compensate for any imperfections because the cabinets take precedence. You don't distort a straight cabinet to fit a crooked wall.

Here, I'll discuss the methods I use to install cabinets when conditions are less than perfect, and believe me, they usually are.

Know the Room Conditions

Every installation begins with a check of the floor and the walls for the carpenter's guiding principles: plumb and level, straight and square. I use a straightedge and a level to see how the floor goes. The goal is to locate high and low spots because one of these spots will be the starting point for the cabinet layout, ultimately determining the height of the countertop.

I also use the straightedge to check the walls for straight and plumb. If there is a corner, I check it for square. Although serious flaws are uncommon, minor problems like spackle buildup often appear.

Marking the Wall and the Floor

To get over the fidgets of starting the job, I mark the cabinet layout on the wall. Marking the layout helps me visualize the finished job.

To begin with, I decide whether to use the high or low spot on the floor for my starting point. Choosing the high spot probably means that only one base cabinet will sit directly on the floor; all the others will be shimmed up. Using the low spot means that most of the cabinets will have to be scribed to fit the irregularities of the floor (more about scribing later). It's easier to use the high spot because it's easier to shim up than to cut off, but the determining factor is countertop height. Usually a countertop is 3 ft. from the floor.

MARKING THE BASE-CABINET
LINE. **Starting from the high or
low spot on the floor, the height
of the base cabinets is marked
on the wall, then the mark is
transferred around the room
with a water level. The line is
also a reference point for laying
out the upper cabinets.**

Countertops themselves are normally
1½ in. thick, so the base cabinets are 34½ in.
high. I mark this height on the wall above
either the high or the low spot on the floor,
whichever I've chosen as the starting point.
Then I transfer that mark around the walls
using a water level (see the photo above). I
use the water level to mark the cabinet
height at each corner, then I strike a
chalkline between the marks. If you don't
have a water level, a conventional spirit
level and a straightedge will do.

After the base-cabinet line is marked on
the wall, I mark the location of the individual
cabinets. I usually don't mark full plumb lines
(the vertical lines) for each cabinet; I just
make check marks along the base-cabinet
line to indicate the width of each cabinet.

The face-frame stiles on most cabinets

project beyond the sides ⅟₃₂ in. to ¼ in.,
which allows the stiles of two cabinets to
be joined tightly without the sides of the
cabinets bumping together. I mark each
cabinet's actual size (its width from stile to
stile) on the wall and then subtract the
amount the stiles protrude to locate the
back of the cabinet accurately.

I also use the base-cabinet line as a reference for laying out the upper cabinets.
The space between the upper cabinets and
the countertop is usually between 16 in.
and 18 in. When measuring up from the
base-cabinet line, I add 1½ in. for the
countertop. Then I mark the wall to indicate the bottom of the upper cabinets. I
double-check to see that the top of the
upper cabinets is the same height as the
top of any full-length cabinet, like a

broom closet or a pantry unit. If it isn't, I adjust the layout of the upper cabinets.

Next, I mark the location of each upper cabinet, again with either check marks or full-length lines. Most of the time the upper cabinets are the same width as the base cabinets below them, and their edges align vertically. Cabinets must line up where an appliance, such as a refrigerator, protrudes into the upper-cabinet space. And by the way, you shouldn't add anything to the space indicated on the plans for an appliance. A 30-in. stove or refrigerator as called out on the plan will fit a 30-in. opening.

Some cabinets, such as those over refrigerators and stoves, don't come down as low as the other upper cabinets. And some cabinets, such as desk units, sit lower than the other base cabinets. I measure these cabinets and mark their locations.

Next I find the studs and mark their locations on the wall because I'll be fastening the cabinets to the studs. I mark stud locations with straight lines. Studs can be sounded out (where you tap the wall and listen for the higher pitch that occurs when you strike a stud) and probed for with a hammer and a nail, or they can be located with an electronic stud finder. If you use the hammer-and-nail approach, be sure to punch the holes where they'll be covered by cabinets.

It's okay to fasten a base cabinet to only one stud. Upper cabinets, however, are better off attached to two studs. Sometimes a cabinet isn't wide enough to catch two studs. I either attach narrow cabinets to their neighbors, or I might add blocking in the wall where it will be covered by a cabinet. I use a reciprocating saw to cut a hole in the drywall, then I insert a glue-covered piece of 1x that will span the hole. This block is the backing that I'll attach the cabinet to, so I make sure the hole is in the right place behind the cabinet.

When I work alone, I find it awkward to hang upper cabinets first. By installing the base cabinets first, I can use them to support the upper cabinets.

Which Cabinets Come First?

The most important consideration when deciding which cabinets to set first, the uppers or the bases, is comfort. Some manufacturers suggest hanging the upper ones first because you can stand closer to the wall when the base cabinets aren't in the way. If you hang the upper cabinets first, it's sometimes recommended that you nail a 1x2 ledger strip on the wall to support the upper cabinets while you fasten them to the wall. It's a good idea if the backsplash will later cover the nail holes. But you wouldn't want to nail a ledger strip on a finished wall.

There are lots of ways to hold upper cabinets in place as you install them. You can buy or make various jacks and props, but it's been my experience that when hanging upper cabinets first, it's better to have two people doing the work—one holding, one fastening.

When I work alone, I find it awkward to hang upper cabinets first. By installing the base cabinets first, I can use them to support the upper cabinets (more on this method later). Plus the base cabinets are more complicated because they have to be fitted to both the wall and the floor, so I start with them.

Start From a Corner

It's much easier to start in a corner and work out of it than to put yourself in one. Most corner cabinets have their backs cut on a 45° angle, so setting them into an out-of-square corner is easy. If the cabinet has a square back, spackle buildup will probably have to be sanded down, but there are times when the only thing to do is cut away the drywall or plaster to get a square-back unit in place.

Because most corner cabinets have cutaway backs, they tend to shift around and are difficult to set in place. One way to shore up corner cabinets is to attach cabinets to each side and then push all three into place as a unit.

Another thing about corner cabinets with cutaway backs is that they often require a ledger strip along the wall to support the countertop. I nail a piece of 1x stock along the base-cabinet line to support the countertop in the corner.

Scribing a Cabinet

When a base cabinet—corner or otherwise—is installed, it must be set level and plumb. If the floor isn't level, there are two ways to get that base cabinet level and plumb—shim it or scribe it. Shimming is much easier; I just slip shims under the cabinet until it's level and at the proper height (see the photo at right). When the top is level, I check all the sides; as long as the cabinet is square, the sides should be plumb no matter how I place the level. Exposed shims and gaps are often covered by a vinyl base; sometimes there's a separate toe-kick board that's scribed to fit the contours of the floor. If I'm installing base cabinets over a wood floor, I hide the shims and the gaps with shoe molding.

If the top of the cabinet is above the layout line even before I shim it, scribing is necessary. To scribe a cabinet to the floor, I bring the cabinet as close as I can to where it belongs in the kitchen, then shim it level. I set my scriber (or pencil compass) to the amount the cabinet extends above the line and scribe the cabinet at the floor (see the drawing at right). I cut the bottom of the cabinet at the scribe line. When I replace the cabinet, it sits level with the base-cabinet line.

When the side of a cabinet is exposed, it must fit perfectly against the wall. The side panels of many cabinets project beyond the back panels. These cabinets are easy to scribe to a wall. First, I level the cabinet, then set the scriber to the widest space between the cabinet and the wall and scribe both sides. I remove the cabinet, cut the sides to the scribe lines, then reinstall it. In some kitchens a decorative end panel is

SHIMMING A CABINET. Shims are used to level a cabinet, but they also bring cabinets that sit in low spots of the floor up to the proper height. Here, the end cabinet of a peninsula is leveled.

SCRIBE THE CABINET AT THE FLOOR

A cabinet that sits higher than the base-cabinet line can be trimmed to fit. First the cabinet is shimmed level, then it's marked, or scribed, the distance the cabinet sits above the base-cabinet line. After that amount is cut off the bottom of the cabinet, the cabinet will sit even with the base-cabinet line.

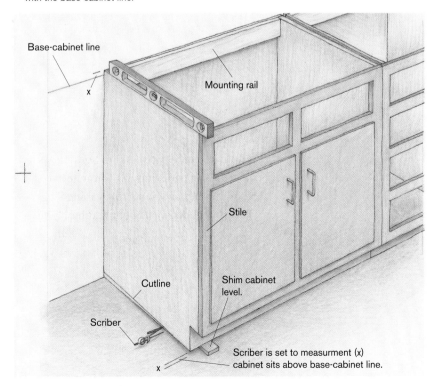

Base-cabinet line

Mounting rail

Stile

Cutline

Shim cabinet level.

Scriber

Scriber is set to measurment (x) cabinet sits above base-cabinet line.

FITTING AN END PANEL. Some cabinets have a separate end panel that should be scribed to fit tightly against the wall. With the panel clamped in place, the author uses a pocketknife to hold a strip of wood for scribing. The wood strip, like a scriber or compass, holds the pencil a set distance from the wall. The scribe mark is made on masking tape.

CUTTING THE END PANEL. The author uses a handsaw to get a clean cut along the scribe line. A slight back cut ensures that the face of the end panel will fit tight to the wall.

used to dress up the exposed side of a cabinet. Such panels are usually slightly oversize so that they can be scribed to the wall (see the photos above). If the cabinet has a flush back, however, scribing is impossible, so straightening the wall or shimming the back and covering the gap with molding is the only choice.

Installation Information

Now that I've talked about laying out and fitting cabinets to the floor and the wall, here's how I go about installing a kitchen. First I put the corner cabinet in place, shim it level with the base-cabinet line and, if necessary, scribe the cabinet to fit. Then I fasten the cabinet to the wall by driving screws through the mounting rail into the wall studs. The mounting rail is a horizontal piece of wood at the back of the cabinet.

Screws need to bite into studs at least ¾ in., so I use 2½-in.- or 3-in.-long drywall screws. But you may prefer to use wood screws, which have thicker shanks, or use the screws supplied by the manufacturer. If there's a gap between the mounting rail and the wall right where I want to run a screw, I slip a shim into the gap to keep the back of the cabinet from distorting when I put in the screw.

After the first cabinet is in place, I bring the second one to it, level it, get the face frames flush by lining up the top and the bottom of the cabinet's stiles, then I clamp the stiles together.

When the stiles are flush and tight with each other, I fasten them with screws (see the left photo on the facing page). I always drill pilot holes and countersink the screws. Usually two screws in each stile are

JOINING CABINETS. **Cabinet stiles are clamped flush and joined with wood screws before the cabinets are installed. Two wood screws hold the cabinets together, one near each hinge.**

ALIGNING CABINETS. **A straightedge placed along a run of cabinets shows which cabinets must move in or out. Here, a cabinet is pried away from the wall and shimmed out.**

sufficient. When the doors are closed, the screws are hidden, but I still try to make them inconspicuous when the doors are open by putting the screws close to the hinges. Once the adjoining stiles are screwed together, I screw the cabinet to the wall.

I install each succeeding base cabinet the same way—level it, shim or scribe as required, fasten the stiles, and then screw it to the wall. As the run of cabinets grows, I put a straightedge across the front of the cabinets to make sure they're in line (see the right photo above). I make any adjustments at the wall by tightening or loosening screws and adding shims.

Installing a Sink Base

Sink base cabinets with back panels may be more difficult to install because they might have to be bored for plumbing and electrical lines. If the cabinets on each side of the sink base are in position—even temporarily—I use them as reference points from which to measure the locations of pipes and wires. If the surrounding cabinets aren't in place, I mark the sink base–cabinet layout full size on both the wall and the floor. Then I can measure the pipe and wire locations from the layout lines.

If I drill holes in the back of the cabinet from behind, I complete them from the finished side to avoid tearing out the veneer. A little tearout isn't a big deal because the plumber usually puts a finish plate around the opening that covers a rough cut.

FASTENING A BACKER STRIP.
This strip of wood acts as a spacer to hold the corner cabinets far enough apart so that their drawers don't bump into each other.

cabinet's stile will be determined by the space required for the next-to-last cabinet when it's replaced.

Once all the scribing and trimming is complete, I put the last cabinet in place, then push the next-to-last cabinet in place with a pry bar. I use wax paper between the stiles to help the cabinet slide in without marring the finish.

Installing Filler and Backer Strips

When a run of cabinets doesn't quite fill the space between walls, filler strips are used. A filler strip is simply a board of the same kind of wood and finish as the cabinets, and it gets screwed to a cabinet's stile to fill a gap. Sometimes cabinets can be ordered with wider stiles to make up the difference, but fillers are more common.

To scribe a filler strip, I first screw it onto the cabinet stile, move the cabinet as close as possible to its final position, then I scribe, using the widest gap as the amount to cut off. I almost always leave a filler strip on a cabinet and cut the strip in place.

Backer strips are frequently installed at inside corners to keep cabinets far enough apart so that drawers or drawer handles don't bump into each other. Because the cabinets have to be separated by the thickness of the drawer front and the hardware, fastening a backer strip to the abutting cabinet will increase the clearance (see the photo above). We'll run into an inside corner later when I talk about peninsulas. But right now, I've still got to hang the upper cabinets.

Installing Upper Cabinets

Like the base cabinets, upper cabinets should be installed level and plumb, with sides parallel and stiles screwed together. All of the cabinets should be fastened to the wall using the same screws as those used for the base cabinets. I like to drive two screws in the top mounting rail and two into the bottom

Some sink base cabinets have no back panel; obviously it won't be necessary to drill holes if the pipes and the wires come through the wall. But sometimes they come up through the floor. And that's when the layout lines on the floor come in handy.

Installing Between Walls

When a run of base cabinets fits between walls, the dimensions may work out, and the cabinets will fit exactly. But more often than not, the cabinets will require some fitting.

If the total dimension of the cabinets is just slightly more than the space to be filled, I put all the cabinets in except the last one, and I leave the next-to-last cabinet unattached; that is, I don't screw it to the wall yet. I measure the space left for the last cabinet. Then I remove the next-to-last one and put the last one back in plumb and level. I scribe it to fit the return wall. The amount of material to be scribed off the last mounting rail. I fill gaps between the wall and the cabinet with shims as needed.

When hanging big, heavy upper cabinets, I lighten the load by removing all doors and shelves, and I reinstall whatever I've removed when all the cabinets are set. Removing the doors before hanging the cabinets also makes it easier to clamp the stiles together before driving the screws.

Instead of holding the cabinets in place as I try to fasten them to the wall, I typically use some plywood props (see the drawing below) or adjustable cabinet jacks (see the photo below). I made two different-size props from ¾-in. plywood; one prop is 17¼ in. high for a 16-in. spacing between upper and base cabinets; the other is 19¼ in. high for an 18-in. spacing (16 in. and 18 in. are the two most popular spacings between upper cabinets and base cabinets). The finish space between upper and base cabinets is 16

in. or 18 in.; the additional 1¼ in. on each prop makes up for the countertop that's not yet in place. The missing ¼ in. is shim space. I put a prop on a base cabinet and rest an upper cabinet on the prop. I use long shims to adjust the height of the upper cabinet to the layout line. (Some base cabinets are open on top, so I lay a piece of plywood on top of these cabinets and use the shorter props.)

Just as I installed the base cabinets, I start with a corner cabinet and work my way out. Each succeeding cabinet is put into place on the plywood prop and shimmed level. Then I clamp and screw the stiles together. Finally I screw the cabinet to the wall and remove the prop. The fronts of the upper cabinets should also be checked with a straightedge and adjusted at the wall line, again either by tightening screws or backing them out and adding shims.

Continued on p. 159

Hold Cabinets in Place With Plywood Props

Cabinet prop If you set base cabinets first, use a prop to support the uppers as you attach them to the wall. The prop's height (17¾ in. or 19¼ in.) equals the space between upper and base cabinets (16 in. or 18 in.) plus 1½ in. for a countertop minus ¼ in. for shim space.

Shim upper cabinet plumb and level.

Shim as needed

Prop rests either directly on base cabinet or on a piece of plywood if cabinet is open on top.

17¼ in. or 19¼ in.

¾-in. plywood

Cabinet jacks consist of square steel tubes that slide inside each other; a cabinet sits in cushioned angle iron.

Installing European Cabinets

BY TOM SANTARSIERO

Cabinetry manufactured in Europe brought a new look and installation system to the United States. European cabinets are frameless—they have no face frame—and the shelf pins, the hardware mounting screws, and the dowels that join the carcases are drilled on 32-mm centers. Although many American cabinet manufacturers have incorporated the European look and construction system into their lines, few have fully incorporated its installation system.

European cabinetry has its own suspension and support hardware that makes installing cabinets fast and efficient, even if you work alone. Upper cabinets are hung from a steel rail that you screw to the wall studs. Base cabinets stand on adjustable leveling legs. Thanks to this hardware, plumbing and leveling cabinets are much simpler.

When laying out a European kitchen, I snap three level lines on the walls. One line indicates the top of the base cabinet; one line indicates the bottom of the upper cabinets, and the third line is for the upper cabinets' hanging rail. The height of this rail varies from brand to brand.

The hanging rail is a length of steel about 1¼ in. wide with an offset bend along the top edge. I predrill ¼-in. holes at 5 cm o. c. (about 2 in. o. c.; European cabinetry is all metric). I screw the rail to the wall through these holes with #14 2½-in. pan-head screws.

I install the upper cabinets first. They hang on the channel in the hanging rail via a pair of adjustable hooks (see the photos at right) that protrude from the back of each cabinet. Two setscrews on each hook adjust the wall cabinets. One screw moves the cabinet in and out; the other moves the cabinet up and down. With this system, one person can easily hang and adjust wall cabinets.

When the hanging rail is above the cabinets, crown molding conceals it. If the hanging rail runs behind the cabinets, I notch the back of the cabinets to fit over the rail. However, end cabinets with visible side panels aren't notched; the hanging rail stops against the inside edge of a visible side panel.

Once the upper cabinets are aligned, I bolt them together using joining bolts supplied by the manufacturer. Most European cabinets have partially bored holes inside along the front of the side panels. I clamp the cabinets together, finish drilling the holes and then pass the bolts through. The

HANGING AN UPPER CABINET. A hanging rail screwed to the studs supports upper cabinets that have adjustable leveling hooks. This system allows one person to install cabinets.

bolts are similar to small carriage bolts with a threaded cap or socket. All of the European cabinets I've seen come with these bolts. If the cabinets you're installing come without bolts, you can use short drywall screws.

Base cabinets have leveling legs that slip into plastic sockets on the bottom of the cabinet. The legs usually come with each cabinet, along with caps that cover adjustment access holes in the cabinet floor. To level and plumb a cabinet, I either use the access holes to turn the legs with a screwdriver (see the photo below), or I turn the legs by hand.

Europeans don't fasten base cabinets to the wall. The thinking is that because base cabinets are joined together and attached to countertops and appliances, the cabinets won't move. Also, Europeans take their cabinets with them when they move, so fewer screws going in during installation means fewer screws to take out on moving day.

So that my cabinets stay put, I fasten them to the wall. How I fasten them depends on the brand of cabinet I'm installing. True European cabinets are a bit shallower than the typical 2-ft.-deep face-frame cabinet. When I install European cabinets, I space them away from the wall slightly so that they'll be the right depth for a conventional countertop. Some manufacturers supply special particleboard blocks with their cabinets that are screwed to the wall and to the cabinet, serving as both a spacer block and a rigid means of attachment.

If the manufacturer doesn't supply blocking, I screw a 2x4 cleat to the wall at the level line and fasten the cabinets to the cleat. I use a length of predrilled metal angle inside each cabinet to keep the wall-mounting screws from pulling through the back panel.

Toe-kick material, usually particleboard covered with plastic laminate or veneer to match the cabinets, comes in long lengths about 7 in. wide. I rip it to the proper width. If the finish flooring is not in place, I rip the toe kick narrow enough to accommodate the flooring. Or better yet, I cut and install the toe kick after the flooring has been installed. A vinyl sealer strip (similar to weatherstripping) comes either attached or loose to seal the bottom edge of the toe kick to the floor.

After cutting the toe kick to length, I join inside and outside corners with plastic end caps. If corners join at angles other than 90°, I miter the toe kicks and glue the joints. The toe kick is grooved on the back to accept knock-in clips that grip the leveling legs. To install the clips, I lay the toe kick face down on the floor in front of and aligned with the cabinets, and then I mark the location of every other leg and pop in the clips. The clips consist of a T-shaped knock-in and a U-shaped clip that slides over the knock-in. This combination allows some side-to-side adjustment of the toe kick

once it's pressed onto the legs. End caps then snap onto the kick ends.

Island and peninsula cabinets are freestanding and are likely to tip and sway. To anchor these cabinets to the floor, I make L-shaped plywood brackets. The vertical side of the L is about two-thirds the height of the toe kick. I use these brackets in pairs, usually two pairs per cabinet. I screw one bracket to the floor and the other to the bottom of the cabinet, installing them so that the vertical faces of the brackets ride against each other. Then I set the cabinets in place, level them, join them, and screw the brackets together.

TOM SANTARSIERO is a cabinetmaker and president of The Kitchen Design Center in Montclair, N.J.

ADJUSTING THE LEG. You don't have to shim or scribe European cabinets because they rest on legs that are adjusted up or down with a screwdriver. The toe kick clips onto the legs; the clips are also adjustable.

SECURE CABINETS TO THE FLOOR WITH BLOCKS

To keep peninsula or island cabinets from moving, attach them to blocks that are screwed to the floor and located according to the layout lines or masking tape.

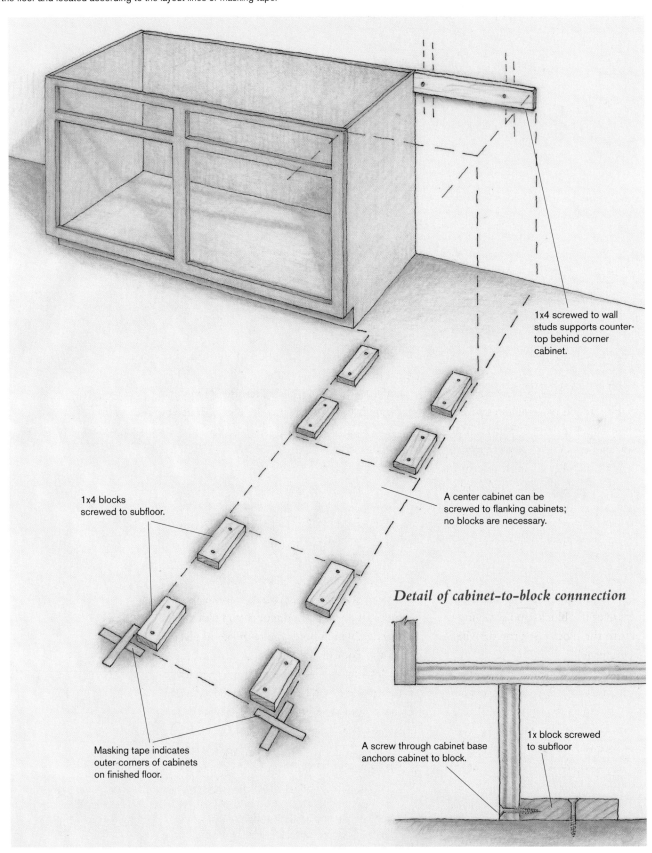

1x4 screwed to wall studs supports counter-top behind corner cabinet.

1x4 blocks screwed to subfloor.

A center cabinet can be screwed to flanking cabinets; no blocks are necessary.

Masking tape indicates outer corners of cabinets on finished floor.

Detail of cabinet-to-block connnection

A screw through cabinet base anchors cabinet to block.

1x block screwed to subfloor

USE TEMPLATE TO DRILL HOLES

Both templates have stop blocks that register against the edges of drawers and doors. The drawer-pull template has a centerline that you align with the centerline of the drawer face, and the door-pull template is self-aligning and reversible for use on a right- or left-hand door.

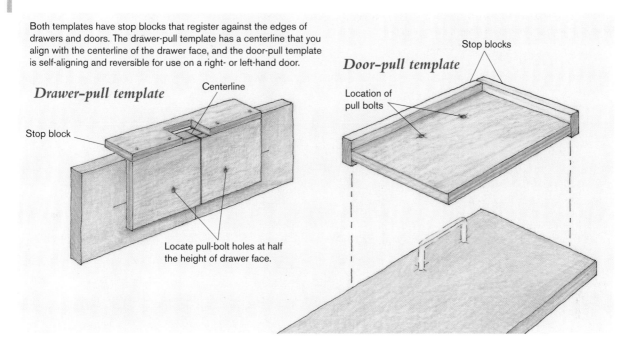

Drawer-pull template

Stop block

Centerline

Locate pull-bolt holes at half the height of drawer face.

Door-pull template

Stop blocks

Location of pull bolts

Continued from p. 155

Islands and Peninsulas

When the kitchen plan includes an island or a peninsula, I make a full-size layout on the floor and check the squareness of the corner with the old 3-4-5 triangle. If the finish floor isn't down yet, I snap chalklines. But if the finish floor is in place, I don't want chalk everywhere, so I use masking tape to show where the cabinets go.

An island or a peninsula should be secured to the floor, and I do it by screwing 1x blocks to the floor, then placing the cabinets over the blocks and screwing the cabinets to the blocks (see the drawing on the facing page).

Using my layout lines, I measure in from the edge of the masking tape or chalkline (which represents the outside of the cabinet) and mark the thickness of the cabinet's base. The new marks indicate where to screw the blocks down. Usually I just use a 6-in. to 8-in. block of 1x4 in each corner. Before I screw the cabinet to the blocks, I shim or scribe the cabinet so that it's plumb, level, and at the same height as the other

cabinets. When an island or a peninsula cabinet is placed over the blocks, it can't be shifted side to side, and when the screws go through the cabinet into the blocks, it can't be lifted either.

Hardware and Handles

After I've replaced all the doors and the drawers, I install the hardware. If the holes for the pulls have been predrilled, it's easy enough to screw the hardware on. But if I need to drill the holes myself, and there are a lot of holes to drill, it's best to make a template (see the drawing above). I use a piece of plywood and glue a stop block at its edge, which holds the template in place on the door or the drawer.

I sometimes use masking tape to mark the hole centers. Masking tape makes pencil marks more visible, but I double-check the marks by holding the handle up to them. I use a sharp scratch awl or punch to mark the hole, then drill it through. The center punch keeps the drill bit from wandering.

TOM LAW lives in Westminster, Md. His video on installing kitchen cabinets is available from The Taunton Press.

Hanging Kitchen Cabinets
Smooth and Solo

BY MIKE GUERTIN

Installing kitchen cabinets is one of my favorite projects. Whether I'm working on a new home or on a remodeling project, cabinet installation signals that the end is in sight. And installing the right cabinets transforms an empty space into a functional, good-looking kitchen.

Even factory-made stock cabinets, though, can be fussy to install. Walls are rarely straight or floors flat. A two-person crew with basic tools requires at least a day to install an average-size kitchen. But thanks to a few specialty tools and some techniques I've developed through many years spent working alone, I can do the same work by myself.

Good planning and joining cabinets together prior to installation are two important strategies. Tools such as a laser level, face-frame clamps, and a cabinet lift save time while also improving the accuracy of my work. Throughout the process, I do everything possible not to damage the new cabinets.

Dings Don't Have to Happen

On most projects, a lot of work has gone into getting the kitchen ready for the cabinets. The cabinets are a finish item, and I take every precaution not to let them become damaged during installation, starting as soon as they are delivered. Even if the cabinets arrive on the job before I am ready for them, I unbox them immediately to make sure everything I ordered was delivered and to inspect them for damage. Before installing the cabinets, I number (on painter's tape) and remove the doors, the shelves, and the drawers to protect them from damage. Removing these parts also lightens the boxes and makes them easier to handle. I don't reinstall any parts until the kitchen is complete.

Put the Plans on the Floor

For me, part of planning a smooth installation is drawing the cabinet layout as well as important plumbing and electrical information on the floor and the walls. I draw the layout on the floor early in the construction process to help other tradesmen and myself proceed. This system speeds the installation process and helps me to avoid mistakes.

On the floor, I mark three lines parallel with the walls: the face of the wall cabinets, the face of the base cabinets, and the face of the rough toe kick. Then I mark the location of the individual base cabinets, wall cabinets, and appliances. I write the cabinet size code in each box and label the appliances and their sizes.

With all this information written on the floor, I can determine if I need filler strips

Continued on p. 167

MARK THE TOP OF THE BASE CABINETS AND THE BOTTOM OF THE UPPERS. I use a laser level to mark the walls at the ends of each cabinet run. Then I snap chalklines to guide base- and wall-cabinet installation. Plan to shim the base cabinets off the subfloor the thickness of the finished flooring so that the 1½-in.-thick countertop will be 36 in. above the finished floor.

START WITH AN ACCURATE MAP. Lay out cabinet details on the floor. Here, I taped resin paper over an old linoleum floor to show details more clearly. Mark the face of the wall cabinets, the face of the base cabinets, and the face of the rough toe kick. Also mark the locations of any individual cabinets and of the appliances.

FIND THE STUDS. A stud finder locates framing members quickly. I indicate the stud locations with a tick mark along the chalklines. The marks still will be visible when the cabinets are in place.

Install Blocking to Anchor Cabinets

You can fasten wall cabinets just to the studs, but horizontal blocking installed between the studs makes for a more secure installation. In new homes or gutted remodels, I install 2x4 or 2x6 blocks between studs. Make sure to locate blocking behind the cabinet's top mounting rail. When installing cabinets on existing walls (as shown here), I cut through the wallboard where the top mounting rail will land. I remove the wallboard and install 2x4 blocks with 3-in. screws. Then I cover the blocks with drywall and finish the seams with tape and compound.

Cabinet Lift

Hanging a run of wall cabinets by yourself isn't a problem if you use a cabinet lift ($525*; www.e-zspreadnlift.com). Available at rental centers, this tool also can be used to roll base cabinets into position.

Face-Frame Clamps

Keeping the face frames of adjacent cabinets aligned while you screw them together is done easily with these special clamps ($71.50 a pair*; www.adjustableclamp.com). The clamps have protective pads to keep new cabinets from being scratched and a drill guide to keep pilot holes straight. The guide flips out of the way, allowing you to drive the screw without removing the clamp.

Join Wall Cabinets on the Floor

USE CLAMPS TO DRAW THE STILES TOGETHER. I use three screws in stiles 24 in. or taller and two screws in those shorter. Drill a ⅛-in.-dia. pilot hole through both stiles and a shallow ³⁄₁₆-in. hole into only the first stile to counterbore each trim-head screw. If possible, I locate the screws so that they'll be hidden by door hinges.

ALIGN THE CABINETS WITH A STRAIGHT-EDGE. Before joining the backs of the cabinets, I put a straightedge across the top to make sure the tops are level and the fronts are straight. Then I shim between the side panels at the rear, and drive screws to keep the ganged cabinets straight. The cabinets now can be installed as a single unit.

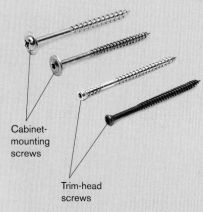

Cabinet-mounting screws

Trim-head screws

DON'T USE DRYWALL SCREWS

Many cabinet companies now supply mounting screws, but years ago, we were left to our own devices. Like many installers, I made the mistake of hanging cabinets with drywall screws, which simply aren't strong enough to support loaded cabinets. These days, I use only special cabinet-mounting screws, preferably those with broad washer heads for full shoulder support (www.mcfeelys.com). To join stiles, I use trim-head screws. The smaller heads can be hidden easily by hinges, plugs, or wood putty.

Preassembled Wall Cabinets Hang as One Unit

1 **CRANK IT UP.** Cabinets make the lift top heavy, so I roll the lift close to the wall before cranking up the ganged cabinets and positioning them against their layout lines. Don't risk dropping the cabinets; clamp them to the lift's table until they are screwed to the wall.

DRILL HOLES FOR WIRING. With the lift holding the cabinet close to the wall, I can drill holes to wire undercabinet lights exactly where they need to be.

DRIVE SCREWS INTO STUDS AND BLOCKING. Cabinet-mounting screws require pilot holes. I drive screws into the studs above the top panel of the cabinet, below the bottom panel, or through the back. When blocking is installed, I drill holes 2 in. from the side panels through the mounting rail and about 12 in. apart. With the unit secured to the wall by at least four screws, I remove the lift and drive the remaining screws.

Hang Cabinets With a Ledger Instead of a Lift

If you don't have a cabinet lift, you can screw a temporary ledger board along the chalkline to support the back of a wall unit, and wedge a wood prop in place to support the front while you drive installation screws. But I prefer to have a helper, especially for longer runs of cabinets.

Smooth Move: Preinstalled Crown Molding

I think it's easier to apply crown molding to the cabinets with the preassembled unit on the floor. To do this, however, I first have to lift the cabinets into position and mark the bottom of the crown on each end of the bank of cabinets and at all cabinet joints. Then I can lower the cabinets, screw blocking to the top rails, and install the crown by screwing through the blocking and into the crown from behind. With this installation technique, no nail holes need to be filled with color-matched putty.

Plywood Strips and Shims Set Base Cabinets to the Right Height

1

KEEP THE TOPS FLUSH AND THE FRONTS STRAIGHT. Join the base cabinets together with trim screws through the stiles. Shim between and screw together the panels in the back. Use a straightedge across the front of ganged base cabinets to keep the tops flush and the fronts straight. If the cabinets are imperfect, I sometimes have to plane the tops down to get surfaces flush.

2

USE A GAUGE STICK TO PAD OUT THE FLOOR. Due to fluctuations in the subfloor, the plywood strips won't all be the same thickness. I rip 2-in.-wide strips of ¼-in., ½-in., and ¾-in. plywood and use a 34¼-in. gauge stick (the height of the cabinets less the countertop) to determine which size strip to use. I place strips at each end of a run of cabinets and anywhere cabinets are joined.

3

4

SET BASE CABINETS ON THE STRIPS, THEN SHIM. After setting a gang of base cabinets into position on the plywood strips, I use shims to make sure they are sturdy and level.

SHIM FOR WAVY WALLS. I drill pilot holes at each stud location and drive screws to secure the cabinets. Shims fill the hollows between the mounting rails and the walls.

Continued from p.160

and can identify any potential conflicts, like an off-center range outlet. The layout also shows the electrician and plumber where to locate rough-ins for appliances and fixtures. I also indicate on the floor and the walls where pipe runs occur to avoid driving any cabinet-mounting screws into them.

Accurate Elevations Help You to Get the Right Heights

On the walls, I mark stud, blocking, and utility locations as well as the top of the base cabinets and the bottom of the upper cabinets. I factor in the thickness of the finished flooring before these elevations are marked.

Stock base cabinets are 34½ in. tall (1½-in.-thick countertops bring the finished elevation of the base cabinets up to 36 in.). If you install the base cabinets on the subfloor and then cover the floor with ¾-in.-thick hardwood flooring, the countertop height will be short. So when I mark the elevation of the top of the base cabinets, I add the height of the finished flooring. In this case, I added ⅞ in. for a tile floor.

I always measure the elevation from the lowest spot I can find on the subfloor and use a laser level to mark the elevations at the ends of cabinet runs. Then I snap a chalkline or connect the points with a long spirit level. I also find the elevation of the bottom of the wall cabinets and use a stud finder to locate and mark the studs along both elevation lines.

When I install the base cabinets, I set them on plywood strips to shim them to the proper height. In fact, I cut plywood strips that are both thicker and thinner than I need and use them to make up for low and high spots in the subfloor. I cut the strips to equal the distance from the rough toe-kick line to the wall (around 22 in.). I also set a strip at each end of a run of base cabinets and everywhere two cabinets meet. Later, when the base cabinets are installed, I use cedar shims to level and make fine ad-

justments to raise the tops of the cabinets to the chalkline.

Wall or Base Cabinets First?

Professional kitchen installers debate whether the wall cabinets or the base cabinets should be mounted first. There's no right or wrong sequence, only preferences.

For many years, I installed the base cabinets first and laid boards over them to serve as a platform to rest the wall cabinets on during installation. But after damaging the face frames on a few base cabinets with my belt buckle and tools dangling from my belt, I changed to mounting wall cabinets first and haven't looked back.

Before I install the wall cabinets, I use a long spirit level, referencing the wall-cabinet positions marked on the floor, to draw plumb lines for the sides of the wall cabinets. This ensures that the wall cabinets will align with the base cabinets.

Gang the Cabinets Together, and Forget About Wavy Walls

Walls are never flat. Even walls framed with engineered studs have bumps and dips at drywall seams. Sometimes cabinets aren't perfect, either. The side panels may be slightly out of square with the face frame, or a backing panel may not be flat across the rear. Imperfections in walls and cabinets make aligning the faces of cabinet runs difficult, particularly when cabinets are installed one at a time. I overcome these problems by ganging cabinets together before mounting them to the wall. This approach is faster and more precise than mounting cabinets individually.

Cabinets can be assembled resting upright on the floor, on their backs, or elevated on a bench. I gang a run of cabinets by screwing together the face-frame stiles and the backs of the cabinets. The trick is to clamp a straightedge along the top front of the cabinets while you screw them together. The front face and the top edge of the run need to be straight. Once the backs of the cabinets are joined, they will stay aligned.

I locate screws where they are least likely to be seen: behind the hinges or in the drawer spaces on base cabinets. If a screw is needed where it can't be hidden, I countersink trim-head screws and cover them with color-matched putty. Screws joining the backs of the cabinets can be driven through the cabinet side panels above the top panel, where they'll never be noticed. I use three screws to join stiles 24 in. or taller and two screws in anything shorter. Two screws are plenty to hold the cabinet backs together. Once screwed together, the individual boxes essentially become one long cabinet.

When I install the cabinet run as a unit, I still have to check the whole run for level using both a spirit level and the elevation lines. I make adjustments once for the whole run of cabinets instead of making many adjustments for each individual cabinet. I usually can move long runs of base cabinets into place by myself, but I sometimes need help with wall cabinets.

Wall Cabinets Get a Lift

Two people easily can lift a gang of three to six wall cabinets when the doors and shelves have been removed. But I work alone a lot, so I rely on a cabinet lift. For me, the cabinet lift has been worth every penny I spent on it, but if you're doing only one kitchen-cabinet installation, you usually can find a lift at a rental center. The lift's table supports up to 6 ft. of ganged cabinets. For longer cabinet runs, I screw a plank to the lift's table.

I roll the cabinets to the wall while they are still low on the lift, then crank them up. This keeps the center of gravity down and makes the lift less likely to tip. When I'm 3 in. from the wall, I raise the cabinets up to the mounting line, mark and drill pilot holes

for mounting screws, and cut openings for utilities and undercabinet-lighting wires.

A cabinet lift isn't necessary to mount wall cabinets; it just makes the job easier. For short runs of cabinets, you can screw a temporary 1x3 ledger to the wall to support the cabinets. If you use a ledger, drill pilot holes and twist screws into the holes at both ends of the cabinet run before lifting it to the wall. The ledger will help as you balance the cabinets with one hand and drive the screws with the other. Long runs of cabinets can be lifted onto a ledger by two people. One person can hold the top against the wall while the other drives the screws.

I also gang together the base cabinets. After shimming the ganged base cabinets to the appropriate elevation, I fasten them to the wall at each stud, using shims to fill any hollows.

Reinstalling the doors and drawers is the last thing I do on a project. I wait until the countertops are set, the plumbing is connected, everything is painted, and the flooring is installed. Waiting until the end of the project protects the cabinet doors and drawer fronts from collateral damage as the project is completed.

Note—prices are from 2005.

MIKE GUERTIN is a builder and remodeler in East Greenwich, R.I., and a contributing editor to *Fine Homebuilding.*

Corner Details

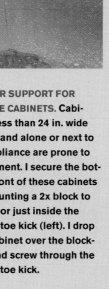

A FACE FRAME TAKES THE PLACE OF A CORNER CABINET. Angled base cabinets for inside-corner sinks are expensive. Rather than buy an unnecessary box, I order an extra face-frame panel and a door from the cabinet company and use them to connect the base cabinets on both sides of the sink (below). The side panels of the adjoining cabinets and the painted drywall become the inside walls of the cabinet. I mount blocking to the sides of the adjacent cabinets and along the walls to support a plywood bottom panel with holes drilled for the plumbing. To support the countertop, I screw cleats to the walls. If the inside-corner cabinet will house a sink, I leave it open. If it is for storage, I make it a lazy Susan.

BETTER SUPPORT FOR SINGLE CABINETS. Cabinets less than 24 in. wide that stand alone or next to an appliance are prone to movement. I secure the bottom front of these cabinets by mounting a 2x block to the floor just inside the rough toe kick (left). I drop the cabinet over the blocking, and screw through the rough toe kick.

Dressing Up Plywood Cabinets With Face Frames

BY JOSEPH BEALS

FACE FRAMES COMPLETE A CABINET. The author fits a face frame to a plywood carcase, giving the cabinet the appearance of solid-wood furniture.

GUIDELINES FOR DESIGNING FACE FRAMES

Start with a basic width of 1¾ in. for rails, stiles, and partitions, and vary it according to the rules below.

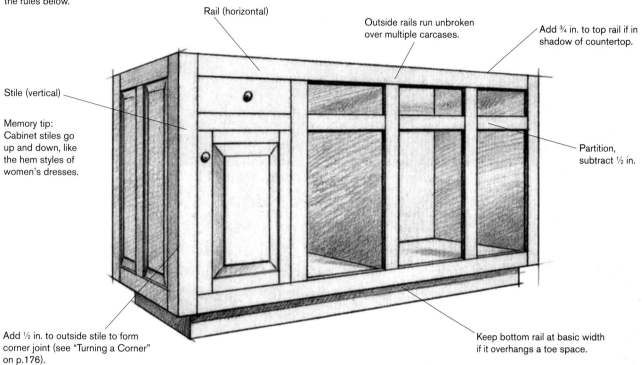

Rail (horizontal)

Outside rails run unbroken over multiple carcases.

Add ¾ in. to top rail if in shadow of countertop.

Stile (vertical)

Memory tip: Cabinet stiles go up and down, like the hem styles of women's dresses.

Partition, subtract ½ in.

Add ½ in. to outside stile to form corner joint (see "Turning a Corner" on p.176).

Keep bottom rail at basic width if it overhangs a toe space.

One of the first face frames I built was a nightmare at every step. It was a maple behemoth, more than 11 ft. long, for a row of cabinets I had built at the job site. When I glued up the frame in my shop, the dowel joints would not line up until I fairly beat them together. I applied the finished frame on site just as a thunderstorm blew in. I spread white glue on the back of the frame and used two hands, two knees, and my forehead to hold it in place. A lightning bolt took out the power at about the third nail. As I set the frame by kerosene lamp, I decided face frames must be the nastiest job invented.

I have made plenty of face frames since then, and they don't seem nearly as difficult anymore. I now make them with mortise-and-tenon joints and attach them to carcases with biscuits or with counterbored and plugged screws.

How a face frame is made is no more important than how it's designed. Face frames should be a subtle element in the composition of a cabinet. A face frame that draws attention to itself through awkward proportions or wild grain isn't doing its job.

And no matter how face frames are made, they all do the same thing. A solid-wood face frame provides a finished front on casework that's usually made of some manufactured material such as plywood or fiberboard. The frame covers the raw edges, provides a place to hang doors, fit drawers, and attach trim. Face frames are appropriate for a variety of practical, built-in, and freestanding furniture.

Design Face Frames Like Doors

Parts of a face frame are best put together as if they were a conventional door frame: Outer stiles should run full height, with top and bottom rails let in between. Internal partitions should follow the same pattern (see the drawing above).

These rules serve well in most instances, but they should be modified when a pair of face frames are joined end to end. The joint between them will look best if the top and

Continued on p.174

Three Common Ways to Build Face Frames

Face-frame joints don't need to be particularly strong, but they should go together easily and be simple to align. Mortise-and-tenon joinery is traditional (see a description of my approach p. 175), but face frames can also be assembled with dowels, biscuits, or pocket screws.

DOWELS

Pros: Doweled face frames are easy to lay out because you don't need to figure in tenon lengths.

Cons: To prevent frame pieces from rotating, each joint requires two dowels, which can be difficult to align accurately. Once drilled, dowel holes can't be adjusted to compensate for even the smallest alignment mistakes during assembly. If used with yellow glue, doweled joints must be pressed tight at one go: a lapse of a minute or less will let a dowel seize with the joint open.

BISCUITS

Pros: Biscuit joints are the fastest and easiest joint to make. They align quickly and positively.

Cons: Kerfs for the smallest standard-size biscuit will break through and show on edges of stock narrower than 2⅜ in. If a molding detail will be added to the inside of the face frame, biscuits may be the most convenient joinery choice.

POCKET SCREWS

Pros: Pocket screws on the back of the frame make a fast and simple joint.

Cons: Joints are difficult to align perfectly flat and can't be adjusted in any practical manner during assembly without pulling out screws. A dedicated jig is needed to drill screw holes.

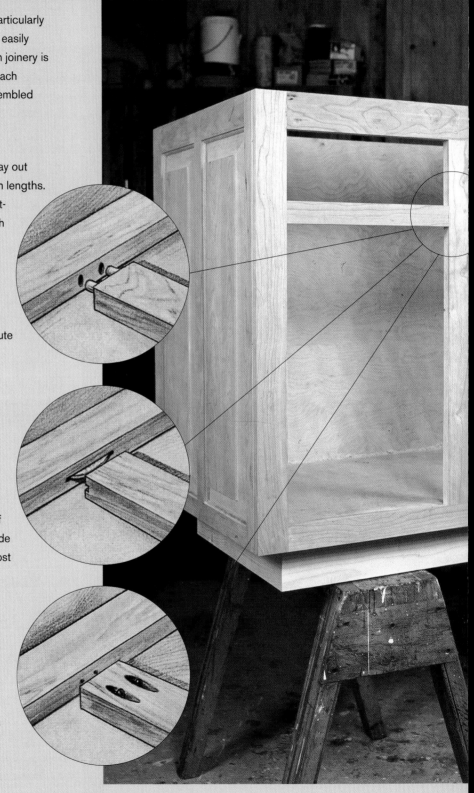

It's often easier to apply face frames while cabinets are still in the shop, but very large or long cabinets are a different story. When a number of smaller cabinet components are put together on a job site, they can be joined with a common face frame. In that situation, frames can be attached to the cabinets with screws or nails.

PLUGGED SCREWS

Pros: Plugged screws are useful when clamping a biscuit joint is not an option. They are the equal of biscuits for strength and overall convenience, and can be used with biscuits for better alignment. Use 1⅝-in. black drywall screws through a ¹³⁄₁₆-in.-thick face frame. They grip well in plywood and do not require a pilot hole.

Cons: The plugs show if the cabinet is finished bright.

NAILS

Pros: The oldest and simplest method is glue and nails, especially for painted work. Nail holes are small and can be filled easily.

Cons: Nails will sometimes wander sideways in a plywood edge, shifting the face frame. Occasionally, a nail will split the plywood or pop out of a cabinet side. Nailed frames are difficult to align exactly without biscuits.

Continued from p. 171

bottom rails butt into each other, rather than into side-by-side stiles. This will give the illusion of a continuous frame, which looks better.

It's important to use straight-grained, stable stock for face frames. Wild grain should be avoided, even when the rail or stile is fastened along its length, such as along a cabinet bottom. It will draw the eye to a pattern that probably has no symmetry or other resolution. The frame should not compete visually with the doors and drawers it surrounds.

There are no best dimensions for the various rails, stiles, and partitions, just some guidelines to keep them visually balanced. I mill rough 4/4 stock to $^{13}/_{16}$ in., but standard ¾-in. stock is fine. The parts should be neither so wide as to appear clumsy nor so narrow as to seem fragile. The proportions of smaller parts such as drawer partitions should be reduced to keep them from looking oversize. For a face frame that will house flush-mounted doors and drawers, I find 1¾ in. to be the most satisfying width for ordinary stiles, and I derive other component dimensions from it.

Outside stiles need to be wider at corners because they form a joint. To make both appear 1¾ in. wide and maintain symmetry around the corner, one must be cut down to 1 in. wide or less. Working with such a narrow piece is not worth the effort, especially if grooved for a panel. I widen the front stile to 2¼ in. and make the side stile 1½ in. wide. (For more on how to get around a corner, see "Turning a Corner" on p. 176)

You Have Several Assembly Choices

There are at least four ways to make a face frame: with dowels, biscuits, pocket screws, or more traditional mortise-and-tenon joinery. Your choice will probably depend on what tools you have on hand and which method you have experience with. For me, the best approach is the old-fashioned way—the mortise and tenon—even if it takes a little longer and is a little more complicated. (The first three methods are explained in more detail on p. 172)

Mortise-and-tenon joints are strong, very reliable, and easily made. They give positive, foolproof alignment of parts. To cut mortises, I use a small slot mortising machine. You could use a router, which is also very fast and accurate.

I make the mortises about ⅜ in. deep and about $^{5}/_{16}$ in. wide. It's not necessary to make them deeper because a face frame is not subject to particularly severe loading. They should be easy to put together but without too much play (see the photos showing my approach on the facing page).

When all the joints have been cut, I dry-fit the face frame and compare it to measurements on my drawings and the carcase. It helps to imagine the finished cabinet and overlay that mental picture on the face frame, in case something brutally obvious has slipped through the design process. If all is well, I glue it together.

I brush yellow glue in the mortises and on the tenons and fit the frame together across sawhorses (see the bottom center photo on the facing page). I clamp across all joints with just enough pressure to bring the tenon shoulders home tight, checking once again to make sure the joints are flat. Adjustments can be made by shifting a clamp or moving it to the opposite side. However, unlike a door, a face frame does not need to be perfectly flat. Because it's relatively thin, the frame will be fairly limber and will be drawn flat when fitted to the carcase. I also check each joint for square and lateral alignment, adjusting them with a hammer and block if necessary.

I measure diagonals to check the face frame for square (see the top photo on the facing page). This is crucial, but easy to forget. To square a slightly racked face frame, I skew each clamp slightly. If that doesn't work, I add a clamp across the long diagonal to pull it into place. Despite every care, the square of the door and drawer openings on

My Way of Making Face Frames

ONLY PERFECT RECTANGLES HAVE EQUAL DIAGONALS. The author compares diagonals to make sure the face frame is square. Angling the clamps corrects minor problems.

USE MORTISE-AND-TENON JOINERY FOR A STRONG, EASILY ALIGNED JOINT. To save time, cut the tenon shoulders on the tablesaw without changing the blade height.

BEFORE GLUE-UP, DRY-FIT THE WHOLE FRAME. This ensures all pieces will go together smoothly when coping with glue that sets quickly and an armload of clamps.

SAWHORSES MAKE CLAMPING UP EASY. They'll let you fit clamps on both sides of the frame for even clamping pressure.

Attaching Face Frames

BISCUITS ARE BEST. Although strong, biscuits can be difficult to align when the face frame hangs over the edge of the cabinet. Instead of resetting the fence on his biscuit joiner, the author uses a spacer block the thickness of the overhang to align the tool.

CLAMP-UP IS A CINCH WITH THE CARCASE ON ITS BACK. Face frames attached with biscuits need to be clamped. Sawhorses make it easy to reach all the edges of the carcase and face frame.

TURNING A CORNER

As seen from the top, face frames can be joined at a cabinet corner in several ways.

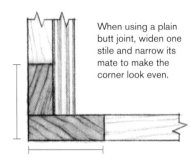

When using a plain butt joint, widen one stile and narrow its mate to make the corner look even.

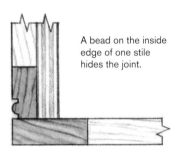

A bead on the inside edge of one stile hides the joint.

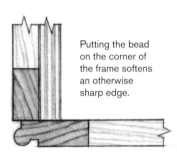

Putting the bead on the corner of the frame softens an otherwise sharp edge.

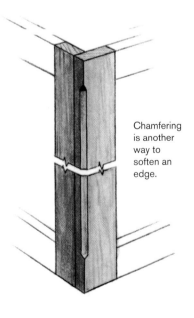

Chamfering is another way to soften an edge.

a complex face frame may not agree with the overall squareness of the frame. When this happens, I split the difference.

Attach Face Frame to Carcases

Whenever possible, I attach the face frame in my shop because all my tools are nearby, and clamping a frame to a cabinet is much easier when the cabinet can be parked on a couple of sawhorses. Attaching them on site is an option if the carcases and frames are too big to carry as a single unit. Attaching a face frame to carcases after they've been set in place is my last option, though there are circumstances when it's the best method.

No matter where you end up attaching face frames, the single most demanding detail is keeping the top edge of the bottom rail flush with the inside of the cabinet bottom. (One exception is when the cabinet bottom becomes a door stop.) The veneers on most cabinet-grade plywoods are very thin and will not withstand much planing or sanding. The top edge of the bottom rail must, therefore, be fastened dead flush or a fraction proud to permit finishing to a smooth joint. This joint has always been particularly important to me. I think it's a sign of sloppy work when it's not flush, but others may not be so obsessed.

Shop installation with biscuits and clamps–

When I attach face frames in the shop, I use biscuits almost exclusively (see the top photo on the facing page). The biscuit joint is strong, accurate, and doesn't show. Also, biscuits are invaluable along the bottom rail, which demands accurate positioning. However, it's foolish to trust the biscuit to align everything perfectly because there can be some occasional play in the slots. Even with biscuits, you should expect to make adjustments.

In some materials, such as medium-density fiberboard, biscuits may be the only practical attachment because screws hold poorly in the edge and tend to split the material. Although biscuits allow me to eliminate screws entirely, the disadvantage is that I need to use clamps (see the bottom photo on the facing page). Clamps tie up the carcase for at least an hour, and they always get in the way of cleaning off glue that squeezes out of the joints.

On-site installation with plugged screws–

For a very long run of cabinets, on-site installation of face frames has some benefits. Long runs of cabinets look better when united with a single face frame, but attaching them all in the shop and moving them to the site later is impractical. Multiple cabinets should be set in place individually, then fastened together to ensure they're square, plumb, and aligned.

Shop installation of face frames is convenient because the cabinets can lie on their backs, which gives full access for clamping. On site, after the cabinets are set against the walls, clamping access disappears. In this application, counterbored, plugged screws are hard to match for strength and overall convenience. Once they're in, the attachment is done. Screws grip well in plywood and do not require a pilot hole in the plywood edge.

To hide the screws, I use plugs cut from the same stock as the face frame. For bright finished work, I try to match grain pattern and color as well. After the glue dries, I strike off most of the excess plug with a chisel and watch how the grain runs. If the grain runs down into the plug, some of the plug can pop off below the surface, leaving a tedious repair job. To avoid it, I finish paring off the plug from the other direction.

Plugged holes vanish under paint, but even with careful grain and color matching, that little circle is always visible under a bright finish. This isn't necessarily offensive, but it requires that screw holes be carefully and symmetrically aligned. I find that there is something pleasing about a thoughtful, geometric pattern of plugs along the edges of a face frame.

JOSEPH BEALS is a custom woodworker in Marshfield, Mass.

Refacing Kitchen Cabinets

BY REX ALEXANDER

By the time she called me, Caroline McCary had already decided that her 32-year-old maple kitchen had to go. Caroline had antiqued the cabinets to a dark green a few years earlier (see the top photo on the facing page), and now she was tired of them. What she had in mind was a whole new set of cabinets.

Caroline runs a beauty parlor in her house and had heard about me from one of her customers. But the customer hadn't mentioned the fact that I reface kitchens— just that I build new ones. In fact, Caroline and her husband, Robert, didn't even know that refacing the cabinets in veneer was an option for them. But when I realized the cabinets were sound structurally, and the layout was sensible, I knew their kitchen was a perfect candidate for a veneer face-lift. And that would mean big savings for the McCarys.

I can make old cabinets look new (see the bottom photo on the facing page) for only two-thirds the price of new ones. What's more, the veneering process is far less disruptive for the customer than tearing out existing cabinets and installing new ones.

There are other advantages with the face-lifting process: First, you're recycling old cabinets, so you can feel good about taking some of the strain off the local land-

SHOP DEMONSTRATION. In his shop, the author cuts veneer roughly to size before demonstrating the refacing technique. The cabinet is from the kitchen shown on the facing page.

fill; and second, you're reducing your customer's exposure to the formaldehyde given off by the particleboard and plywood used in new cabinets. At the same time, a veneer face-lift is an opportunity for the homeowner to add some of those kitchen accessories that make life easier—things like self-closing door hinges, full-extension drawer slides or pull-out shelves, and lazy Susans. I get these items from Direct Supply (1055-36th St. SE, Grand Rapids, Mich. 49508; 800-878-8704).

A FACE-LIFT CANDIDATE. Caroline McCary had worked in her kitchen for 32 years before deciding that the original maple cabinets, now antiqued to a dull green, needed replacement.

SAME VIEW, NEW FACE. Working with existing cabinet carcases and face frames, the author transformed Caroline's kitchen with oak veneer, new doors, and new drawer fronts.

The veneering process can transform a kitchen in a matter of a week or two. Specialized tools are few. And when applied with care, the veneer is both attractive and durable. Some of the work—like filling and sanding the face frames and finishing the new veneer—is done on site. Other work—such as making new doors, drawer fronts, and end panels—takes place back in my shop. When all these elements are combined in the kitchen, the results can be dramatic.

Choosing Veneers

Wood veneers of almost all native American hardwoods, and of some imported species, are available from many wood suppliers. Veneers come in a variety of widths, from ¾-in. strips all the way to 24-in.-wide sheets. Veneer is available in at least two preglued varieties—pressure sensitive (see the sidebar on pp. 180–181) and heat sensitive—as well as in the traditional types

Continued on p. 182.

Another Option: Pressure-Sensitive Veneer

BY HERRICK KIMBALL

My approach to veneer refacing includes basic steps that most kitchen-cabinet refacers are likely to follow: the removal of cabinet doors and the repair of imperfections in the existing frames; the application of ¼-in. hardwood plywood end panels; and finally, the actual veneering. But I use pressure-sensitive veneer—or what's called peel-and-stick veneer—instead of the type treated with a heat-activated adhesive.

I use 10-mil-thick veneers with an adhesive backing made by 3M® (3M, 3M Center, St. Paul, Minn. 55144-1000; 888-364-3577). I buy it in 2-ft. by 8-ft. sheets. I simply cut the veneer to size, apply a bonding agent to the cabinet, peel off the backing paper, and stick the veneer to the surface I'm refacing. There is, however, one major caveat: pressure-sensitive veneer is very much like contact cement. That is, once it's stuck, there's not much chance of moving or adjusting it. If the veneer you apply goes on crooked, you'll need a sharp chisel and exceptional patience to get it off.

All the material I use for kitchen refacing—doors, plywood end panels, drawer fronts, and veneer—is prefinished by my supplier. That saves me a lot of time. There are many places to buy material, but the company I use is Concepts in Wood (4021 New Court Ave., Syracuse, N. Y. 13206; 315-463-8084).

VENEER THE STILES FIRST

Once any repairs have been made to the face frames, and the surface has been sanded with 60-grit or 80-grit paper, I get ready to apply the veneer. The pressure-sensitive veneer sticks best to smooth, nonporous surfaces like old-fashioned metal cabinets. But let's face it—few surfaces are in perfect shape, so I use a bonding agent made by 3M called NF30. This is a water-based contact adhesive that is neither flammable nor noxious smelling. Just before I put on the veneer, I go over the frames with a damp cloth to remove any dust. Then I paint on a coat of NF30 with a disposable foam brush and let it dry.

I prefer to veneer the inside edges of the stiles and rails as well as their faces. The entire face frame looks like it's new—even when the doors are opened. Fortunately, the veneer I use is flexible enough to wrap around a corner, and I

don't have to cut separate pieces for faces and inside edges. I cut the strips, allowing ¼ in. extra in width and ½ in. extra in length (I trim that excess off later). I start with the vertical pieces of veneer, so after cutting the pieces I apply a coat of NF30 to the stiles, including the inside edges (see photo 1). For the moment I don't coat the rails with any adhesive.

Before I apply the veneer to the stiles, I make a reference mark on the top and bottom rails. These marks will show me how much veneer must overhang the face to fold around the corner and cover the inside edge of the stile. With the marks made and the veneer cut, I peel the backing paper from the top of the veneer strip and lightly stick the veneer to the stile so that the inside edge is aligned with the reference mark (see photo 2).

Then, with one hand holding the piece taut and with the veneer lined up with the bottom reference mark, I press the top firmly into place. Then I slowly peel the backing paper down and off the veneer, pressing the veneer to the face frame as I go. To ensure a good bond, I apply pressure with a hand roller or a stiff putty knife that has been covered in cloth.

The veneer must be sliced horizontally at both top and bottom rails so that it can be folded around the inside edge of the face frame. Using the rail as a guide, I make these cuts with a sharp utility knife. Once the cuts have been made, the veneer is folded around the edge (see photo 3) and

SAVING A TIRED CABINET. Beginning at left: A water-based bonding agent is applied with a disposable foam brush (1) and allowed to dry for a few minutes; a strip of veneer is lined up with a reference mark on the rail of the cabinet, applied to the stile (2), then bonded with a roller; the veneer is cut where it overhangs the cabinet rails, then it's folded around the edge of the face frame (3); excess veneer on cabinet stiles is trimmed with a sharp utility knife and a square (4).

smoothed to ensure a good bond. Because a roller won't fit into corners, I smooth inside edges with the shank of a fine-point nail set. Any excess veneer inside the cabinet is trimmed with a utility knife and sanded smooth.

I trim excess veneer extending onto the rails of the face frame. Because no bonding agent has yet been applied to the rail, the veneer can be peeled off with relative ease. I use a square against the rail as a guide and make the cut with a utility knife (see photo 4). As a last step, I trim off any extra veneer that hangs below the bottom of the frame. The stiles should now be complete.

THE RAILS ARE NEXT

Horizontal surfaces are handled in much the same way: first the bonding agent, then the veneer and, finally, a roller. I find the exact length of the rail veneer simply by holding up a strip of veneer between the two veneered stiles and marking the strip. I make the marks with a utility knife and then cut the veneer on a cutting board with a square. Once cut to exact length, the rails are applied in the same way—with

one notable difference. Instead of marking the face frame to show the correct overhang for the inside edges, I apply pieces of masking tape to the stiles and mark the tape. That makes removing the marks a snap.

When rails and stiles are veneered, I sand outside corner edges carefully with 120-grit paper. Then I stain any bare wood and spray on a couple of coats of aerosol lacquer. Where the veneer wraps around the edges of the face frames, it can crack slightly. If that's the case, I use 150-grit paper to knock down any high spots, then stain and spray finish the area.

On larger surfaces, the pressure-sensitive veneer can be unwieldy. Here's a tip: those bulletin-board push pins can substitute for an extra pair of hands while you scribe a sheet of veneer to the wall.

HERRICK KIMBALL is a remodeling contractor in Moravia, N. Y.

Continued from p. 179

with no glue at all. I use heat-sensitive veneer, which I apply with a clothes iron, and I've found it is durable enough to withstand the wear and tear of normal kitchen activities. In fact, in 15 years of kitchen face-lifts, I have not had a single callback because veneer loosened or was torn off during normal use.

But keep one thing in mind: The choice of wood can greatly affect the price of a kitchen face-lift. I use ¼-in. plywood for end panels and door panels most of the time, and I've found it cost effective to use either birch or red oak. These plywoods are available in the northern Michigan lumberyards that I frequent, and they are economical. If you want something different, your supplier probably can order it. But ordering special plywood may be more expensive, and you'll have to buy solid lumber of the same species for drawer fronts and door frames. That matching solid lumber can cancel out the economies of veneer refacing.

Are the Cabinets Worth Saving?

Cabinetry that is still sound structurally can provide the right foundation for new veneer—but some cabinets aren't worth the effort. I look for well-built carcases and face frames. The bottoms, sides, and backs of the cabinets should be in good condition and anchored to one another solidly. Adjustable shelves should work. I also check that face frames are firmly attached to the cabinet carcases, or can be reattached easily, and that the face-frame joinery is flush and secure.

A set of kitchen cabinets, of course, is made up of a number of smaller units that are assembled when the kitchen is installed. If there are gaps between the face frames on adjoining cabinets, I usually can pull the cabinets together with drywall screws. But there are danger signs when inspecting a kitchen for a possible face-lift: ¼-in. plywood cabinet bottoms that are bowed, loose, or falling apart; or face frames that are toenailed together. You might have to put more work into rehabilitating a kitchen like this than is profitable—for you or the customer.

The drawer joinery and glide operation should also be checked closely. Many older kitchens are blessed with hardwood drawers held together with dovetail joints. These older drawers often run on hardwood glides that may need only a little paraffin. Many other kitchens will include drawers of fir or pine with stapled lock joints that have failed over the years. Some of these drawers can be reinforced and strengthened, but others will have to be replaced.

Although the McCarys' cabinets were sound, the existing cooktop and range hood were near death, so they had to be removed, along with the base cabinet in which they were installed. I replaced the old cooktop with a new drop-in range flanked on both sides by narrow tray cabinets. In addition, we slated the old built-in wall oven for the scrap heap. In the cabinet opening that resulted from the oven's removal, I planned a pair of tall cabinet doors that would open to reveal two pull-out shelves for pots and pans. Finally, we agreed that I would install a pivoting blind-corner shelving system to make better use of an existing corner cabinet. None of these cabinet changes altered the kitchen's layout. But the McCarys did want to extend the cabinet peninsula to house a built-in dishwasher.

They wanted simple, easy-to-clean frame-and-panel doors of red oak. They chose matching red oak for moldings, end panels, and face frames. To finish off the room, Caroline wanted the soffit over the upper cabinets removed and 2¾-in. crown molding installed in its place. A plastic-laminate countertop with bullnose wood trim would complete the transformation.

The choice of wood can greatly affect the price of a kitchen face-lift.

Make Doors and Drawers or Buy Them?

I started compiling the lists and the drawings that would make the rest of the job easier. I drew a floor plan of the existing kitchen and added the pertinent changes. And I made elevation drawings of the cabinets (1-in. scale) on graph paper to show actual openings for all doors and drawers. These drawings were helpful back in my shop, 20 miles away from the McCarys' kitchen.

There are many pieces that go into a kitchen face-lift, and I make accurate lists of all of them.

I took this process in several steps, beginning with the end panels. I also listed the lineal footage for the crown molding, the bullnose countertop trim, and the baseboard, and I had my assistant double-check all measurements.

This is also the time to think about any special hardware that will be needed later—things like new drawer slides and pulls. I put in my order for that hardware, along with the plastic laminate and substrate for the countertop, so that the supplies would be on hand before the kitchen installation began. With these initial tasks completed and supplies en route, I could concentrate on door and drawer-front construction.

Although I like to make my own doors and drawer fronts, you can also order them from a supplier and install them yourself. There are many such companies (see "Sources of Supply" at right). Some suppliers can produce drawers and doors—as well as the veneer you will need—all finished and ready to install.

D-Day for Installation

One big advantage of a veneer face-lift is that the actual installation can be carried out quickly. In a small, uncomplicated kitchen, I can get most, if not all, of the work done in three days. On the first day I remove the countertops, the doors, and the drawers; install the new end panels; and veneer and stain the face frames. And I'm still home in time for supper. On the second day I lacquer the frames and apply new doors and drawer fronts. That leaves the third day for installing the countertops and the moldings. Larger kitchens may take five days to complete once we get on the site; the McCarys' kitchen took a little longer than that because of extra cabinets and molding they wanted and because I, or my assistant, often worked there alone.

When the doors, the drawer fronts, and other parts and supplies were ready, we loaded our tools and converged on the McCarys' house. I had given the McCarys plenty of notice, so they had time to clean out the cabinets. I also prefer to have everything off the countertops, the refrigerator and stove out of the way, and all of the plumbing dismantled (if the countertop is to be replaced). Any patching or painting of walls or ceilings also should be done in advance.

Homeowners usually are around the house during the installation. So I keep dust and the general mess under control by blocking off door openings to the rest of the house and by using an exhaust fan to control dust and any finishing odors. It's also handy to have a Shop-Vac® on site.

When it's time to start, I remove the doors, the drawers, the countertop, the false drawer fronts, the valances, the cabinets that won't be used, and anything else that may hinder the veneering and finishing process. Then it's time to make sure individual cabinet units are fastened to each other securely. I plane any uneven spots in adjoining face frames and close any gaps between cabinets with drywall screws. If the cabinets can't be screwed together, I fill gaps with wood filler and sand down the surface.

Other work on the face frames may include filling in around new appliances with new wood or cutting portions out of existing frames so that new hardware will fit into place. In the McCarys' kitchen, for

Sources of Supply

The veneers used in kitchen refacing are widely available—check the yellow pages or call your local lumber supplier. There also are many companies that make cabinet doors and drawer fronts. Your lumber supplier probably can direct you to one in your area.

example, a new pivoting blind-corner shelf system called for a 14½-in. opening—2½ in. more than what was there. I had to cut the stile to accommodate the new shelf before any veneer was applied.

After these alterations have been made, I start by applying the new end panels. I cut the panels ⅛ in. oversize in width so that they can be scribed to walls that may be slightly out of plumb. The edge of each panel should be flush with the face frame so that the veneer will iron on smoothly to both surfaces. End panels that are ¼-in. plywood may be attached with construction adhesive and hot glue—the hot glue holds the panels in place while the adhesive sets. If the new end panels are of frame-and-panel construction, they can be attached with screws from the inside of the cabinet.

SCUFF SANDING. The author demonstrates the veneer technique in his shop on a cabinet originally part of the McCarys' kitchen. The first step is to sand the face frames with 120-grit paper to remove dirt, grease, and any other residue. Sanding also scuffs the surface to provide a good hold for the veneer that will follow.

ROUGH CUTTING THE VENEER. Alexander roughly measures strips of veneer and cuts them to length. On the job site, he cuts all of the strips for one cabinet, puts the veneer inside the cabinet, and moves on to the next one until he has worked his way around the kitchen.

Applying the Veneer

Before applying the veneer, I scuff sand the face frame with 120-grit paper in an orbital sander (see the top photo at left), then wipe the frame clean. The Porter-Cable #330 Speed-Bloc® sander is perfect for this operation because it allows you to sand into tight corners, and the sander won't fall out of your hand.

My veneer applicator is nothing more than a standard household iron that I plug in and set between perm-press and wool. The iron warms up while I cut the veneer roughly to size. Once the veneering begins, I like to keep at it without interruption, and that means having all the veneer precut and the other tools I will need close at hand. The tools include a utility knife with a sharp blade, an edge-trimming knife (available from Tapes and Tools, P. O. Box 1195, High Point, N.C. 27261; 336-884-5371), a flexible 10-in. drywall knife, and a 3-in. J-roller. My roller comes from Woodcraft Supply Corporation (P.O. Box 1686, Parkersburg, W.Va. 26102-1686; 800-225-1153).

As a rule, most kitchens require both 2-in.- and 3-in.-wide veneer strips. I buy mine unfinished in rolls; the material is easy to cut with sharp scissors. I work my way around the kitchen, cutting all the rail and stile pieces an inch or two longer than they need to be and putting the pieces in the cabinet for which they are intended (see the bottom photo at left). Where two 1½-in. face frames meet, 3-in. veneer can be used to cover both surfaces at once. Should a kitchen have areas that need more than 3-in. coverage, I use two pieces of 2-in. veneer and iron them on at the same time.

When I've got the pieces of veneer cut, it's time to apply them with the iron, which by now is warmed up. I iron with a slow, steady movement (see the top photo on the facing page). Stopping the iron may scorch the veneer, and while scorch marks can sometimes be sanded out, the damaged

IRONING ON VENEER. **After the iron has warmed up, the veneer is bonded to the face frame by heat. The iron should not be held too long in any one spot, or the wood will be scorched. The author also is careful not to iron down areas that will later be trimmed—like the short section of veneer extending onto the cabinet rail immediately above the iron.**

veneer often must be replaced. First I veneer the stiles (the vertical members of the face frame) and allow the veneer to hang over the inside and outside edges (I'll trim it later). I also allow the veneer to lap onto any adjoining rails (horizontal members), although I'm careful not to iron that part down yet. That excess, too, will be trimmed a little later.

Once the veneer has been ironed on, I roll it out to ensure a good bond (see the photo at right). Then I use the edge trimmer to slice off the excess on the edges (see the top photo on p. 186). A word of caution about that process: It's a good idea to keep an eye on the direction of the wood grain. Even though the veneer is thin, it can tear out if you try to slice against the grain. I read the grain on the veneer just as I would if I were planning a piece of solid lumber.

After veneer has been applied to the stiles, it's time for the rails. That veneer goes on the same way—overlapping the edges and the stiles. But I pay close attention not to iron the rail and stile veneers together quite yet. Once veneer is bonded to both

ROLLING OUT THE VENEER. **After the veneer has been ironed on, the author uses a roller to ensure a good bond. A few quick passes over the veneer are all it takes.**

rail and stile, I use the 10-in. drywall knife as a straightedge to cut the excess veneer at the rail-stile joint (see the bottom photo on p. 186). Because the drywall knife is flexible, I can register it against the inside edge of a stile and at the same time bend the knife over the face of the rail. I cut both layers of veneer at once. With the excess cut and peeled away, the rail veneer fits snugly against the stile veneer, and both can be ironed and rolled.

Once the veneer has been applied and trimmed, I sand all the edges. The bottom edges of the bottom rails are usually hard to

sand because most toe kicks are only 3 in. or 3½ in. high—not enough room for the sander. I simply use a file in those tight spots and round over the edge slightly.

The veneer is now in place, the joints have been cut, and all of the edges have been slightly rounded. Next I test for any voids where the iron might have missed the heat-sensitive glue on the back of the veneer. Tapping lightly over the surface of the veneer with two fingers in a rhythmic motion, I listen for a hollow sound, which tells me the veneer has not held. These areas are ironed and rolled again to ensure adhesion. I also test all the veneer edges to make

sure they are secure and have been rounded over. I flick the edges with my finger to check for any looseness. After re-ironing and rolling any spots that need it, I sand the face frame with 220-grit paper.

Finishing the Face Frames

With the veneer firmly in place, it's now time to prepare the kitchen for finishing. I discard the veneer scraps and vacuum the cabinets, paying particular attention to the face frames. Because I spray my finishes, I also mask off all areas in the kitchen that might be damaged by finish overspray.

I like water-based finishes, especially if I'm doing the face-lift during winter. The new generation of water-based lacquers are manufactured without the volatile organic compounds (VOCs) that make nitrocellulose lacquer so dangerous outside a spray booth. And the water-based materials dry very rapidly, allowing me to apply multiple coats in a single day. I use Hydrocote® stains and finishes (Hydrocote Company, 1000 Somerset St., Bldg 3B, New Brunswick, N.J. 08901; 800-229-4937).

When I'm ready to apply the finish, I bring in my air compressor and lightly spray on any stain that might be required. I stain small sections at a time and wipe them down as I go. Spraying stain is quick, but hand application may be best when overspray would damage wallpaper or other surfaces. While the stain is drying (about one hour), I busy myself with other tasks like installing glides to drawers or hinges to doors. When the stain is dry, I begin applying the lacquer. I apply two light coats at a time and do that three times, so there are really six thin coats of lacquer in all. Between each of the three applications, I sand the face frames with 320-grit paper.

After the lacquer has been applied, it's time for another inspection of the face frames. Air pockets resulting from poor glue adhesion will really stand out now. They can be made to lay flat by heating them with a hair dryer set on high, followed by a quick roll.

Installing Drawers and Extras

With finishing out of the way, all of the hardware that makes a kitchen efficient and fun to use can be installed. That might include pull-out shelves, blind corner systems, or special tilt-up shelves for heavy kitchen equipment like mixers. I also fit new drawers and drawer glides and set any new cabinets that I've made.

At this point the drawers are just boxes—without their fronts. With the new drawer boxes in position, I drill two holes in the front of each box so that I can attach the drawer fronts. The holes are 1 in. from the inside front edges and centered top to bottom. To the outside of the drawer, I apply double-stick carpet tape to hold the drawer front in place while I make sure it fits. Then I use drywall screws to attach the face to the box.

Drawers that are in good condition need only new fronts. More often, however, older drawers don't have separate drawer fronts—the existing front also has a lip edge. If that's the case, as it was at the McCarys, I chuck a flush-trimming bit with a pilot bearing in my router and cut the lip off. New fronts can then be applied. Occasionally, a drawer also will need some type of reinforcement. If the drawer sides are pulling away from the front or the back, several repair methods may be used. Small wood screws may be enough to hold the sides together. Reattaching the sides with pneumatically applied staples or brads also may work. Another technique is to glue small triangular pieces into inside corners to reinforce failing joinery.

New Doors, Countertops, and Trim

Most homes have carpeted living rooms. This is a perfect staging area for the next part of the installation—hanging new cabinet doors. I finish the doors in my shop before taking them to the kitchen for installation. Once at the job site, I line up doors face down on the carpet where the finish won't be damaged and, in assembly-line manner, install the hinges. Each door is then moved from the living room to the kitchen and applied to the appropriate cabinet.

Because the door hinges I use are fully adjustable (up and down and side to side), I simply open the hinges, eyeball their placement on the inside edge of the face frame, and screw them in place. Once the doors are hung, I use a jig (available from most woodworking suppliers) to drill all the holes for knobs or pulls in both doors and drawers. I also use felt cushions on inside edges of doors and drawers.

After that, crown molding, soffit trim, and baseboard all can be cut and nailed into place. The top perimeter of the McCarys' cabinets was accentuated with 2¾-in. crown molding that was glued and nailed to a 1x that had been screwed to the top edge of the cabinets. I also dress up the toe kicks by gluing ¼-in. oak plywood to the recessed surfaces. It is sometimes appropriate to make the toe kick as unobtrusive as possible, and I do that by painting a strip of hardboard flat black and gluing it in position. In other situations, I apply baseboard right over the toe kick—as was the case on one cabinet at the McCarys.

Because my shop can be far from a customer's house, it's easier to construct the countertop right on the job site. In the McCarys' kitchen, I used ¾-in. high-density particleboard as the countertop substrate and covered it with plastic laminate. The countertop was edged with a ¹³⁄₁₆-in. oak bullnose trim that I made on the shaper. After scribing the counter to the walls, I secured it from below with drywall screw. Then I glued and brad-nailed the bullnose trim into place and finished up by filling all nail holes.

REX ALEXANDER is a cabinetmaker, specializing in kitchens. He lives in Brethren, Mich.

TIP

Occasionally, a drawer will need some type of reinforcement. If the drawer sides are pulling away from the front or the back, small wood screws may be enough to hold the sides together. Also try reattaching the sides with pneumatically applied staples or brads, or glue small triangular pieces into inside corners to reinforce failing joinery.

Choosing Kitchen Countertops

BY SCOTT GIBSON

Yearning for the good old days? Take a close look at an old kitchen. Even well-appointed houses were likely to have kitchens that look utilitarian, even stark, when compared with what contemporary cooks expect. Counter space often was provided by a built-in cabinet or dresser with a wood top, or even just a big table. Not these days. We want countertops that delight the eye, stand up to heat, keep out food stains, are easy to clean, and are more durable than the deck of a battleship.

Amazingly, a variety of materials, both natural and man-made, manages to fit the bill: plastic resins, sheet metal, wood, stone, ceramic tile, concrete, even slabs of quarried French lava. Prices range from less than $5★ per sq. ft. for plastic-laminate countertops to $300★ per sq. ft. for granite as rare as blue Brazilian bahai.

In addition to their many practical contributions, countertops also make a big visual and tactile impact. The huge variety of materials—each with its own range of characteristics and cost—allows a kitchen countertop to fit neatly into just about any lifestyle and architectural tradition. Spending thousands of dollars isn't hard to do, but far more economical alternatives also exist. The only trick is wading through all the options.

★Note—prices are from 2001.
Cost estimates are gathered from manufacturers, retailers, and installers as well as Repair & Remodeling Cost Data by RSMeans. Prices vary by region.

SCOTT GIBSON is a freelance editor who works from his home in Maine.

Butcher Block: Built-in Cutting Boards

Butcher block is one of the few totally natural kitchen-countertop materials. Typically made from strips of hard maple, 1½-in.-thick butcher-block counters are glued up to expose wear-resistant edge grain. They can be ordered in sizes up to 12 ft. long and 4 ft. wide for about $30* to $35* per sq. ft. Butcher block can be ordered through local lumberyards and home centers as well as a few large manufacturers. One of them, John Boos® & Company, also makes end-grain tops 4 in. thick in sizes up to 60 in. by 38 in. for about $85* per sq. ft.

Among its advantages as a countertop material: It's easy to work and install, has a visual warmth and pleasing resilience, and can be used as a cutting board. Scratches, scorch marks, and other signs of wear and tear can be counted as character, or scraped and sanded away. One drawback is that wood is susceptible to water damage, so butcher block used around the sink should be carefully sealed.

CHOP WHERE YOU LIKE. Maple butcher block exudes a visual warmth many other materials lack (above). Standard thickness is 1½ in., although 4-in. thick end-grain block is available (left).

End-grain butcher block

Edge-grain butcher block

Pros: Resilient, easy to work, relatively durable, can be used as cutting board, surface can be repaired.

Cons: Will scorch, not as easy to keep clean as some other materials, can stain if unsealed, susceptible to moisture damage around sinks.

Cost: $30* to $85* per sq. ft. uninstalled (shipping, if applicable, extra).

Concrete: High Style, Potentially High Maintenance

Samples from
Cheng Design

Glass and steel fragments
decorate this sample.

Marbleized patterns are typical in
the work of Buddy Rhodes.

From a design perspective, few countertop materials are as malleable as concrete. Cast upside down in molds or formed in place, concrete counters can be made in virtually any shape and thickness. Made correctly, they are hard, durable, and heat- and scratch-resistant. But cast without proper reinforcement and the correct mix of materials, concrete counters have been known to develop severe cracks as they cure. Even the best of them will stain if not assiduously maintained.

Counter fabricators often cast standard countertops 1½ in. to 2 in. thick, using structural steel and polypropylene fibers to minimize cracking. Fabricators exert considerable control over the look of the finished product. Some add pieces of glass and metal to the mix, then grinds the surface to create beautiful, multicolored patterns. The work of concrete pioneers like Fu Tung Cheng and Buddy Rhodes further reveal concrete's versatility.

Concrete's Achilles' heel as a countertop is that it stains easily. "The bottom line is that your concrete counter is going to end up staining no matter what you do," says Eric Olsen, a Berkeley, Calif., writer who collaborated with Cheng on a book on the topic. "That's part of its charm."

Pros: Versatile, heat resistant, durable, colors and textures easily customized.

Cons: Can stain.

Cost: $60* to $75* per sq. ft. for prefabricated countertops (shipping and installation extra).

SITE-CAST COUNTERS ARE ANOTHER ALTERNATIVE. Oregon builder Thomas Hughes cast this counter upside down in his client's garage from garden-variety portland cement and aggregates.

Tile: Design Flexibility, Durability, Low Cost

As a countertop material, ceramic tile offers nearly as much design flexibility as concrete. Tile is available in a huge variety of colors, patterns, textures, sizes, and prices, from mass-produced 4-in.-sq. field tile to hand-painted works of art. Installed prices start at about $15* per sq. ft. for a basic counter and go up from there. Loose field tile starts at less than $2* per sq. ft.

Glazed ceramic and porcelain tiles have a glasslike outer layer that makes them long-wearing, highly heat resistant, and nonabsorbent. Tile can be set on a mortar bed or over cement backerboard with thinset mortar. Because it is easy to cut, tile can be formed into counters of just about any shape and size. Damaged tiles can be chiseled out of a counter and replaced.

The downside? For one, tile is really hard. Fragile wine glasses and thin china won't fare well in careless households. You'll need cutting boards on tile surfaces, and because tile counters are made of many pieces, the surface is unlikely to be perfectly flat. Tile's major shortcoming is the grout between the tile. Left untreated, cement-based grout stains easily, and it can be hard to keep clean.

Epoxy grout is one solution. It's good at resisting stains. But epoxy grout yellows with time, especially when exposed to sunlight.

Cement-based grout can be sealed to provide some protection. The National Tile Contractors Association says a water-based acrylic sealer (such as AquaMix®, see "Sources of Supply" on p. 199) is less likely than solvent-based sealers to be eroded by household degreasers and cleaners. The bottom line: The smaller the grout joint, the less maintenance you have.

Pros: Versatile, inexpensive, heat resistant, durable, high stain resistance.

Cons: Grout may stain, surface not perfectly flat.

Cost: Materials, including substrate, adhesive, and border tile, from $7* and up per sq. ft. Installation adds $8* to $10* per sq. ft.

HARD-WEARING AND STAIN RESISTANT. Ceramic tile, available in hundreds of colors and patterns, offers great design flexibility at a relatively low cost. But watch for grout stains.

Solid Surfacing: A 35-Year-Old Wunderkind in the Kitchen

Few products have had more influence in kitchen design in the past 35 years than DuPont®'s Corian®. What was then the world's first solid-surface countertop material now has many rivals. Avonite®, Gibraltar®, Surell®, Pionite®, Swanstone®, and Fountainhead® all are brand names for essentially the same stuff: polyester or acrylic resin plus a mineral filler called ATH, or aluminum trihydrate. Solid surfacing comes in plain colors, patterns that resemble stone and, more recently, translucent versions that are glasslike in appearance.

Regardless of brand, solid surfacing has a long list of attributes that make it a nearly ideal countertop material. Solid surfacing is the same material all the way through. Minor surface blemishes—a scorch mark, for example—can be sanded out. It's nonporous, so it's easy to keep clean. And it's highly stain resistant. Solid surfacing can be fashioned into a sink and then glued to the countertop for a seamless, leakproof installation without any crevices or edges to catch and hold food and debris. It can be worked with regular woodworking tools, and solid surfacing comes with a long guarantee, usually ten years. It's typically sold only to certified fabricators who have taken a manufacturer's training course.

Countertops are most often formed from ½-in.-thick sheets. Edges are formed by building up layers of identical or contrasting material and milling the profile with a router. Sheets 30 in. and 36 in. wide run to 12 ft. in length. Solid surfacing is expensive—roughly $50* to $100* per sq. ft.—and it's a plastic, so not as appealing to some homeowners.

Pros: Nonporous and nonstaining, easy to clean, repairable, durable, wide range of colors and patterns available, integral sinks possible.

Cons: High cost, should be protected from high heat, sharp knives.

Cost: Typically installed by certified fabricator, $50* to $100* per sq. ft.

Corian

Avonite

Surell

PLASTIC THAT LOOKS LIKE STONE.

Stainless Steel: The Pros Like It for a Reason

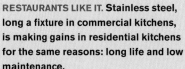

RESTAURANTS LIKE IT. Stainless steel, long a fixture in commercial kitchens, is making gains in residential kitchens for the same reasons: long life and low maintenance.

Once found only in commercial kitchens, stainless-steel counters are gaining ground at home, too. Boston architect Ann Finnerty chose a combination of stainless steel and maple butcher block when she redid her own kitchen four years ago. "I wanted a material that was common and not too precious and not too expensive," she says. Working with a local fabricator, Finnerty chose stainless steel with a plain edge and no backsplash. Finnerty likes the fact that stainless steel is easy to clean.

"When it's new especially, fingerprints show up like crazy," Finnerty says. That problem fades as the surface gets more wear and develops a patina.

Like stone and concrete countertops, stainless steel can't easily be modified on site. Countertops are usually fabricated from templates, often in 16-ga. material. Sheet metal is glued to a substrate of medium-density fiberboard. Sinks can be welded in.

Expect to pay $60* to $80* per sq. ft. But edge details, sinks, and overall complexity can change prices dramatically. Mark Ponder, an estimator at Weiss Sheet Metal, which made Finnerty's counters, cautions that generalized prices can be misleading. A plain 10-ft. long counter with a simple sink and a 4-in. backsplash might cost $1,200*, he said—a price that does not include the substrate, shipping, or installation. Linda Bergling of The Stainless Steel Kitchen, a large Midwestern fabricator, says her shop charges about $160* per running foot of counter with backsplash. But the stainless is already laid up on a substrate and ready to go in.

Counters are typically made from 304 stainless with a #4 brushed finish, the same stuff used in restaurants and commercial kitchens. Length is usually limited to 10 ft., widths to 4 ft., although larger sheets can be ordered. Stainless can be cleaned with a mild detergent or baking soda or vinegar diluted in water, Bergling says, but bleach should be avoided. Some foods—including mustard, mayonnaise, lemon juice, and tomato ketchup—that sit on the counter may cause a white surface discoloration that can be rubbed out with a Scotch-Brite® pad.

Counters also can be fashioned from copper, zinc, and nickel. But prices are usually higher, and these metals require more maintenance.

Pros: Nonporous and nonstaining, resistant to heat, durable, easy to clean.

Cons: Can dent.

Cost: $45* to $65* per sq. ft. for uninstalled straight runs; $80* to $90* installed.

Slab Stone: Durable, Heat Resistant, and Popular

Granite

Soapstone

PRICEY BUT IN HIGH DEMAND. Natural stone is the current favorite of high-end countertop choices. It offers high heat resistance and durability and a wide variety of colors and textures, such as this red-slate bar top with a honed finish (bottom photo on the facing page).

Slab stone, especially granite, is cold to the touch, heavy, hard to work, and expensive. It's also so popular, says former stone-restoration contractor Fred Hueston, that it's now going into spec houses selling for $100,000*. "It's the big one now," says Hueston, owner of the National Training Center for Stone and Masonry Trades in Longwood, Fla. Granite comes from all over the world, in a variety of colors and patterns. Prices show big regional differences, starting at $40* to $50* per sq. ft. (possibly lower in some areas) and commonly running to $80* to $100* per sq. ft. installed.

Sold in two thicknesses (¾ in. and 1¼ in.), granite is resistant to heat and scratches. Most countertop material is polished, but it also is available in a honed (matte) finish, usually for a little more money. Slab size is usually limited to 10 ft. in length, 5 ft. in width.

Although resistant to acidic foods such as lemon juice, Hueston says, granite will stain. It's especially susceptible to oil. Penetrating sealers, commonly called impregnators, can keep out oil and water. Hueston prefers sealers containing fluoropolymers (the same chemical used to make Scotchgard®).

Other stone options include slate and soapstone. Both come in smaller slab sizes than granite (roughly 6 ft. long and between 30 in. and 40 in. wide) and in not nearly the variety of colors. Prices of these two types of stone are similar, $65* to $80* per sq. ft., not including installation or shipping.

Blue gray and lightly variegated when newly installed, soapstone oxidizes and darkens with time to a rich charcoal. It is extremely dense, with better stain resistance than granite. But soapstone is also soft. Soapstone is usually treated with mineral oil. Scratches in soapstone can be sanded out.

Slate runs in a wider but still limited color palette: blacks, greens, reds, grays, and muted purples. Like soapstone, slate is relatively soft, although scratch marks can be buffed out with fine steel wool, says Daphne Markcrow of Vermont Structural Slate Company^{SM} in Fair Haven, Vt. Vermont slate needs no sealers, she says, and no maintenance, although slate mined in different regions may be more absorptive. Hueston says slate, which is formed in layers, will occasionally delaminate.

Pros: Wide variety of colors and textures, heat resistant, very durable (stain and scratch resistances vary).

Cons: High cost, some types may stain, slab size may be limited. Can delaminate.

Cost: $50* to $100+* per sq. ft. fabricated and installed.

Slate

Composite

Although many countertop materials are familiar, a variety of newer, man-made materials also is available.

Silestone is a composite of 93 percent quartz, resin binders, and pigments. It is made in Spain and sold in the United States through a network of distributors. A similar material is made by DuPont under the Zodiaq® brand name. Prices vary by region and by the color of the material, but Silestone says that installed prices are between $45* and $70* per sq. ft. It is nonporous and never needs to be sealed, the company says, and it's more resistant to food stains than the natural stone it closely resembles. Silestone is available in 35 colors and three thicknesses— $\frac{7}{16}$ in., $\frac{13}{16}$ in. and $1\frac{1}{8}$ in.

Trespa® is a Netherlands-based company that makes three types of composite architectural panels. Two of them—TopLab® and Athlon®—are potential kitchen countertops. Athlon is essentially super-thick high-pressure laminate. It's made from phenolic resins reinforced with cellulose fiber and manufactured under high pressure and temperature. Its top decorative layer is melamine-impregnated paper, and it is available with either a smooth or slightly textured finish. Standard sheet sizes go up to 6 ft. by 12 ft., with thicknesses ranging from ¼ in. to 1 in. One thing that makes Athlon attractive is its price: In a ½-in. thickness, Athlon is less than $7* per sq. ft. It can be worked with standard carbide tools, and it doesn't need sealing. TopLab is usually used in laboratory settings because of its resistance to chemicals, scratches, and stains. Prices are slightly higher. Pionite makes a similar material called thick phenolic-core laminate.

In the market for something truly unusual? How about French lava with a kiln-fired enamel coating that the manufacturer says is impervious to stains and heat? Pyrolave comes in sheets up to 4 ft. by 8 ft., in two thicknesses—1¼ in. and 1½ in. Custom colors are available in addition to the 30 stock colors the company offers. Installed prices range from $220* to $350* per sq. ft.

Pyrolave

Lava

Pros: Hard, stain resistant, heatproof.

Cons: Extremely high cost, limited availability.

Cost: $220* to $350* per sq. ft. (installed).

OOH LA LA! Ancient French lava from Pyrolave is an expensive and alluring countertop choice. Other nonstandard choices are quartz composites, resin composites, and fiber cement.

Trespa resin composite

Resin Composites

Pros: Scratch and stain resistant, low cost.

Cons: Limited color choice, damaged by heat.

Cost: $7* to $10* per sq. ft.

Fiber cement

Fiber-cement countertops—sold under the SlateScape®, Fireslate2, and Colorlith® brand names—are manufactured in Germany, imported to the United States, and sold through authorized fabricators. Fiber cement has the bulk of quarried stone, but it can be less expensive: $30* to $40* per sq. ft. in 1¼-in. thickness. Fiber cement is currently available in four colors and five thicknesses. It has good resistance to heat and has high compressive strength. Like other cement-based products, this material stains easily unless it is sealed properly—and that takes regular maintenance. The company suggests pure tung oil two or three times a year to augment the penetrating sealer applied by the fabricator.

Fiber Cement

Pros: Relatively low cost, heat resistant, durable, high strength.

Cons: Can stain (requires periodic resealing), limited color selection.

Cost: $30* to $70* per sq. ft. uninstalled (shipping extra).

Quartz Composites

Pros: Nonporous and non-staining, scratch and heat resistant, durable.

Cons: Relatively high cost.

Cost: $45* to $75+* per sq. ft. installed.

Silestone quartz composite

Zodiaq quartz composite

Plastic Laminate: Old Standby Still Rules

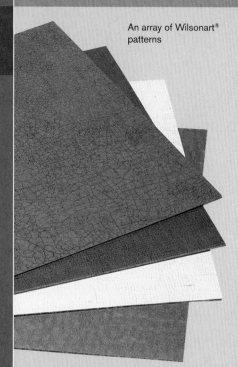

An array of Wilsonart® patterns

High-pressure laminate is the family minivan of the countertop world: It's practical and economical, and you'll never brag you own it. Still, laminate is the choice in as many as three-quarters of all new kitchens in the United States. Standard high-pressure laminate, roughly ¹⁄₁₆ in. thick, is a sandwich of kraft paper impregnated with phenolic resin and topped by a decorative layer of melamine-protected paper. In sheet form, laminate is glued to a particleboard substrate, either on site or in a fabricator's shop. A thinner version is manufactured into a ready-made countertop with a rounded front edge and an integral backsplash called a post-formed counter.

Laminate is available in dozens of colors and patterns for $2* or less per sq. ft. in sheets up to 12 ft. long and 5 ft. wide. Post-formed counters, ready to drop into place, may be $5* or less per sq. ft. at big home centers. There are fewer colors to choose from, and post-formed counters are for straight runs only; curvaceous kitchen designs won't work.

Most kitchen countertops are made of general-purpose laminate, but laminate is also available in high-wear, extra-thick, and fire-retardant versions. In addition to its low cost, laminate has many other attributes. Hard and durable, laminate is highly stain resistant and stands up well to everyday use. However, heat and sharp knives damage the surface, and any water getting into seams may degrade the substrate.

A variety of new edge treatments has eliminated one of laminate's long-standing aesthetic weaknesses: the dark line formed where the top of the counter meets the front edge. Edging made from wood, solid-surface material, or beveled laminate can make that seam all but invisible but at a higher cost.

Laminate's real breakthrough in recent years has been in the top decorative layer. Digital printing and metallic inks have resulted in higher-fidelity reproduction, allowing manufacturers to create uncannily accurate patterns of materials such as wood, stone, and fabric.

Pros: Inexpensive, relatively durable, easy to clean, needs no regular maintenance, wide range of colors and patterns available.

Cons: Damaged by sharp objects and heat, not repairable.

Cost: Uninstalled post-formed counters, $5* per sq. ft., $1.50* per sq. ft. for sheet laminate. Installed, $8* to $11* for post-formed, $10* to $17* for laminate sheet.

THE WORKHORSE. Today's high-pressure laminate is aided by innovations in digital printing.

Sources of Supply

American Fiber Cement Corp.
800-688-8677
www.americanfibercement.com
Fiber cement

Aqua Mix
800-366-6877
www.aquamix.com
Tile and installation

Avonite
800-428-6648
www.avonite.com
High-pressure laminate/solid surfaces

Buddy Rhodes Studio Inc.
877-706-5303
www.buddyrhodes.com
Concrete

Cheng Design
510-849-3272
www.chengdesign.com
Concrete

Corian
800-426-7426
www.corian.com
High-pressure laminate/solid surfaces

DuPont Zodiaq
877-229-3935
www.zodiaq.com
Quartz composites

Gibraltar
800-433-3222
www.wilsonart.com
High-pressure laminate/solid surfaces

infotile
www.infotile.com
Tile manufacturers and distributors

John Boos & Co.
217-347-7701
www.johnboos.com
Butcher block

Freshwater Stone + Brickwork
207-469-6331
www.freshwaterstone.com
Slab stone

National Tile Contractors Association
601-939-2071
www.tile-assn.com
Tile and installation

Pionite
800-746-6483
www.pionite.com
High-pressure laminate/solid surfaces

Pyrolave
919-788-8953
www.pyrolave.com
Kiln-fired lava

Silestone
800-291-1311
www.silestoneusa.com
Quartz composites

Swanstone
800-325-7008
www.theswancorp.com
High-pressure laminate/solid surfaces

The Hardwood Lumber Co.
800-798-1269
www.hadwood-lumber.com
Butcher block

The Stainless Steel Kitchen
574-259-1060
www.stainlesssteelkitchen.com
Stainless steel

Tile Council of North America[SM]
864-646-8453
www.tileusa.com
Tile and installation

Trespa North America Ltd.
800-487-3772
www.trespanorthamerica.com
Resin composite

Vermont Soapstone Co.
800-284-5404
www.vermontsoapstone.com
Slab stone

Make Your Own Laminate Countertops

BY STEVE MORRIS

THE SUBSTRATE IS CRITICAL. To ensure accuracy, the author fabricates the substrate where it will be installed. Here, he's truing a particleboard edge by guiding a router against a straightedge.

Choosing a kitchen countertop is a big deal. The surface has to be durable, attractive, and complementary to the kitchen's style. The decision becomes more difficult when you consider cost. You can spend thousands of dollars on the countertops for an average kitchen, but you don't have to. Fabricating and installing a laminate countertop can save you loads of money.

The popularity of expensive countertop materials like granite, solid surface, and engineered stone makes it easy to overlook the appeal of plastic laminate. But laminate countertops still have the durability and beauty to compete with more expensive options, and there are more colors and patterns to choose from than with any other material.

Making your own laminate countertops doesn't require many tools, and the price of materials—laminate, particleboard, and contact cement—is insignificant. You can make countertops in a garage or in a basement, or you can work outside if the weather is nice.

Start With a Custom Fit

One benefit of laminate countertops is that they can be made to fit large, oddly shaped areas without seams. Sheets of laminate are available as large as 5 ft. by 12 ft. But before I get to the laminate, I have to build a substrate. The substrate is the structural part of the countertop to which the laminate is glued. Whether I am fabricating a large, oddly shaped kitchen countertop or a small bathroom-vanity top, I prefer to prepare the substrate in place—right in the kitchen, in this case (see the left photo on the facing page). This way, I can be sure the finished countertop will fit correctly.

Particleboard is the best material to use for the substrate, and fortunately, it is the least expensive. Plywood is too grainy, and medium-density fiberboard (MDF) is too heavy. Particleboard is strong enough to do the job and provides a smooth surface for

Endless Choices and Unbeatable Prices

These days, everyone wants kitchens full of granite and stainless steel because they are durable and attractive. But before you write off laminate as a choice for your kitchen countertops, consider this: Among only a few major laminate suppliers, there are hundreds of styles and colors to choose from. From the look of stone, metal, and glass to wood-grain patterns and solid colors, there is a style and color to complement any kitchen or bathroom. Laminate is available in different grades, including fire-rated, chemical-resistant, and abrasion-resistant materials. Laminate is durable and easy to work with. The edges take a number of interesting treatments, including simple bevels and wood nosings. And laminate costs as little as $2* per sq. ft. Add the cost of the substrate, the glue, and your time, and laminate countertops still cost a fraction of the alternatives.

Laminated edges have the look of solid-surface material.

Wood nosing can be made to match the cabinets.

A half-round nosing softens the countertop edge.

W alls can be bowed, and corners aren't always square. If you measure, mark, and cut the particleboard substrate in place, you can make sure that the countertop fits the cabinets and the walls.

SCRIBE NOW, NOT LATER. The substrate should fit flush against the wall, and the overhang should be consistent along the length of the cabinets. Scribe and cut the particleboard to fit the walls now to avoid having to cut the finished countertop during installation.

IF YOU CAN'T AVOID A JOINT, try to plan the least-obtrusive places to join the particleboard pieces that will make up the countertop. Overlapping two pieces allows you to mark the exact location of the joint. You can cut particleboard to size with a circular saw. For smooth, straight edges, run the saw against a straightedge guide.

laminate. I use 1¹⁄₁₆-in. particleboard to make my countertops.

If the kitchen is large enough to set up sawhorses and if the room can be sealed to contain dust, I work right in the kitchen. Otherwise, I set up outside. I measure from the walls to the edges of the cabinet frames and add ¾ in. Later, when I add wood strips to the edges, the overhang will increase to 1½ in. If the cabinets have full-overlay doors and drawer fronts, the result will be a finished overhang of ¾ in. (see the drawing on p. 204).

I cut the particleboard with a circular saw guided by a straightedge. Then I put the substrate in place to make sure it fits

well. This often means scribing the particleboard to the walls. It is safer to cut the scribes on the blank substrate than to cut the laminated top during installation.

I avoid joining sheets of particleboard when I can. Sometimes, however, joints are inevitable. Preparing the substrate in place allows me to determine the best spots for joints. Even with thorough filing and sanding, particleboard joints can show up in finished countertops. For this reason, I try to hide the joints in corners or under the top cabinets.

Particleboard sheets are joined with biscuits and countertop bolts. On a 2-ft. joint,

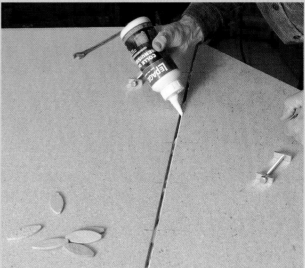

BISCUITS AND BOLTS WORK TOGETHER. Mark biscuit locations every 6 in. A pencil line across the joint is all you need to align the biscuit joiner. Bond each joint with yellow glue. Hidden on the underside of the substrate, countertop bolts clamp the joint together.

I use four biscuits and two bolts. The T-shaped mortises for the bolts are cut free-hand with a router and a ½-in. straight bit. The biscuits help with surface alignment, and the bolts pull the joint together. I then file and sand the top of the joint to make sure it is smooth.

Build a Stronger Countertop

To provide strength and to make the countertop look 1½ in. thick, I reinforce the edges with 3-in.-wide strips of particleboard. Along the front and along any exposed edges, the strips are glued and nailed flush and are sanded smooth with a belt sander.

In the back, where the countertop meets the walls, the strips are recessed about ¼ in. Any area at which the countertop overhangs the cabinets by more than 6 in., such as a bar top, is doubled up entirely.

Attaching ¾-in. by 1½-in. hardwood strips to the front edge of the substrate is the next step. The wood strips stiffen the surface, which is helpful when installing long countertops. The wood also gives the vulnerable front edge of the countertop some extra hardness and durability, and it accepts contact cement better than the porous cut edges of the particleboard.

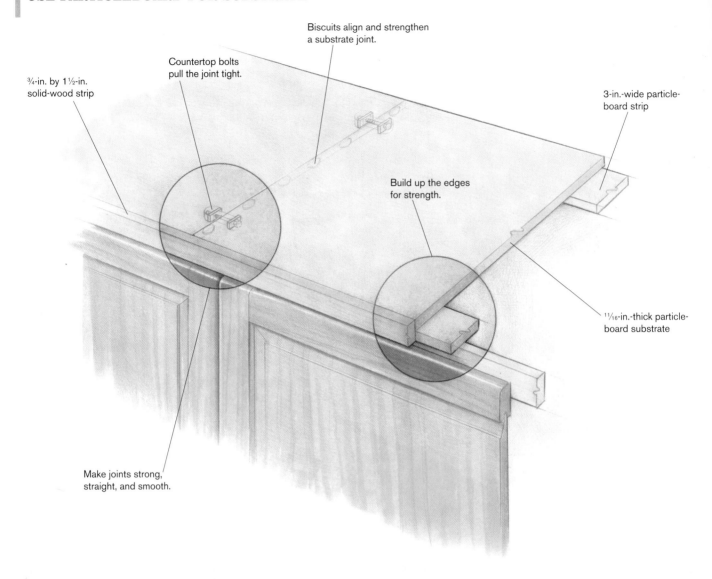

Biscuits align and strengthen a substrate joint.

Countertop bolts pull the joint tight.

¾-in. by 1½-in. solid-wood strip

3-in.-wide particle-board strip

Build up the edges for strength.

1¹⁄₁₆-in.-thick particle-board substrate

Make joints strong, straight, and smooth.

DOUBLE UP THE PERIMETER. Build up the edges with particle-board strips. On the edges that will be laminated, attach the strips flush with the top. On the back edges, recess the strips about ¼ in. to ease any scribing that has to be done. Glue and nail solid-wood strips along the front edge. The wood strips stiffen longer surfaces and accept contact cement better than the cut edge of particleboard.

Be Careful With the Laminate

Until it is glued to the substrate, plastic laminate tears and cracks easily. It is important to treat large pieces carefully. I leave the laminate rolled up in the box until I am ready to work with it. Laminate can be cut in various ways, but I use a laminate trimmer or a small router with a sharp laminate bit. A dull bit will chip the laminate.

The laminate is first cut oversize, then trimmed after it is glued to the substrate. I clamp the sheet of laminate to a large table or a sheet of plywood and cut 3-in.-wide strips for the edges. Then I cut the top pieces of laminate on the prepared substrate, where I can follow the shape of the countertop. The cutoffs must be supported, or they will crack.

Joining pieces of laminate is tricky. Never rely on the factory edge of the laminate to be straight. If you are joining large sheets, use a laminate trimmer or a router with a straightedge and trim both pieces to make sure they are straight and square. Cut edge strips to length with a miter saw. Sandwich the laminate strip between two scraps of particleboard, and make the cut through the particleboard and the laminate.

Laminate the Edges First

Contact cement is sticky, so work slowly when you are gluing the laminate. Once you glue down a piece of laminate, you probably won't be able to get it off.

I use latex contact cement because it is nontoxic and nonflammable (www.lepage products.com). Both the laminate and the substrate get two thin coats of contact cement. Two thin coats dry faster than one thick coat. Because the particleboard will absorb some of the contact cement, the first coat is used to seal the pores, while the second coat remains on the surface, where I want it. Allow the contact cement to dry completely between coats and before applying the laminate to the particleboard.

Three Tips for Working With Laminate

Use Venetian-blind slats as spacers between the substrate and laminate sheets to make sure the laminate is aligned properly before the two glued-up surfaces are allowed to touch.

For a clean-cut laminate edge, first cut a longer strip than you need. Then put the end of the strip between two scraps of particleboard and cut it with a miter saw.

Laminate warmed up with a heat gun or a hair dryer is easy to bend. Pull the laminate gently while applying heat. At first the laminate will resist, but after a few minutes, it will bend.

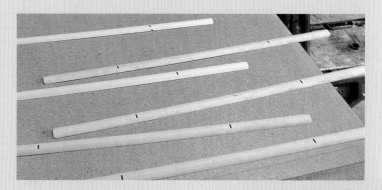

Venetian blinds make great spacers.

A laminate sandwich makes for clean cuts.

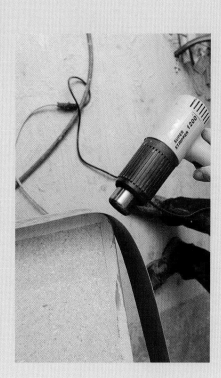

Heat laminate to make it flexible.

Laminating the Countertop

Get the front edges done first, then turn to the top. Once the glued-up laminate and substrate meet, it's difficult to separate them. Starting with oversize pieces of laminate and aligning the top on spacers helps to prevent mistakes.

EDGES FIRST. After adhering a laminate edge strip along the front edge of the countertop, trim it flush. A bearing-guided, flush-trimming bit gets the job done.

LATEX DOESN'T STINK. Use a roller to apply two coats of latex contact cement to the substrate and the laminate. Make sure the contact cement is dry on both surfaces before gluing them together. Spacers keep the two adhesive-coated surfaces apart while you position the large top sheet of laminate. When you're ready, remove the spacers, starting in the middle of the countertop and working out toward the edges.

The edges are laminated and trimmed first. After the edge strips all are applied, I press them to the substrate with a roller. I use a heat gun to bend edge strips into and around radiused corners. Heating the laminate helps to prevent cracking as it bends. Pushing a heated edge piece into a curved inside corner is more difficult than turning an outside corner. Any voids that are left between the laminate and the substrate will be filled with epoxy before the top laminate goes on.

To trim the edge pieces flush, I usually use a bearing-guided, flush-trimming bit, which can be chucked in a laminate trimmer or a small router. After the edges are trimmed, I give the top of the substrate a final check to make sure it's flat and smooth. Slight irregularities near the front edge—between the particleboard, the wood edging, and the laminate—can be removed with a file or a belt sander.

Align the Top Sheet Carefully

Before applying contact cement to the top of the substrate or the laminate, these surfaces should be dusted with a brush or air hose to remove debris. Even a tiny piece of debris will show through the laminate.

To line up large sheets of laminate without letting them touch the glued-up substrate,

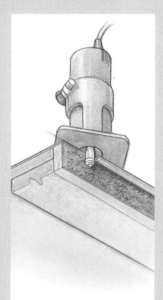

FINAL STEPS. Press the laminate to the substrate with a roller to ensure a good bond. Check the surface for air bubbles as you go. Then trim the top flush with the edges. Finish up by smoothing the top and bottom edges and all corners with a wood or laminate file.

I use Venetian-blind slats as spacers. The laminate is placed on top of the spacers and positioned as it will lay on the substrate. Starting in the middle of the countertop, I work my way toward the ends, removing the spacers and pressing down the laminate. To ensure a good bond, I use a roller to press the laminate to the substrate.

If I find an air bubble, I heat the laminate from the bubble to the nearest edge to create an exit for the air. If that doesn't work, I can drill a small hole (⅟₁₆ in.) through the bottom of the substrate to get the air out from under the laminate.

The oversize sheet of laminate then can be trimmed around the edges of the countertop. Use a light touch with the laminate trimmer or router to avoid marking or scratching the laminated edges. Because the cut edges of the laminate can be sharp, the last thing I do is lightly file the top and bottom edges and all the corners with a hand file.

Note—prices are from 2004.

STEVE MORRIS is a finish carpenter and kitchen installer in Sarnia, Ontario, Canada.

Drawer Design Strategies

BY GARY ROGOWSKI

It's always a wonder to me when I come across an old piece of furniture with drawers that slide as sweetly as they did the day they were made. How is it possible for old drawers to work so well? Odds are they have been weighted down, filled to overflowing, pushed, pulled, slammed home, tipped over, and otherwise abused by several generations of owners. Yet if a drawer is well-made, it will fit snugly in its opening and open and close effortlessly, regardless of the season. And it will continue to work that way for a long time.

With so many ways to put a drawer together, which way is best? There's no simple answer, but there are some basic considerations that can help you choose the right corner joint, materials and method of supporting the bottom.

The object is to build a strong, stable, attractive drawer in a reasonable amount of time. How you do this will depend on your skills, tastes, and the function of the piece that you are building. I built the drawers shown at left to showcase a number of the best possibilities for drawer construction in a fine case piece. These methods aren't the last word on drawer construction, but they should provide a good starting point.

Function: Make It Strong and Stable

When I'm working out the design for a piece of furniture that will include a drawer, I think first about function. A file cabinet or tool-box drawer obviously needs to be stronger than a drawer that will hold only socks or a few pencils. And, generally, the deeper a drawer is the stronger it needs to be.

Drawer joints, like all woodworking joints, derive their strength either from the amount of long-grain glue-surface area shared by the two joined parts or by the way the parts interlock mechanically.

Dovetails make the strongest joints– In a chest of drawers, most any well-made joint will be strong enough because the weight the drawers will have to bear is minimal. But stuff a drawer with reams of paper, a dozen handplanes or a blender, assorted bowls, and a Cuisinart®, and you've upped the ante.

In situations where I know a drawer is going to have to stand up to some heavy use, I like to use a dovetail joint. Through, half-blind, and sliding dovetails (see the sidebar on p. 210) will stand up to almost any use or abuse imaginable. Short of destroying a drawer, you're not likely to see a well-made dovetail joint fail. So choosing one of these three joints becomes a question of aesthetics and efficiency.

A simpler joint in the back– Often a drawer is held together with two kinds of joints: something a little fancier in the front where it will show and something simpler in the back where strength, not appearance, is the primary consideration. In the chest shown at left, I joined the backs of the top four drawers to the sides with sliding dovetails because they're strong, and I can make them quickly with a router.

There's one situation in which you can't use a sliding dovetail at the back of a drawer: when you want to capture a plywood drawer bottom on all four sides, as I did on the bot-

tom drawer in this chest. For that drawer, I used dado-rabbet joints at the back corners. The dadoes run from top to bottom on the drawer sides, just in from the ends. The back is rabbeted to engage the dado and is flush with the back end of the sides.

Quartersawn lumber is best– Another functional consideration is stability: how much the drawer will move with seasonal changes in humidity. A drawer that's swollen shut is obviously useless, but one with a huge gap at the top isn't very attractive. So I try to use quartersawn lumber for the sides and backs of drawers whenever possible. It's much more dimensionally stable than flatsawn stock and less likely to warp or twist.

Regardless of whether I'm using quartersawn or flatsawn lumber, I make sure the drawer stock is thoroughly seasoned. I also try to let it acclimate in my shop for a few weeks before working it.

Choosing wood for sides, back, runners– For drawer sides and backs, I generally select a wood that's different from the fronts. Secondary wood saves a little money. And there's no need to waste really spectacular lumber on drawer sides or backs. I use a wood that moves about the same amount seasonally as the drawer fronts and is long-wearing. I also use this secondary wood for the drawer runners. This prevents the sides from wearing a groove in the runners or the runners from wearing down the sides.

Using a secondary wood for the sides of a drawer also can set up an interesting contrast when the drawer is opened, especially with a lighter-colored wood.

Aim for a thin drawer side– Drawer-side thickness is a concern for both structural and aesthetic reasons. What you're trying to achieve is a drawer that's light, strong, and well-proportioned. For this chest, I used ⅜-in.-thick drawer sides for the top pair of drawers. I added ¹⁄₁₆ in. thickness to the sides and back of each descending drawer. Graduated drawers distinguish this piece from

THROUGH DOVETAIL

Pros: Very strong, great mechanical strength and large long-grain to long-grain glue area. The hand-cut through dovetail is aesthetically strong, too. End grain shows on the drawer face, providing a pleasing contrast in some furniture styles.

Cons: The end grain exposed on the face may be inappropriate on more traditionally styled pieces. Comparatively speaking, the dovetail is a time-consuming joint to cut, and it takes practice before you can cut it well. Router jigs used to make through dovetails are relatively expensive, and the resulting joint can look too uniform.

HALF-BLIND DOVETAIL

Pros: As with the through dovetail, half-blind dovetails are very strong and look great, too. And because the joint doesn't show on the drawer face, it's ideal for even the most formal and traditional drawers.

Cons: Even more time-consuming and finnicky to cut by hand than through dovetails. Routed half-blind dovetails look routed because of the minimum width of the pins. Most jigs don't allow flexible spacing of pins and tails.

RABBETED HALF DOVETAIL

Pros: Simple to cut (one pass on the router table for each drawer component), simple to clamp, and quite handsome. When pinned with dowels, it's a mechanically strong joint.

Cons: Not as strong as through- or half-blind dovetails and without the traditional cachet. All glue-surface area is end grain to long grain, a weaker connection than long grain to long grain.

SLIDING DOVETAIL

Pros: Very strong, easy to cut once set up. Can be made so the joint is visible at the top edge of the drawer or so the joint is hidden (stopped).

Cons: Difficult to fit and assemble. The fit should be a bit loose when the joint is dry because glue will start to bind the joint almost immediately. You'll need to work fast once you've applied the glue.

BLIND-DADO RABBET

Pros: Good production joint. It's quick to cut on the router table once it's set up. With a dedicated bit, setup is quick, too. Joint is hidden from front and looks nice if done well.

Cons: Time-consuming to set up unless you have a dedicated bit, which is expensive. Only fair mechanical strength and all glue-surface area is end grain to long grain. Side edges of drawer front are vulnerable to chipping if they're not beveled slightly.

production work; each drawer has sufficient strength and pleasing proportions.

Aesthetics: Make It Attractive and Appropriate

The next consideration is appearance. A nailed rabbet joint, for example, may work perfectly well but just wouldn't make it in a reproduction American highboy. All of the joints I used in this chest of drawers are attractive, but some are more refined than others. So the choice of joinery, especially at the front of the drawer, may hinge on the expectations or tastes of the client and the style of the piece.

To my eye, the through dovetail, the half-blind dovetail, and the rabbeted half dovetail work better aesthetically with this piece than do the sliding dovetail or blind-dado rabbet. But for drawers in a kitchen island or a child's bureau, I'd probably go with the sliding dovetail or the blind-dado rabbet because neither of these furniture pieces requires fancy joinery.

Efficiency: Can I Make It Quickly and Easily?

Ease and speed of construction are related concerns, especially if you make your living as a furniture maker. As a professional, I have to weigh the time it takes to cut and assemble a joint against what it adds to the piece. I also have to know whether the client is willing to pay for the extra labor. If you're an amateur woodworker, time probably is less of a concern, but there will still be projects you just want to finish.

The relative difficulty of making a particular joint also may be a consideration. If you've never cut dovetails by hand before, it's probably a good idea to practice before you start cutting into those figured-maple drawer fronts.

If you have no desire to cut dovetails by hand, a number of router jigs will cut dovetails that are just as strong or stronger than hand-cut ones. But with a few exceptions, they all give you dovetails that look rigidly uniform and machine-made. These may not be the right choice on a piece of furniture that traditionally would have had hand-cut dovetails. And even if routed dovetails work for you aesthetically, there's a learning curve for most of these jigs. So while there may be some gain in efficiency over time, you shouldn't plan to buy a jig on Saturday to speed you through your dovetails on Sunday.

A router can help you make other good-looking, simple joints that are plenty strong. The sliding dovetail and the blind-dado rabbet on the bottom two drawers of this chest fit the bill on all counts.

Supporting Drawer Bottoms

Corner joinery is only one facet of drawer construction. There's also the question of how to support the drawer bottom. What's wrong with a simple groove cut near the bottom of the drawer sides? Not a thing for most work (see the drawing on p. 212), but if you check out a really first-rate antique, chances are good that the drawer will be riding on slips (see the drawing on p. 213).

Drawer slips are strips of wood glued to the bottom inside faces of the drawer sides. They sit flush with the bottom of the side and are grooved to accept a drawer bottom. Designed to increase the running surface of the drawer, slips prevent the drawer side from wearing a groove in the runner. They also prevent a thin drawer side from being weakened by a groove. I used drawer slips on two of the drawers shown on pp. 212–213: one with a plywood bottom and one with a rabbeted, solid-cedar bottom.

Slips are more than just functional additions to a drawer. They add a measure of finish and formality that catches your eye. I didn't add any decorative elements to the slips in this drawer, but you could bead the top inside edge of the slip, cove it, or round it over to add more visual interest, as shown in the drawings on p. 213.

Continued on p.214

Bottom Construction

MIX AND MATCH

You can support a drawer bottom in grooves cut in the drawer sides or in slips glued to the sides. Drawer bottoms can be made of plywood or solid wood. Either material is compatible with either method of support. Your choice will be based on time, cost, and the piece's function.

Fully enclosed plywood panel (left)

Solid raised panel in a groove

GROOVES

Grooved drawer sides provide plenty of support for most drawer bottoms, as long as the drawers aren't going to carry a lot of weight. Sides should be sized proportionally to the width of the drawer.

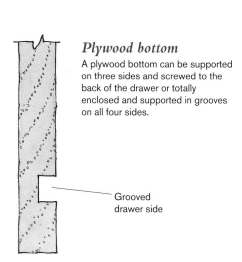

Plywood bottom

A plywood bottom can be supported on three sides and screwed to the back of the drawer or totally enclosed and supported in grooves on all four sides.

Grooved
drawer side

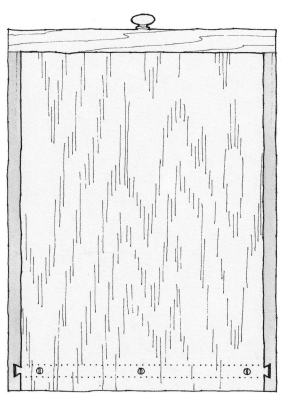

Plywood panel in a drawer slip

Rabbeted solid panel in a drawer slip

SLIPS

Drawer slips add strength and rigidity and increase the drawer's bearing surface on the runners. Slips can be simple, grooved pieces of wood, or they can be made more decorative.

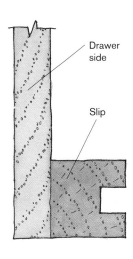

Drawer side

Slip

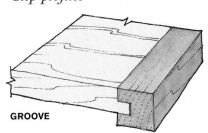

GROOVE

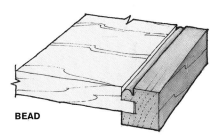

BEAD

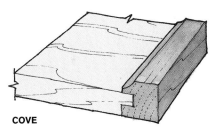

COVE

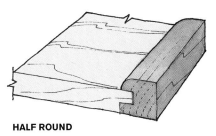

HALF ROUND

Slip profiles

Solid-bottom profiles

Tongue

Rabbet

Raised panel

Solid bottom

A solid bottom can be cut to a tongue profile, rabbeted, or raised. Because solid wood expands and contracts seasonally, the panel should be oriented so that its grain runs across the drawer. The screw hole at the back of the drawer bottom should be elongated (see inset drawing at left).

Continued from p. 211

Plywood or Solid Wood?

The other big decision is whether to make the drawer bottoms from plywood or from solid wood.

Plywood is stronger but not traditional–
Plywood has many advantages over solid wood, but for some purists, it is simply unacceptable.

Plywood is dimensionally stable, so you don't have to take wood movement into consideration. It is stronger for a given thickness than solid material, so you can use a thinner piece: ¼-in. plywood is thick enough for a drawer bottom (I usually use a ½-in. panel if it's solid wood). This also makes plywood a good choice if you're concerned with weight.

One problem with using plywood is that the actual thickness of a ¼-in. sheet is about $\frac{7}{32}$ in. That means that if you rout a ¼-in. groove in a slip or in your drawer sides, the plywood panel will flop around. Instead, I use a $\frac{3}{16}$-in. bit and make two passes. I get a perfect fit, but it takes more time. Of course, there are dado sets available that will plow a $\frac{7}{32}$-in. groove, but you can't always run the groove the length of the drawer piece. On some drawer fronts, for instance, you need a stopped groove.

Installing solid-wood bottoms–For solid-wood drawer bottoms, the grain must run side to side in the drawer, rather than front to back, so wood expansion won't push the drawer apart and shrinkage won't create a gap at the sides. I usually either rabbet or raise a panel on a solid-wood drawer bottom so the edge is thinner than the rest of the field (see the solid-bottom profiles on p. 213). This lets me plow a smaller groove in the drawer sides. The result is a strong, sturdy panel that will not weaken the drawer slips or sides excessively.

A rabbeted panel can be slid in with the raised portion facing either up or down. When I use drawer slips and a rabbeted panel, I put the panel in with the raised portion up, mark the panel, remove it and then plane, scrape and sand the panel so it's flush with the drawer slips. With the more traditional raised panel, I position the panel bevel-side down.

Keeping the drawer bottom in place–
I don't glue drawer bottoms in place. It's easier to repair a drawer if the bottom just slides right out. To keep solid-wood drawer bottoms from sagging, I screw them to the drawer back with a single pan-head screw and elongate the hole so the bottom can move (see the drawing detail on p. 213).

In spite of its strength, a ¼-in. plywood panel is quite flexible, so I usually drive two or three screws into the drawer back. Otherwise, the bottom will sag (see the right drawing on p. 212).

Another possibility for plywood is to enclose it on all four sides (see the top left photo on p. 212). Because plywood is dimensionally stable, there's no need to leave the back open.

GARY ROGOWSKI is a contributing editor to *Fine Woodworking*.

Credits

The articles in this book appeared in the following issues of *Fine Homebuilding* and *Fine Woodworking*:

Photos: p. iii by Anatole Burkin, © The Taunton Press, Inc.; p. iv (left) by Tom Begnal, © The Taunton Press, Inc.; (right) by Marc Vassallo, © The Taunton Press, Inc.; p. v (left) by Michael Pekovich, © The Taunton Press, Inc.; (right) by Scott Gibson, © The Taunton Press, Inc., p. 2 by Anissa Kapsales, © The Taunton Press, Inc.; p. 3 (top) by Andy Engel, © The Taunton Press, Inc.; (bottom) courtesy DuPont.

p. 4: Engineering a Bookcase by Jeff Miller, *Fine Woodworking* issue 190. Photos by Tom Begnal, © The Taunton Press, Inc.; except pp. 6 (right), 7 (top and inset bottom), 8 (top), 9 (top), 10–11 by Michael Pekovich, © The Taunton Press, Inc.; Drawing by Stephen Hutchings, © The Taunton Press, Inc.

p. 13: Biscuit Basics by Tony O'Malley, *Fine Woodworking* issue 165. Photos by Asa Christiana, © The Taunton Press, Inc.; Drawings by Jim Richey, © The Taunton Press, Inc.

p. 22: A User's Guide to Plywood by Roland Johnson, *Fine Woodworking* issue 177. Photos by Steve Scott, © The Taunton Press, Inc., except pp. 23 & 24 by Michael Pekovich, © The Taunton Press, Inc.; Drawings by Bob La Pointe, © The Taunton Press, Inc.

p. 31: Six Ways to Edge Plywood by Mario Rodriguez, *Fine Woodworking* issue 156. Photos by William Duckworth, © The Taunton Press, Inc., except pp. 31, 32 (top), 33 (top), 34 (top) & 35 (top) by Kelly J. Dunton, © The Taunton Press, Inc.; Drawings by Vince Babak, © The Taunton Press, Inc.

p. 39: Shelving, Plain and Simple by M. Felix Marti, *Fine Woodworking* issue 113. Photo on p. 31 by M. Felix Marti, © The Taunton Press, Inc.; photo on p. 40 by Alec Waters, © The Taunton Press, Inc.; Drawing by Kathleen Rushton, © The Taunton Press, Inc.

p. 42: Shaker Wall Shelf by Peter Turner, *Fine Woodworking* issue 129. Photos by Zachary Gaulkin, © The Taunton Press, Inc.; Drawings by Jim Richey, © The Taunton Press, Inc.

p. 46: Arts and Crafts Wall Shelf by Nancy Miller, *Fine Woodworking* issue 193. Photos by Anissa Kapsales, © The Taunton Press, Inc.; Drawings by Christopher Mills, © The Taunton Press, Inc.

p. 54: Bookcase Made With Biscuit Joinery by Peter Turner, *Fine Woodworking* issue 126. Photos by Anatole Burkin, © The Taunton Press, Inc.; Drawings by Heather Lambert, © The Taunton Press, Inc.

p. 61: A Choice of Three Bookcases by Philip C. Lowe, *Fine Woodworking* issue 133. Photos by Marc Vassallo, © The Taunton Press, Inc., except p. 61 by Boyd Hagen, © The Taunton Press, Inc.; Drawings by Bob La Pointe, © The Taunton Press, Inc.

p. 71: A Bookcase That Breaks the Rules by Gary M. Katz, *Fine Homebuilding* issue 154. Photos by Roe A. Osborn, © The Taunton Press, Inc., except pp. 74 & 75 by Dean Della Ventura, © The Taunton Press, Inc.; Drawings by Bob La Pointe, © The Taunton Press, Inc.

p. 80: A Classic Bookcase in the Craftsman Style by Gary Rogowski, *Fine Woodworking* issue 136. Photos by Marc Vassallo, © The Taunton Press, Inc.; Drawings by Vince Babak, © The Taunton Press, Inc.

p. 85: Knockdown Shelves in a Day by Steve Latta, *Fine Woodworking* issue 158. Photos by William Duckworth, © The Taunton Press, Inc.; Drawings by Michael Gellatly, © The Taunton Press, Inc.

p. 90: Updated Arts and Crafts Bookcase by Gregory Paolini, *Fine Woodworking* issue 179. Photos by Andy Engel, © The Taunton Press, Inc., except p. 92 by Rodney Diaz, © The Taunton Press, Inc.; Drawings by Bob La Pointe, © The Taunton Press, Inc.

p. 98: Outfitting a Clothes Closet by Gary M. Katz, *Fine Homebuilding* issue 124. Photos by Roe A. Osborn, © The Taunton Press, Inc.

p. 106: Built-In Basics by Tony O'Malley, *Fine Woodworking* issue 166. Photos by Michael Pekovich, © The Taunton Press, Inc.; Drawings by Bob La Pointe, © The Taunton Press, Inc.

p. 118: Engineering an Entertainment Center by Brooks Tanner, *Fine Woodworking* issue 159. Photos by Mark Schofield, © The Taunton Press, Inc.; Drawings by Bruce Morser, © The Taunton Press, Inc.

p. 126: Entertainment Center in Quartersawn Maple by Peter Turner, *Fine Woodworking* issue 139. Photos by Anatole Burkin, © The Taunton Press, Inc.; Drawings by Bob La Pointe, © The Taunton Press, Inc.

p. 138: An Inside Look at Kitchen Cabinets by Scott Gibson, *Fine Homebuilding* issue 127. Photos by Scott Phillips, © The Taunton Press, Inc., except p. 139 by Scott Gibson, © The Taunton Press, Inc.

p. 148: Installing Kitchen Cabinets by Tom Law, *Fine Homebuilding* issue 85. Photos by Rich Ziegner, © The Taunton Press, Inc.; Drawings by Christopher Clapp, © The Taunton Press, Inc.

p. 160: Hanging Kitchen Cabinets Smooth and Solo by Mike Guertin, *Fine Homebuilding* issue 174. Photos by Brian Pontolillo, © The Taunton Press, Inc., except p. 161 (top left) by Nat Rea, © The Taunton Press, Inc., & p. 162 (bottom left) courtesy E-Z Spread N' Lift Industries.

p. 170: Dressing Up Plywood Cabinets With Face Frames by Joseph Beals, *Fine Woodworking* issue 128. Photos by Strother Purdy, © The Taunton Press, Inc.; Drawings by Tim Langenderfer, © The Taunton Press, Inc.

p. 178: Refacing Kitchen Cabinets by Rex Alexander, *Fine Homebuilding* issue 82. Photos by Scott Gibson, © The Taunton Press, Inc., except p. 179 (top) by Warren Harris, © The Taunton Press, Inc.

p. 188: Choosing Kitchen Countertops by Scott Gibson, *Fine Homebuilding* issue 143. Photos by Scott Gibson, except p. 189 (bottom) by Andy Engel, © The Taunton Press, Inc., p. 190 (bottom right) by Charles Miller, © The Taunton Press, Inc., p. 191 by Roe A. Osborn, © The Taunton Press, Inc., p. 192 courtesy DuPont, pp. 194–195 courtesy Vermont Structural Slate Co., & p. 196 (bottom) courtesy Pyrolave.

p. 200: Make Your Own Laminate Countertops by Steve Morris, *Fine Homebuilding* issue 166. Photos by Brian Pontolillo, © The Taunton Press, Inc., except pp. 200 (right), 201 (top) & 206–207 (middle) by Scott Phillips, © The Taunton Press, Inc., & p. 201 (bottom) courtesy Wilsonart; Drawings by Bob La Pointe, © The Taunton Press, Inc.

p. 208: Drawer Design Strategies by Gary Rogowski, *Fine Woodworking* issue 117. Photos by Vincent Laurence, © The Taunton Press, Inc., except p. 208 by Phil Harris, © The Taunton Press, Inc.; Drawings by Jim Richey, © The Taunton Press, Inc.

Index

The New Best of Fine Woodworking Series

A collection of the best articles from the last ten years of Fine Woodworking

Designing Furniture

The Best of Fine Woodworking
From the editors of FWW
ISBN 1-56158-684-6
Product #070767
$17.95 U.S.
$25.95 Canada

Small Woodworking Shops

The Best of Fine Woodworking
From the editors of FWW
ISBN 1-56158-686-2
Product #070768
$17.95 U.S.
$25.95 Canada

Working with Routers

The Best of Fine Woodworking
From the editors of FWW
ISBN 1-56158-685-4
Product #070769
$17.95 U.S.
$25.95 Canada

Building Small Projects

The Best of Fine Woodworking
From the editors of FWW
ISBN 1-56158-730-3
Product #070791
$17.95 U.S.
$25.95 Canada

Designing and Building Cabinets

The Best of Fine Woodworking
From the editors of FWW
ISBN 1-56158-732-X
Product #070792
$17.95 U.S.
$25.95 Canada

Traditional Finishing Techniques

The Best of Fine Woodworking
From the editors of FWW
ISBN 1-56158-733-8
Product #070793
$17.95 U.S.
$25.95 Canada

Working with Handplanes

The Best of Fine Woodworking
From the editors of FWW
ISBN 1-56158-748-6
Product #070810
$17.95 U.S.
$25.95 Canada

Working with Tablesaws

The Best of Fine Woodworking
From the editors of FWW
ISBN 1-56158-749-4
Product #070811
$17.95 U.S.
$25.95 Canada

Workshop Machines

The Best of Fine Woodworking
From the editors of FWW
ISBN 1-56158-765-6
Product #070826
$17.95 U.S.
$25.95 Canada

Workstations and Tool Storage

The Best of Fine Woodworking
From the editors of FWW
ISBN 1-56158-785-0
Product #070838
$17.95 U.S.
$25.95 Canada

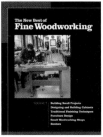

Traditional Projects

The Best of Fine Woodworking
From the editors of FWW
ISBN 1-56158-784-2
Product #070839
$17.95 U.S.
$25.95 Canada

Hand Tools

The Best of Fine Woodworking
From the editors of FWW
ISBN 1-56158-783-4
Product #070840
$17.95 U.S.
$25.95 Canada

Spray Finishing

The Best of Fine Woodworking
From the editors of FWW
ISBN 1-56158-829-6
Product #070875
$17.95 U.S.
$25.95 Canada

Selecting and Drying Wood

The Best of Fine Woodworking
From the editors of FWW
ISBN 1-56158-830-X
Product #070876
$17.95 U.S.
$25.95 Canada

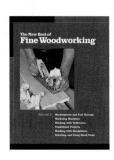

The New Best of Fine Woodworking Slipcase Set Volume 1

Designing Furniture
Working with Routers
Small Woodworking Shops
Designing and Building Cabinets
Building Small Projects
Traditional Finishing Techniques

From the editors of FWW
ISBN 1-56158-736-2
Product #070808
$85.00 U.S./$120.00 Canada

The New Best of Fine Woodworking Slipcase Set Volume 2

Working with Handplanes
Workshop Machines
Working with Tablesaws
Selecting and Using Hand Tools
Traditional Projects
Workstations and Tool Storage

From the editors of FWW
ISBN 1-56158-747-8
Product #070809
$85.00 U.S./$120.00 Canada